Pitt Latin American Series

THE FILM INDUSTRY IN BRAZIL

THE FILM INDUSTRY IN BRAZIL

Culture and the State

RANDAL JOHNSON

University of Pittsburgh Press

Published by the University of Pittsburgh Press, Pittsburgh, Pa. 15260
Copyright © 1987, University of Pittsburgh Press
All rights reserved
Feffer and Simons, Inc., London
Manufactured in the United States of America

Library of Congress Cataloging-in-Publication Data

Johnson, Randal, 1948–
   The film industry in Brazil.

   (Pitt Latin American Series)
   Bibliography: p. 247
   Includes index.
   1. Moving-picture industry—Government policy—
Brazil. I. Title. II. Series.
PN1993.5.B6J624 1986   384'.8'0981   86-4025
ISBN 0-8229-3538-4

To my parents

CONTENTS

TABLES

Acknowledgments

PRIMARY RESEARCH FOR this study was carried out in Rio de Janeiro and São Paulo during the academic year 1980–1981 with the support of postdoctoral fellowships from The Tinker Foundation and the Social Science Research Council. Subsequent trips to Brazil in 1982, 1984, and 1985 allowed me to collect additional information.

The completion of the project owes much to the generous help, comments, and suggestions of many people in both Brazil and the United States. In Brazil, the current director of Embrafilme, Carlos Augusto Calil, deserves special recognition for providing invaluable documentation. Others who contributed to the study in many different ways are: Inácio Araújo, Sérgio Augusto, Luiz Carlos Barreto, Jean-Claude Bernardet, Vera de Oliveira Brandão, Elenice de Castro, Carlos Diegues, Eduardo Escorel, Michel do Espírito-Santo, Arnaldo Jabor, Jair Leal Piantino, Aníbal Maccheroni, Hilda Machado, Jorge Peregrino, Francisco Ramalho, Jr., Antônio Amâncio da Silva, Nelson Pereira dos Santos, Carlos Roberto Rodrigues de Souza, João Luiz Vieira, and Ismail Xavier. I must also recognize and thank the staff of the Fundação Cinemateca Brasileira (São Paulo), the library of the Museu Lasar Segall (São Paulo), the Biblioteca Nacional (Rio de Janeiro), and the Cinemateca of the Museu de Arte Moderna (Rio de Janeiro).

In the United States, special thanks go to Professor William P. Glade, who served as senior consultant to the project for the Tinker Foundation, and to Julianne Burton and Emile McAnany, who read and commented on portions of the manuscript. Also thanks to Robert Stam, Steven Topik, and Thomas J. Trebat for their encouragement and always thoughtful comments.

Portions of this study have appeared in different forms in "Brazilian Cinema Novo," *Bulletin of Latin American Research* 3, no. 2 (copyright, Pergamon Press 1984), 95–106; *Cinema Novo x 5: Masters of Contemporary Brazilian Film* (Austin: University of Texas Press, 1984), pp. 1–12; and "State Policy Toward the Film Industry in Brazil," Technical Papers Series, Office for Public Sector Studies, Institute of Latin American Studies, University of Texas, Austin, 1982. All are used with permission.

Note: English translations of film titles are given the first time they appear in the text, but not in tables nor appendixes.

THE FILM INDUSTRY IN BRAZIL

INTRODUCTION

Much has been written in recent years about the relationship between the state and the economy in Brazil, and much has been said about the important social function of the state.[1] Yet relatively little has been written on the relationship between the state and cultural production. The Brazilian state has historically served as a patron, guarantor, regulator, repressor, and, at times, producer of culture. Writers, for example, have long depended on the state not only for prestige and patronage, but also, and more immediately, as an employer.[2] The Brazilian publishing industry, furthermore, is frequently subsidized by such state organizations as the Instituto Nacional do Livro (National Book Institute), set up in 1937 by Getúlio Vargas as a means of incorporating intellectuals into state policy. Although the state's intervention in the cultural arena can be traced back to the colonial period, with the establishment of libraries, educational institutions, and more or less direct patronage of the arts, such intervention—along with similar state intervention in the economy—increased rapidly in the twentieth century, especially under the governments of Getúlio Vargas (1930–1945, 1951–1954) and since the military coup d'état of 1964.

State activity in the cultural sector is not limited to erudite culture. The characterisics of Rio de Janeiro's famed samba schools (escolas de samba) and their colorful carnival parades (desfiles) have to a large extent been shaped by government policy. In the 1930's the city of Rio de Janeiro created a Department of Tourism (RIOTUR) "to promulgate the cariocan carnival and organize the performances and contests of the samba clubs in particular. RIOTUR took official charge of the clubs' contests which had been

3

patronized by cariocan newspapers. Certain rules and requirements were set . . . Themes of the parades might deal only with
historical or patriotic Brazilian motifs. An official list contained
the criteria in terms of which experts appointed by RIOTUR
would judge each parade."[3] Soccer networks are linked to the
federal government through the Vargas-created National Sports
Council, and even *umbanda* groups, once outlawed, at times receive state support.[4] If we define "state" as including a variety of
public authorities at the federal, state, and local levels, then state
intervention in culture is indeed pervasive.

Over the last fifty years, the Brazilian state has gradually developed a policy of protection and support of the national film
industry. The policy has not grown out of a carefully planned,
well-conceived design, but rather has evolved according to pressures derived from successive crises in the industry. During the
last decade, Brazilian cinema, partially because of state support,
has attained unprecedented levels of technical quality and has
achieved fairly broad international acclaim with such films as
*Dona Flor and Her Two Husbands, Bye Bye Brasil, Gaijin, Xica,
Pixote,* and *They Don't Wear Black-Tie,* among others, all of
which were at least partially financed by Embrafilme (Empresa
Brasileira de Filmes), the government film agency. Under Embrafilme's aegis, Brazilian cinema has maintained a multiplicity of
themes and styles and has captured an ever-increasing share of its
own market as well as limited foreign markets.

Despite Brazilian cinema's undeniable critical and cultural
success, state policy toward the industry has in some areas been
so short-sighted that it has led, in the late 1970s and early 1980s, to
the most severe economic crisis of the industry's recent history.
The exhibition sector has been particularly hard hit, witnessing a
net decrease of over 48 percent in the number of 35mm theaters in
operation between 1975 to 1984. Brazil has become one of the
countries with the fewest number of theaters, in relation to the
country's population, in the world.

Although most of the crises Brazilian cinema has undergone
over the last two decades have been economic, there have also
been political crises, as filmmakers have run afoul of the authoritarian military regime. In March 1982, for example, Roberto

Farias's *Pra Frente Brasil (Onward Brazil)* was chosen best film at the Gramado Film Festival in the southernmost Brazilian state of Rio Grande do Sul. Although it had not yet been released for commercial distribution, *Pra Frente Brasil* had already received extensive attention in the country's newspapers and had been the subject of lengthy discussions and debates by filmmakers and critics as one of the first national films to speak directly of the violence, repression, fear, and torture of the early 1970s under military rule.[5]

The film deals with the arrest, torture, and murder of an innocent man by the repressive apparatus as the country's attention is turned toward Brazil's successful participation in the 1970 World Cup tournament in Mexico. *Pra Frente Brasil,* whose title evokes the propaganda slogans of the Médici regime (1969–1974), evidently touched a raw nerve, for within a week of its exhibition at Gramado it was banned and the director of Embrafilme, which had co-produced the film, was forced to resign. The film dealt with a subject the military regime apparently did not want projected on theater screens across the country, especially in the period before the 1982 elections. The film was released with no cuts later that same year, *after* the elections.

This study will trace the development of the film industry in Brazil, focusing specifically on the evolution and nature of its relationship to the state over the last fifty years. State intervention in the industry has been shaped by a number of factors, each of which will be examined in the course of a historical discussion of the growth of the industry. The most important factor in state support has been the dominant presence in the domestic market of foreign films, which contributed to the industry's chronic undercapitalization and underdevelopment. A number of internal factors are also crucial. State policy, especially as it evolved in the late 1960s and 1970s, was shaped by a dual struggle for hegemony. While different groups within the industry fought for leadership in order to determine the direction of state support, the state itself attempted, through an increasingly aggressive cultural policy, to achieve its own hegemony over the film industry and other cultural sectors in order to create a consensus as to the goals and nature of national culture.

In his seminal *The International Film Industry*, Thomas Guback traces the development of state financial assistance to Western European film industries. He argues that without such assistance, most such industries would exist only under the most precarious and insolvent conditions. By its very nature, the film industry combines both economic and artistic production. A film's viability as a form of artistic expression depends, at least in capitalist contexts, on the availability of production financing, which in turn depends on the film's potential to attract a fairly wide audience and attain success in the marketplace. The artistic aspects of film production in such a context frequently take a back seat to economic imperatives.[6]

While demonstrating throughout his study that state support of film industries in Europe derives primarily from U.S. domination of local markets and the resulting loss of foreign exchange, Guback correctly suggests that the extent and nature of state assistance reflect basic and differing assumptions about the role of the state. In many countries, "there has been the belief which holds the state responsible for the maintenance and perpetuation of national heritage and culture. The authority of the state gives it the mission to preserve and encourage art and culture, for it is the only institution representative of its people and their traditions."[7] According to this view, the state has an obligation to defend the national cultural patrimony through state support of artistic production. On the other hand, this century has seen increased state planning in order to coordinate economic investment and growth in accordance with state-defined national priorities. As Guback observes, "the obligation of the state to preserve and encourage art, and the growth of public control over economic matters, have provided the rationale enabling European governments to become involved in their domestic film industries."[8]

If film industries in Western Europe have been unable to withstand the onslaught of American films without state assistance, the industries of economically weaker, dependent countries have been even less able to do so. In Latin America, only Mexico, Argentina, and Brazil have strong cinematic traditions, and their periods of success, however relative, have by and large been accompanied by considerable state support. When such support has waned, as in Argentina after the overthrow of Juan Domingo Perón in 1955, the strength of the industry has also decreased.[9]

As in Western Europe, state protection and assistance has been necessary in Latin America primarily because of the United States' film industry's domination of local markets. In 1960, the American industry controlled at least 50 percent of all screen time in every Latin American country except Mexico, where the state owned major studios and exhibition circuits.[10] There U.S. films controlled 40 percent. American films occupied 70 percent of screen time in Brazil and 50 percent in Argentina.[11] Unable to depend even on home markets for a return on investments, unprotected Latin American film industries have lacked the capital necessary to sustain continuous production on a large scale. Inevitably, the result has been the underdevelopment of most national film industries.

To fully understand cinema-state relations in such a context, however, one must look beyond the relationship of center to periphery, and the U.S. domination of local markets. Of course one cannot deny or understate that presence, nor can one fail to recognize that the question of the "occupied market" has been central to the development of governmental protectionist policies. But Brazil's relationship of dependence is more complex than that. The foreign control of the Brazilian market is not simply a question of forced imposition. Such control has proved to be in the interest of certain national groups (namely, large exhibition circuits) who benefit financially from cooperation with foreign producers and distributors. These groups are supported by large numbers of Brazilian viewers who have been weaned on foreign films, and oppose any measures that would limit the access of such films to local marketrs. The question, then, is not simply one of an unequal relationship with the dominant power, but rather is a complex play of external *and* internal interests.[12]

To look only at the dichotomy between foreign and domestic influence, furthermore, is to oversimplify relations between the cinema and the state and to focus primarily on a quantitative analysis of the industry's development. In his well-researched study of Latin American film industries, for example, Jorge Schnitman argues that the protectionist policies of the Mexican government have helped create a strong film industry in that country, especially when compared to that of Argentina. That may be true, but what he does not deal with is the quality of Mexican cinema.[13] Mexican critic Alberto Ruy Sánchez, writing on the "ideology of crisis" in the national industry, convincingly reveals state support to be essentially pernicious, creating a situation in which the film itself is the least important aspect of the industry.[14]

Qualitative aspects of film production must also be taken into consideration, and that leads to numerous questions concerning the relationship of cultural production and the state, a can of worms even by conservative estimation. The Brazilian state, especially in its more authoritarian incarnations, is not exactly a benevolent Lone Ranger riding to the defense of helpless filmmaker-settlers. The state has its own interests and its own reasons for intervening, or not intervening, in support of the national film industry, and those interests may not always coincide with those of the industry itself. Cinema-state relations are a two-way street. Since the late 1920s industrial groups or professionals have requested different forms of state protection and aid, and the state has responded in accordance with its own priorities and designs. One must thus also analyze the internal tensions of Brazilian cinema and the diverse articulations between that cinema and the state. Such an analysis clearly transcends the purely economic and the impact of foreign cinemas on the national film industry.

Before discussing these relationships in more detail, we must first digress momentarily to examine the nature of the product we are dealing with. A film is of course a commodity, but not a commodity in the traditional sense of the word. Within the current structure of the film industry (and here I am speaking of all Western, capitalist film industries prior to the video revolution, which is just beginning in Brazil), a film is an abstract commodity in that it is not purchased or sold per se. It does not change hands. The producer makes the film and then entrusts it to a distributor (often part of the same production company, in the case of the U.S. industry), who circulates it to exhibitors. Exhibitors, under normal circumstances, do not own the film, nor, obviously, do they "sell" it to spectators. Exchange value is realized through box-office receipts.[15]

The exhibitor sells the right to admission to his theater, not the film-object itself, which is infinitely reproducible and can be shown in many different places at the same time. The original copy is, in real terms, worth little more than the celluloid it is printed on. The spectator pays for a promise of sensorial gratification or aesthetic pleasure. If seats are not filled for any given showing, then the value of those seats is lost forever. The film is not consumed and removed from the market because of any single showing. It is in the interest of producers and distributors to have the film shown simultaneously in as many different theaters and markets as possible, thus helping to assure an adequate and rapid return on sometimes considerable investments. The cost of film production in the United States has made foreign markets essential to the American industry (although ancillary markets in the U.S.—video, cable television, and the like—have diminished their importance in recent years), and the reproducibility of the film-object has facilitated international distribution.

Along the same lines, a film differs from more traditional commodities in that its production process is difficult to regulate and quantify. Michael Chanan uses the concept of "aesthetic labor" to describe this difference:

In all forms of cultural production, including the new technological media, aesthetic workers retain at least some degree of autonomy—if only that of individual style—of a kind which can be progressively denied to the factory worker as the capitalist reconstructs the labour process by introducing new technology, new means of production and new techniques of management ("scientific management"). This process, by which capital required real control over labour, depends on being able to quantify the labour process, establish fixed times which each part of the job is supposed to take, which the worker must keep up with. But there is no form of aesthetic production where, try so ever hard, this kind of "time economy" can be properly imposed. You cannot predetermine how long a composer should take to write a piece, or a painter to paint a picture. Nor exactly how long it should take to make a film. At the very least, this introduces a degree of uncertainty into the business which increases the risk of the undertaking.[16]

The modes of production, distribution, and exhibition of a film, furthermore, are shaped by a variety of industrial, economic, cultural, aesthetic, and ideological factors.[17] As an industry, the cinema in Brazil is affected by state measures in ways not affecting other art forms. Since it depends largely on imports for virtually all production equipment, as well as raw film stock, it is sometimes dramatically affected by changes in import or exchange policies. Ticket prices are set by government agencies, so the industry has virtually no say in determining the market value of its product. Its development has been hindered by foreign trade accords in which the Brazilian government has agreed to the principle of free flow of motion pictures across international boundaries (GATT, for example). In short, Brazilian cinema, even without direct government protection or intervention, is in many ways dependent on or shaped by the state and its policies.

The cinema is an industry that manufactures a cultural product. Like many other cultural products in Brazil, a film is subject to laws of censorship. Although such laws have changed over the years and have been exercised with more or less flexibility, depending on the political conjuncture, censorship represents an area in which the state, through its coercive apparatus, has ultimate control over what the public sees or does not see. Since there has never been censorship prior to the making of a film in Brazil, as has been the case with the press, it has not directly prevented filmmakers from producing the film they choose. Rather, it exercises control at the level of consumption. The very existence of censorship, especially when imposed in an arbitrary manner, may shape the nature of the subjects dealt with, because banned films cannot offer the producer a return on investments. The result is often a form of self-censorship.

In a capitalist context, most feature-length films are also subject to the whims of the marketplace. In Brazil, the filmgoing public historically has been conditioned by the standards of European and American cinema, which dominated the local market as early as the first decade of the century. These films displayed levels of technical perfection impossible for the incipient Brazilian industry, and with that perfection they imposed certain cultural models of the "proper" or preferred form of cinematic discourse. Audiences became accustomed to that form, and have been reluctant to accept alternative forms, even if produced locally. So Brazilian cinema found itself in a double bind. On the one hand, it has not had the economic wherewithall to equal the technical achievements of advanced industrial countries, and on the other, it has often lacked audience support for introducing different modes of filmmaking.

In his study of Latin American film industries, Jorge Schnitman distinguishes between restrictive, supportive, and comprehensive protectionist policies. A restrictive policy, which includes measures such as screen and import quotas, high import tariffs and customs duties, is designed to give the local industry some breathing room by impeding a complete takeover of the local market by foreign concerns. A supportive policy includes direct state support of the industry in the form of bank loans and credit, prizes, production subsidies and other forms of film financing, assistance in reaching foreign markets, and training of film industry technicians. Restrictive policies provide indirect support of the industry while supportive policies lend direct financial support. A comprehensive state policy includes both restrictive and supportive measures.[18]

State intervention in the film industry in Brazil can be traced back to the early 1930s, when Getúlio Vargas implemented the first of what would turn out to be a long series of restrictive protectionist measures designed to give the industry a modicum of stability for future development. Since that time, and especially in the last twenty years, the state has added supportive measures to its policy, and the state role has evolved from that of regulator of market forces to active agent and productive force in the industry, characterized by what Schnitman would call a comprehensive state protectionist policy. The state began granting production subsidies in the mid-1960s and has, since 1973, invested in the production of commercial films by private production companies.[19]

Multiple factors have shaped the approximation between the state and the film industry in Brazil. First, due to the industry's historical underdevelopment, caused largely by the domination of the domestic market by foreign film distributors, the industry itself has since the early 1930s called on the state for protectionist measures. In this sense, the situation of the film industry is not significantly different from industries in other economic sectors, which have needed state support to guarantee development. In accordance with what is known as the "infant industry argument," the state attempts to stimulate an adequate level of sustained growth in the national industry to enable it to attain satisfactory economies of scale to operate at its optimum and most cost-efficient level, and to compete effectively against established industries from advanced countries.[20] This is one of the economic justifications for state intervention in the Brazilian film industry, although there is some doubt that the policy has been or can be truly successful.

Second, state intervention in the film industry is a continuation and an extension of the historical relationship between artists and the state in Brazil: the Brazilian state has historically acted as a sort of philanthropic agent and patron of the arts. Because of the small market for élite cultural products in Brazil, the state has frequently supported artists and intellectuals through bureaucratic positions, donations, awards, and sinecures. The poet Carlos Drummond de Andrade, in fact, has described Brazilian literature as a literature of "public employees."[21] The state has become, and continues to be, a *locus* around which artists and intellectuals gather for support, recognition, and, ultimately, legitimation.

This brings us to a third determining factor in the relationship between cinema and state in Brazil. The state is not entirely disinterested in its support of intellectuals and artists, and they often become incorporated as part of the state apparatus, living in what Carlos Nelson Coutinho, borrowing from Thomas Mann and Georg Lukács, calls "intimacy in the shadow of power."[22] Brazilian film critic Jean-Claude Bernardet describes this same phenomenon as a "legal space."[23]

In *El ogro filantrópico (The Philanthropic Ogre)*, a book whose title goes a long way toward describing the state's role in relation to cultural production, Octavio Paz discusses the role of artists and intellectuals in Mexican society. He says that as a writer, his duty is to maintain a marginal position in relation to the state, to political parties, to ideologies, and to society itself.[24] To be marginal does not of course imply neutrality, but rather a critical attitude toward society and its institutions. Paz affirms that the state itself should be neutral with regard to questions of art, citing the example of Mexican muralist art, which lost energy following state intervention. And yet at the same time, he calls on the state to increase its "no-strings-attached" financial support of young artists and writers.[25]

The state, by its very nature, determines the parameters within which artists may act; in the case of the cinema these are delimited not only by state mechanisms such as production financing and censorship, but also by the dictates of the marketplace, and the filmmaker has relative freedom as long as he or she stays within these parameters. The state has a monopoly on the use of coercion. It obviously can control what the public sees through the exercise of censorship; however, it would prefer to control cultural production through consensus or hegemony rather than coercion.

The increased state intervention in the film industry which occurred in the mid-1960s and intensified in the early 1970s can be seen as part of a broader state policy designed to attain hegemony and indirect, if not direct, control over many areas of cultural production. It was during this period that the state created the Conselho Federal de Cultura (Federal Council of Culture, 1966), the Instituto Nacional do Cinema (National Film Institute, 1966), Embrafilme (1969), Fundação Nacional das Artes or FUNARTE (National Foundation for the Arts, 1975), and the Conselho Nacional de Cinema or CONCINE (National Film Council, 1976). The state institutionalized cultural production, or "incorporated" it into state policy during this period.

The Brazilian film industry is not monolithic, nor is it particularly united on any given issue other than its own survival. "Brazilian cinema" exists only in the abstract. In concrete terms, there is no single Brazilian cinema that can be analyzed as a unit; rather, there are many cinemas, each of which claims to be the only valid one. Critic Jean-Claude Bernardet gives a perfect example of this divisiveness when he quotes Cinema Novo veteran Paulo César Saraceni and pornochanchada (erotic comedy) director Pedro Rovai. Saraceni calls on the state, through Embrafilme, to support what he calls the culturally serious films made by himself and the remnants of the Cinema Novo group and their followers. He refers constantly to "our films" as being synonymous with "Brazilian cinema." Rovai, on the other hand, wants Embrafilme to stop producing individual films and to finance production companies, much as the state does in other economic areas. When he acerbically refers to films that no one wants to see, that make no money at the box office, and that transmit an "elite, bourgeois" conception of Brazilian culture, he is talking about precisely the same films that Saraceni supports.[26]

It should be added at this point that there have been and continue to be significant sectors of the industry that exist independently of, and frequently in opposition to, state support. Filmmaking in Brazilian cinema's Golden Age (1908–1911) obviously had no state support, nor did the *chanchada* (light musical comedy) during its heyday between 1940 and 1960. More recently, exhibitors, whose interests traditionally have been linked to foreign distributors, have tended to see the screen quota for national films as an unfair burden and an unwanted intrusion in the free enterprise system. Consequently, some of them joined together and have began producing their own films—largely *pornochanchadas*—to satisfy the legal requirements of the quota. These "quota quickies," as they have been called, are generally made on extremely low budgets, are of poor technical quality, and yet are highly successful in that they are aimed at a very specific, urban, male audience. Since these films occupy much of the reserve market for national films, they have become, together with foreign films, one of the major targets of Embrafilme and its supporters.

This study focuses primarily on economic aspects of the development of the Brazilian film industry while at the same time recognizing that the cinema is always seen as having an importance that transcends economics. With the exception of television, cinema is perhaps the most "public" of art forms in Brazil. Discussions of its films frequently occupy entire pages of major newspapers, and changes in state policy toward the industry are debated widely in the press, as well as in the industry. Some of these debates will be outlined throughout this study, since they are often crucial to an understanding of the reasons behind such changes.

Very few sectors of Brazilian society would agree with Octavio Paz that the state should be "neutral" with regard to the kinds of films it finances. Although most would oppose explicit political constraints imposed by the government, they would also oppose government financing of films that offend predominant social values, regardless of how one defines such values. Arguments have arisen throughout the past forty years over the important educational or pedagogical function of the national cinema, and many feel that state support of the industry should be at least consistent with the broader educational goals of the government. Industrial development per se has rarely been an absolute goal among most filmmakers and critics, although exceptions always exist. Given the nature of the industry, however, economic development or stability is frequently a sine qua non of the cinema's other functions.

In its relationship to the cinema, the state thus has a dual role, economic and cultural. Although there are many parallels between state participation in the film industry and that in other economic areas, they are ultimately quite different precisely because of this dual role. Cultural products cannot, in the final analysis, be judged according to economic criteria. A film, as Michael Chanan would say, cannot be quantified to the extent that other commodities can be. One of the conclusions of this study is that the state, through Embrafilme and other organizations, has failed to reconcile its cultural and industrial responsibilities. Although it has helped create what many feel to be the premier cinema in Latin America, it has failed to stimulate an economically stable and self-sustaining film industry.

Underlying the following discussion of the relationship between cinema and state in Brazil are a number of assumptions concerning the nature of the Brazilian state and the regimes that have held power in the post-1930 period.[27] For our purposes it is useful to view state and regime both abstractly and concretely. In abstract terms, the Brazilian state is a dependent, capitalist state, the "expression" of society's dominant mode of production. In concrete terms, it is an institutional framework—a state apparatus—with very specific characteristics, embodying the "historical and social processes that have most influenced the formation of the nation or the society. In this role the state is greater than the sum of regimes over time."[28]

Coexisting with the dependent capitalist state, especially since the 1930s, have been what Cardoso calls "corporative regime types."[29] In this framework, the state and its regimes structure society and social organizations along corporative lines. Individuals participate in the political and social process through state approved and regulated organizations which themselves have varying degrees of autonomy from the central government. Society is thus organized horizontally into classes and vertically into state approved or even state created organizations. That is, society is "organized along both *class and corporate lines*."[30] With these organizations, as with the rest of civil society, the state maintains patron-client relationships. The state, by virtue of its relationships with corporative organizations and other social groups, thus becomes a site of conflict and contradiction and acts within an unstable equilibrium of compromises between opposing social forces.[31]

The corporative structure of Brazilian regimes has shown relative permanence over time. Howard J. Wiarda suggests that the corporative system adjusts to change, but does not itself change. At different times in modern Latin American history, it has had to adjust and expand to encompass rising new groups, but "the structure of society [has] remained hierarchical, authoritarian, elitist, corporative, and closed."[32] Alfred Stepan distinguishes between "inclusionary corporatism," which characterized the Estado Novo of Getúlio Vargas, and "exclusionary corporatism," which describes the Brazilian political system under post-1964 military regimes.[33] The real struggle has been between different conceptions of corporatism. As Wiarda suggests, "In Brazil it was the Left-syndicalist position of Goulart as opposed to the authoritarian-gremialist position of the army."[34] Despite changes in the political system, the Brazilian dependent capitalist state has grown out of a strong patrimonial tradition and has remained, at least over the last fifty years, a state supported by corporative regimes.

In practical terms, this means that the state has become not only a site where opposing social forces struggle for domination, but also a site and source of legitimation. Moreover, in the case of the cinema, the state itself has become, especially since the mid-1970s, a marketplace where filmmakers compete for recognition and, consequently, financing for their film projects. Although I do not argue that the Brazilian cinematic apparatus is a "corporation" per se, this is the context in which cinema-state relations must be seen. The state historically has a propensity to intervene in virtually all areas of society, and society, on the other hand, sees the state as the supreme source of legitimation.

In chapter 1 of this study I discuss the early development of Brazilian cinema, ranging from 1898, when the first Brazilian film was made, to 1930, with the advent of sound and the first attempts at industrialization based on a studio model. I briefly examine the structure of the incipient film industry, as well as the domination of the market by foreign films and other reasons for the industry's failure to develop on a satisfactory scale. Chapter 2 takes the discussion from 1930 to approximately 1950. During this period, a number of attempts at concentrated industrialization were made, starting with the Cinédia Studios in 1930 and ending with Vera Cruz, founded in 1949. This period also witnessed the initial steps in the development of a state policty toward the film industry, which will be discussed in some detail.

Chapter 3 discusses the evolution of state policy from bankruptcy of Vera Cruz (1954) to the creation of GEICINE (1961; Executive Group of the Film Industry), focusing initially on the important film industry congresses held in the early 1950s before shifting to the numerous state organizations created during the fifties to deal with problems facing the industry. The chapter also outlines the rise of new conceptions as to the industrial model Brazilian cinema should follow, and traces some of the tensions and divisions within the industry and how they relate to state policy.

Chapter 4 looks at the activities of GEICINE (1961–1965), which in many ways mark the beginning of a more aggressive state policy toward the cinema, as well as the rise of the internationally acclaimed Cinema Novo movement and its attitude toward state intervention in the film industry and toward the film industry itself.

The Instituto Nacional do Cinema (1966–1975) will be the focus of chapter 5. It first created, on the national level, a program of production subsidies and other measures of a supportive protectionist policy to accompany the restrictive policies that had been evolving since the early 1930s. Policies of the INC were relatively neutral in that they were designed to benefit the industry as a whole.

Chronologically overlapping the discussion of the Instituto Nacional do Cinema, chapter 6 focuses on the reorientation of state policy under Embrafilme (1969) away from neutral policies toward the industry, to ones which favored limited groups within the industry. During this period, and especially after 1973, Brazilian cinema achieved unprecedented levels of technical excellence and international acclaim and began to solidify a strong position in the domestic market while at the same time penetrating foreign markets.

The final chapter examines the severe crisis that has gripped the Brazilian industry since the late 1970s. It focuses on four contributing factors to the crisis: television, increased production costs, the decline of foreign cinemas in the country, and the relationship between the exhibition sector and the state.

1

The Early Development of Brazilian Cinema, 1896–1930

At the beginning of the Republic in 1889, Brazil faced a situation of "classic dependence," functioning as an exporter of agricultural products and as an importer of manufactured goods.[1] The deposition of Dom Pedro II at the hands of a military establishment imbued with positivist, republican ideals followed eighteen months after the abolition of slavery (1888) and foretold the end of the political and economic dominance of the sugar aristocracy in the northeast in favor of the coffee planters of Rio de Janeiro and São Paulo. Coinciding with the Republic was the country's first surge of industrialization, largely in textiles and food production.[2] The export of agricultural goods—coffee from Rio–São Paulo, sugar from Recife, meat and leather products from Rio Grande do Sul to other regions of the country—had led to the development of internal markets for imported manufactured products. The existence of such markets, although poorly integrated with each other, combined with the abolition of slavery and increased European immigration, both of which helped not only to expand the market but also freed capital and constituted a large work force, provided Brazil with an impetus to develop local industry, thus beginning a slow process of import substitution. Demand, however, continued to be satisfied first and foremost by imports and only secondarily by locally produced goods.[3]

In the initial phase of industrialization, local manufacturers tended to produce bulky and low-value goods which cost less to make than to import, and for which only rudimentary technology was needed.[4] Although seemingly logical, such a strategy of industrialization tended to create, in the mind of the consumer, an association between locally manufactured goods and inferior quality. This was true not only with economic goods, but also with the production of symbolic goods, or goods such as films which, although themselves commodities, functioned on both the economic and symbolic planes.

Urbanization occurred as a function of regional agricultural exports as cities attracted the free work force and began to witness the concentration of commercial, political, and administrative activities.[5] Between 1890 and 1920 Brazil's population grew from 14,333,915 to 30,635,605. In 1890 only six of Brazil's cities had a population of over 50,000, and only three a population of over 100,000. By 1920, fifteen cities had populations of over 50,000, six of over 100,000, and one, Rio de Janeiro, of over 500,000 (Rio's population in 1920 was 1,157,873).[6] Prior to the Republic, however, Brazilian cities had hardly been pleasant or salubrious places to live in. Sewage often ran through open gutters in the streets, and diseases such as yellow fever and smallpox were rampant. Rio de Janeiro had been "neglected and run down. In many ways it resembled a colossal, temporary encampment of human hordes who had renounced life's material comforts. It had narrow streets, tiny squares, few trees or gardens, and decadent architecture of incredibly bad taste, tawdry, and ridiculous."[7]

The optimistic atmosphere of the Republic began to change the face of the city. Rio de Janeiro, in the words of a local columnist of the period, was "becoming civilized." President Rodrigues Alves (1902–1906) began a program of urban renewal under the direction of engineers Passos Pereira and Paulo de Frontim. They opened new streets and widened public squares, which not only gave the city a more modern appearance, but also helped officials eradicate disease. The process of modernization and urbanization, although opposed bitterly at the time, was most perfectly symbolized by the opening of the Avenida Central (now Avenida Rio Branco), a broad, tree-lined thoroughfare running from Praça Mauá to the former Senate building (torn down several years ago to make way for a new subway system). The avenue gave cariocas a sense of pride and confidence, a feeling that Brazil was entering the modern age. And it created an atmosphere propitious for the introduction of the cinema.

The new invention arrived in Brazil a short six months after Auguste Lumière first revealed his *cinématographe* in Paris. The first session of what was called the *omniographo* took place on 8 July 1896, in a room on Rio de Janeiro's fashionable Rua do Ouvidor. Although it is not known who imported the first projector, the little evidence available suggests that the *omniographo* was the name given locally to Lumière's invention.[8] Rio de Janeiro had already seen Edison's Kinetoscope, but the *omniographo* had a much greater impact since it projected an image on a wall or screen for viewing by large numbers of spectators, whereas the kinetoscope could be seen by only one person at a time.

Just as the owner of the first *omniographo* is unknown, so too is what film or films were shown on that July evening. One thing is certain: neither the films nor the projector was Brazilian. Consistent with the economic situation of the country as a whole, technological and economic dependence marked the development of cinema in Brazil from its very inception. Within this framework, the exhibition sector naturally developed at a more rapid pace than either the production or distribution sectors. Lacking national films, exhibitors were from the very beginning allied with foreign film producers.

Brazil's dependency has been largely responsible for the underdevelopment of the national film industry. By the second decade of this century, foreign cinemas had established firm control of the Brazilian film market, leaving little space for the national product. Without full access to the admittedly limited domestic market, the film industry could not achieve adequate returns on investments. Consequently, the process of capital accumulation within the industry has been stifled, and continuous production has been difficult. The result has been a chronic lack of continuity within the industry, which frequently developed in isolated and short-lived cycles, often far from the country's major metropolitan centers and, consequently, far from the limited market that did in fact exist. Technologically speaking, Brazilian cinema has had to play a perennial game of catch-up since virtually all equipment used in film production, including raw film stock, has had to be imported.

The country's dependency and peripheral development have

also had ideological and cultural effects. When film production begin in Brazil on a fairly large scale after the turn of the century, the formal uses to which the highly technological cinematic apparatus could be put had already been largely determined. Brazilians imitated European practices, especially those of Lumière, by first filming commonplace events and, subsequently turning to events of local interest. The forms the cinema would take, like the technological apparatus itself, were created in Europe and the United States, and any deviation was considered "incorrect." Brazilians therefore had little if any opportunity to develop an autonomous, national mode of cinematic discourse. As Ismail Xavier notes, "The notion of 'correct' technique assumes the legitimacy of 'universal' values embedded in the equipment and the raw material, themselves products of advanced technology. . . . The technology embedded in the means of production facilitates its equivocal transfer of the economic notion of underdevelopment to the level of culture."[9]

To blame the Brazilian film industry's failure to develop adequately solely on foreign domination of the national market is thus simplistic. Besides the problems mentioned above, a number of internal factors rendered development improbable. Despite conjunctural disadvantages, local filmmakers were fairly successful in the first decade of the century, and their general failure to expand in the area of production was due, in part, to their reluctance or inability to reinvest and develop more complex organizational structures and forms of production, to their failure, with some exceptions, to develop a national market, and to their proprietary attitude toward their own companies, which caused them to resist concentration through joining with other producers or exhibitors. These shortcomings were not limited to the film industry alone, for before 1920 the industrial sector was marginal within the export-oriented economy, and there existed no "operational ideology" of industrial development.[10]

At the same time, the cinema lacked, during this early period, the cultural prestige that could have garnered more substantial support and led to its more satisfactory development in Brazil. It was seen as little more than a mechanical novelty with virtually no relationship to the "arts." Moreover, it had not undergone theoretical elaboration, which might have attracted the attention of intellectual circles. The social position of Brazilian intellectuals during this period was more or less defined by the capacity to import and absorb cultural goods from Europe. This left them little sympathy for, or interest in, national production, other than their own or that of a small group of friends and associates.[11] Finally, the cinema was imported largely by immigrants of low social standing, which did not recommend it to the more affluent sectors of society.[12]

This chapter will examine the Brazilian film industry in the first thirty years of this century, discussing in some detail its successes and failures, before turning to the entrance and dominant role of foreign cinemas in Brazil's domestic market. This will lay the groundwork for a subsequent discussion of the relationship between cinema and state in Brazil. The state had virtually no role in the industry in this early period. Nevertheless, a discussion of the evolution of Brazilian cinema during its early days is necessary for a complete understanding of its more recent development and its relationship to the state.

EARLY PIONEERS OF BRAZILIAN CINEMA

Although exhibition officially began in Brazil in 1896, it was only a decade later that it developed into a firmly established business. Early exhibitors were ambulatory, showing their wares at different places in the city or even traveling to different cities. Early in 1897, for example, Aurélio Paz dos Reis, who had initiated film production in Portugal the year before, exhibited his *Kinetographo Portuguez* to a closed session of journalists and then to the public in Rio de Janeiro's Teatro Lucinda (Araújo, p. 78). The exhibitions of Paz dos Reis's films were sponsored by Costa, Reis e Cia., a firm established by Vicente Reis and orchestra conductor Costa Júnior. They had rented the Lucinda Theater for a period of fourteen months for the presentation of Reis's "revue" *O Filhote*, and they contracted Paz dos Reis to exhibit his films while the theater company rehearsed for its opening. Neither the films nor the company was particularly successful, due in part to the unreliability of electric power, forcing the company out of business in March 1897 (Araújo, p. 81).

During that same month, Spanish prestidigitator Enrique Moya set up an Edison cinematograph on the Rua do Ouvidor. On 11 April 1897, it was seen by 1,400 spectators. On 10 April, the Italian Vittorio di Maio exhibited what he called Edison's *animatographo* in Rio's Teatro Variedades. This gave the city a choice between two cinematic spectacles, although both of them were ambulatory and destined to last only a short time (Araújo, p. 84). Because of the constant repetition of the same "views," as they were called, the novelty of the invention began to wear thin, and Moya was forced to sell his cinematograph, which had been seen by some 52,000 people in two months (Araújo, p. 89). By the time Moya went out of business in May 1897, the cinema's reputation was in danger because of reports of the catastrophic fire at Paris's Bazar de la Charité, in which some two hundred people were killed.

Paschoal Segreto

On 31 July the Italo-Brazilian Paschoal Segreto and José Roberto Cunha Salles (a leader of Rio's numbers racket, the *jogo do bicho*, or animal game) opened the first permanently established exhibition hall in Rio, the Salão de Novidades, with its *animatographo* (apparently, in this case, another name for Lumière's *cinématographe*). The success of the Salão was so great the owners soon sent emissaries to Europe to purchase additional one-reel films. By the end of the year, Cunha Salles ended his partnership with Segreto and set up his own *cinématographe* in the mountain resort town of Petrópolis, leaving Segreto as the undisputed king of film exhibition in Rio de Janeiro.

Paschoal Segreto, who is said to be the model for the character Laje da Silva in Lima Barreto's novel *Recordações do Escrivão Isaías Caminha*, is a key figure in the early development of film exhibition in Brazil.[13] By 1900, in fact, the press had deemed him Rio's "Minister of Entertainment." In partnership with his brothers Gaetano and Afonso, he imported exhibition equipment from France and films from both Europe and the United States. The success of his rechristened Salão de Novidades Paris was so great and of such prestige that on 17 July 1898 he inaugurated a new series of "views" in the presence of Prudente de Morais Neto, the president of the Republic (Araújo, p. 107).

Less than a month after the president's visit, however, the Salão de Novidades Paris was completely destroyed by fire. The building also housed the residences of Paschoal and his brother Gaetano. Fortunately no one was injured, and the animatographo was insured for 50.000$000 (approximately U.S. $7,500), the building itself for 60.000$000 (approximately U.S. $9,000). Gaetano Segreto calculated his losses at 100.000$000 (approximately U.S. $15,000). The Salão did not reopen until 5 January 1899, almost five months after the fire, but Paschoal Segreto spared no expense in creating an environment of great luxury, and his new Salão was illuminated by fifty incandescent lights and four arc lamps (Araújo, p. 109).

Although other ambulatory cinématographes opened during 1898 and 1899, Segreto's Salão continued to be the most popular, possibly because of its constantly renewed repertoire of films. Afonso Segreto made frequent trips to Europe and the United States to bring back the latest in one-reel films to meet the public's demand for novelty. In December 1899 Segreto opened another amusement park and exhibition hall, the Parque Fluminense, which he maintained until 1902 (Araújo, p. 146). By mid-1900, his entertainment empire consisted not only of the Salão Paris and the Parque Fluminense, but also of the Coliseu-Cidade Nova and the Maison Moderne, where, initially, he staged musical concerts (Araújo, p. 123). The empire later expanded to include the café-chantant Moulin Rouge, the Teatro Carlos Gomes, the Teatro São José, the Concerto Avenida, the Parque Novidades (1907), and the Cinematographo Brasileiro in the Exposição Nacional (1908).

Segreto also timidly expanded into São Paulo with the acquisition, in 1901, of the Polytheama-Concerto. In 1907 he opened the café-chantant Moulin Rouge on São Paulo's Largo do Paissandu and in 1908 he leased the Teatro Sant'Anna for two years. By 1913 he owned the Teatro Variedades and the Teatro Apolo. He also opened a wax museum in São Paulo in 1912 with the name Museu Científico Anatômico.[14]

In 1907 the Salão de Novidades Paris was renamed the Pavilhão Internacional. At night the exhibition hall of the Pavilhão would show films of the "free genre," pornographic films prohibited to women and children (Araújo, pp. 210, 272). A journalist of the period wrote that the "free" cinema was frequented by "senators, congressmen, businessmen . . . and prostitutes" (Araújo, p. 321). Anatole France is said to have seen such films in Segreto's Pavilhão in 1909 (Araújo, p. 298).[15] It thus appears that Segreto was not only Brazil's first major film exhibitor, but also its first exhibitor of pornographic films.

Segreto's entertainment centers, however, were not used only for the exhibition of films. The Parque Fluminense featured, among its many diversions, a skating rink, sharp-shooting, balloons, bicycles, roller coasters, swings, and fireworks. The Maison Moderne featured popular singers such as Eduardo das Neves. Other attractions at Segreto's various establishments included "flying women," strongmen, wax museums, theatrical presentations, and male and female wrestlers. In 1908 Segreto opened, at his Pavilhão Internacional, a Japanese cinématographe, showing films made by the Sadayco Company. The following year, in a continuation of his Oriental predilections, he programmed Japanese wrestlers during the intermissions of his film exhibitions (Araújo, pp. 139, 141, 293).

The cinema began to stabilize as a widespread popular diversion in 1907 with the opening of a number of new exhibition halls, including Arnaldo Gomes de Sousa's and Marc Ferrez's Cinematographo Pathé, Jacomo Rosário Staffa's and Ugolino Stamile's Grande Cinematographo Parisiense, and Guilherme Auler's Grande Cinematographo Rio Branco, among many others. A major contributing factor to this stabilization was the Rio de Janeiro Tramway, Light, and Power Company's completion of its electric plant in Ribeirão das Lajes in that same year, providing a more reliable output of energy in the nation's capital.[16] The increasing number of theaters also increased competition between exhibitors, causing a general improvement in the quality of exhibition.

Film Production and the Bela Época

The production sector began to develop only after the exhibition sector had shown reasonable success. Paschoal Segreto was, as might be expected, instrumental in production as well as in exhibition. On a business trip to Europe in 1898, Paschoal's brother Afonso acquired a Lumière camera and shot the first Brazilian film as the ship on which he was traveling entered Guanabara Bay. Over the next few years, the Segreto brothers, working out of their own laboratories, would film public events, presidential outings, and scenes of local interest, exhibiting them almost immediately in their own theaters.

Other enterprising exhibitors quickly followed the Segretos' example of vertical integration of production and exhibition by making their own films to show in their own theaters. Guilherme Auler's William & Cia. made films for his Cinematographo Rio Branco, Staffa and Stamile for their Parisiense, José Labanca and Antônio Leal for their Cinema Palace, Marc and Júlio Ferrez for their Pathé, Joseph Cateysson for the Cassino Nacional and his own Palace-Theater, and somewhat later Francisco Serrador for his Chantecler. The period's leading historian, Vicente de Paula Araújo, mentions little film production independent of the exhibition sector during this early period. The incipient Brazilian film industry continued to grow and prosper throughout the decade, producing some 100 (mostly one-reel) films per year between 1908 and 1911, a period which has since been called the Bela Época of Brazilian cinema.

The denomination of this period as the Golden Age of Brazilian cinema obfuscates, to a certain extent, the reality of the film market at the same time as it simultaneously maintains and propagates the myth of a "paradise lost" of that cinema. Although precise statistics are unavailable for film production and exhibition during this period, and although Brazilian cinema did achieve undeniable success, it seems unlikely that, even then, Brazilian cinema occupied more than a minority position in the market due to the vast numbers of foreign films imported. What was important during this period was that there existed a certain "peaceful coexistence" between Brazilian cinema and foreign cinemas; there was plenty of exhibition time available for both foreign and national films, a situation that would not occur again for several decades.

The most successful production company of the early period of Brazilian cinema was the Photo-Cinematographica Brasileira, formed in 1908 by the Italo-Brazilian Giuseppe (José) Labanca and the Luso-Brazilian Antônio Leal. Prior to that time, Labanca ran a small business selling local and foreign newspapers as well as lottery tickets. Leal, who is often credited with having made Brazil's first feature-length film, was a well-known photographer for the magazine *O Malho* (Araújo, pp. 136, 186). He evidently owned his own photographic studio, and it is thought that he began filming as early as 1905.[17] In May 1907, Leal was contracted, probably by Jacomo Rosário Staffa, to film an operation on Siamese twins. The resulting film, *Operação das Marias Xipófagas pelo Dr. Chapot Prevost (Dr. Chapot Prevost's Operation on Siamese Twins)*, was exhibited shortly thereafter in Staffa's Grande Cinematographo Parisiense (Araújo, p. 198).

The Photo-Cinematographica Brasileria, whose films were shown in the company's own Cinema Palace, quickly became the largest production company in Rio de Janeiro. Labanca and Leal not only made films, but also imported and sold projection equipment and films and claimed to have agencies in Paris, London, and Chile (Araújo, p. 240). Their first major success was Leal's *Os Estranguladores (The Stranglers, 1908)*, depicting a notorious criminal incident that had occurred in Rio de Janeiro. This film, which was probably three reels in length, was given over eight hundred screenings in the first three months of exhibition (Araújo, pp. 256, 258).

In 1909 Labanca built the first Brazilian film studios.[18] In this year alone, Labanca and Leal produced eighteen films in the studios, including successful versions of *Uncle Tom's Cabin* and *The Merry Widow*. But their partnership was to last only two years, and after Leal left the firm, Labanca continued producing films only sporadically. Between 1910 and 1918 he produced only half as many as in 1909 alone.[19] Antônio Leal went on to work for other companies, but never again achieved the success of the Bela Época of 1908–1911.

Another early pioneer of Brazilian production and exhibition was Cristóvão Guilherme Auler, who until 1907 was a furniture maker. On 1 September of that year he inaugurated his Cinematographo Rio Branco, which soon became one of the more fashionable theaters in Rio de Janeiro. Auler's firm, William & Cia.,

specialized in *fitas cantantes* (singing films) in which opera singers would stand behind the screen and attempt to accompany the
movements of the characters' mouths. Like Labanca and Leal,
Auler also made a successful version of *The Merry Widow* (1909).
In a newspaper advertisement published in 1910, Auler claimed
that his version of the story had been seen by 180,854 spectators
(Araújo, p. 324). His most spectacular success, in fact the most
successful film of the first two decades of Brazilian cinema, was
the musical revue *Paz e Amor* (*Peace and Love*, 1910), which
spoofed Brazil's new president, Nilo Peçanha.

After a fire destroyed the Rio Branco, Auler leased Segreto's
Pavilhão Internacional and continued his activity in exhibition.
Between 1909 and 1911 he produced some eleven films, most of
them singing films. Toward the end of 1911, however, Auler declared that his company had been invited to exhibit its "vast repertoire" abroad and that it would begin functioning with other
forms of entertainment (Araújo, p. 370), thus ending another
short-lived attempt at the industrialization of Brazilian cinema.

The vertical integration of this early period's production and
exhibition was more illusory than real. Photo-Cinematographica
Brasileira and William & Cia., to use as examples the two companies just mentioned, made films for only *one* theater each, their
own. Segreto had a number of exhibition outlets in both Rio de
Janeiro and São Paulo, but seemed more concerned with presenting novelty in various forms of entertainment than in consolidating a place in the incipient Brazilian film industry. A comparative
examination of production in Rio de Janeiro and the films exhibited in São Paulo indicates that few films were exhibited outside
of the locale in which they were produced. The exceptions are a
series of films by Afonso Segreto exhibited in São Paulo's Teatro
Sant'Anna in 1908. These films were in all probability the same
ones Segreto had exhibited earlier in Rio de Janeiro's Exposição
Nacional.[20]

One of the reasons for the failure of Brazilian cinema to stabilize on an industrial scale was precisely the inability to develop
and consolidate a broad market for whatever production did indeed exist. Another contributing factor was the general failure to
move toward a concentration of resources. Production companies

normally remained isolated from, and in competition with, each other. None of them had alone the financial strength or will to withstand the massive presence of foreign films in the Brazilian market. The one exception to this rule was Francisco Serrador, and he withdrew for other reasons, namely, because it was evidently more profitable to function as an importer, distributor, and exhibitor of foreign films than to invest the considerable sums necessary to develop a national cinema on an industrial scale.

Francisco Serrador

Serrador, a Spaniard by birth, had arrived in Brazil in 1900.[21] He was not highly educated, but possessed a keen entrepreneurial spirit. He arrived in São Paulo in 1905 and began working as an itinerant film exhibitor, traveling through the interior of the state and in Paraná with a troupe known as the Empresa Richabony. On returning to São Paulo in 1907, he began exhibiting films with surprising success in the Teatro Sant'Anna, which he leased from Paschoal Segreto for a short period. Soon thereafter he leased the Teatro Eldorado, which had been for musical revues, and thus established the first permanent, nonambulatory exhibition hall in São Paulo. The Bijou and the Grêmio São Paulo soon came under his control as well. An anecdote perhaps typifies his strategies. When a circus opened across the street from his theater in São Paulo, rather than changing his own offerings, he simply leased the circus and transferred his theater, which then became known as the Coliseu Campos Eliseos.[22]

His empire expanded further over the next few years as he constructed a new Coliseu and, in partnership with Antônio Gadotti, a new Bijou. He then acquired the Radium and the Íris, two of the principal theaters in São Paulo. In 1908 he hired *carioca* photographer Alberto Botelho as a cinematographer. Botelho had gone to São Paulo in 1907 as a sales agent for the Pathé Frères' representatives in Rio de Janeiro, Marc and Júlio Ferrez, owners of the Pathé theater. Serrador and Botelho made the ideal combination: they would consistently beat the competition to local events of interest, and quickly exhibit the films in Serrador's circuit. Serrador produced, and Botelho directed, the first feature-length film made in São Paulo, *O Crime da Mala* (*The*

Suitcase Crime, 1909), based on a sensational crime of the period. In 1910, after consolidating his position as the undisputed king of exhibition in São Paulo, Serrador turned his attention to Rio de Janeiro, where he soon inaugurated his first *carioca* theater, the Chantecler.

In Rio, Serrador became the leading competitor of Guilherme Auler in the production of singing films. In 1909 and 1910 he produced some forty-four such films, exhibiting them in both Rio de Janeiro and São Paulo.[23] Auler, on the other hand, produced only eleven singing films during the same period. Limited to his own Rio Branco theater, Auler simply could not compete in quantity or quality with Serrador. In fact, he managed to exhibit his films in São Paulo only in his rival's circuit.[24] Auler left the film business in 1911, whereas Serrador went on to create what was often called an exhibition "trust."

In 1911, Serrador's empire continued to expand with the inauguration of the Cinematographo Richebourg and the importation of Brazil's first nickelodeons (Araújo, p. 369).[25] In that same year, he created a new company, the Companhia Cinematográfica Brasileira, which was perhaps the first cinematic venture in the country to attract outside investors and thus go beyond the traditional family or partnership ventures that had characterized the industry to this point (and which to a large extent continues to characterize production to this day). His investors and board of directors included industrialists, bankers, and doctors. The firm was active in the fields of distribution and exhibition, production becoming increasingly a secondary activity.

In 1913 the Companhia Cinematográfica Brasileira announced an increase in its capital from 2.000:000$000 (around U.S. $640,000) to 4.000:000$000 (around U.S. $1,280,000) (*Salões*, p. 222). At that time the company owned two theaters in Rio de Janeiro (the Avenida, which had opened in 1911 to exhibit American Vitagraph films, and the Odeon), eight in São Paulo (Íris, Bijou, Radium, Teatro Rio Branco, Pavilhão Campos Eliseos, Smart, Ideal, Teatro Colombo), two in Santos (Guarany and the Coliseu Santista), one each in Belo Horizonte, Juiz de Fora, Curitiba, and Niterói, in addition to other less important establishments. At the same time, he was constructing the Marconi Theater and the Pathé Palace in São Paulo. His profits in the second half of 1911 and 1912 were on the order of 1.329:990$131 (around U.S. $425,600). The Companhia Cinematográfica Brasileira's income came not only from exhibition, but also from distribution. In 1913 it had some seven million meters of film in circulation throughout the country (Salões, pp. 222–23).

At about the same time that Serrador was consolidating his empire, independent distributors began to appear in Rio de Janeiro. The first film renters appeared around 1911. Pharmacist Honório do Prado, for example, operated the Cinema Jatahy, which rented films by Pathé, Gaumont, Urban Bioscope, and others (Araújo, Bela Epoca, p. 370). And yet even Prado felt threatened by the voraciousness of Serrador, as a newspaper advertisement of the period indicates: "We affirm that soon our establishment will be number one in Rio de Janeiro and that it will not be absorbed by the great tentacles of the trust [read Serrador] that is currently taking over some states" (Bela Época, p. 370). Prado was thus keenly aware of the unequal competition offered by someone like Serrador, who controlled an exhibition circuit that was inevitably attractive to foreign companies wishing to place their films in the Brazilian market. The Cinema Jatahy, however, was not immediately put out of business, and by 1912 had agencies in São Paulo, Minas Gerais, Rio de Janeiro, and Espírito Santo (Bela Época, p. 396). Other exhibitors, such as Stamile, also sold films that they had produced or imported.

Competition among importers, distributors, and exhibitors was intense, but Serrador managed to win out because of his superior business sense. Rather than compete, for example, with the highly organized Pathé organization, Serrador struck a deal that made him Pathé's exclusive agent in São Paulo, Paraná, and other parts of southern Brazil. He became involved in legal battles with Jacomo Rosário Staffa over exclusive importation rights to films of a number of European companies, such as the Danish firm Nordisk (Araújo, Salões, p. 213). By 1912 he controlled distribution rights in São Paulo to the films of the following companies: Pathé Frères, Gaumont, Éclair America, Éclair, Ambrosio, Cinés, Pasquali, Savoia, Itala Film, Film d'Art, Nordisk, Biograph, Vitagraph, Edison, Messter, Lubin, Imp. Film, Wild West, Pharos,

American Kinema, and Realiance. He also claimed to be the only person in São Paulo legally authorized to present cinematic "novelties" (*Salões*, p. 210).

Along with the change in scale of Serrador's company came a change in orientation as well. Emphasis was placed almost exclusively on the distribution and exhibition of foreign films. When asked if the company would also exhibit national films, Silvério Ignarra, one of the Companhia Cinematográfica Brasileira's managers, gave the following answer:

Yes. But the company will look for films with the perfection of foreign films. We will make films of views and aspects of the country's capitals, major cities, and picturesque and important sites of the different states. Once these films have been exhibited here, they will be sent to companies with which we have contracts where they will be exhibited in foreign theaters, thus constituting excellent propaganda for our country. (*Bela Época*, p. 395)

A number of things in Ignarra's statement are of interest. First, one can clearly see that the foreign film has become the standard by which all films are to be judged. Without a large market and without a strong industrial base, Brazilian films could not hope to compete with foreign films in terms of technical quality. Second, Ignarra emphasizes that his company will produce documentaries ("views and aspects"). There is no mention of fiction films.

Serrador, in fact, continued producing films until at least 1930, but the bulk of his production consisted of short documentaries and newsreels, including the *Bijou Jornal* (1910), *Atualidades Serrador* (1925–1930), and the *Revista Serrador* (1927).[26] These newsreels, many of which were made with imported footage, accompanied programs of foreign films in Serrador's exhibition circuit. The rapid expansion of his exhibition circuit, moreover, left even less room in the domestic market for national films. In short, the one person who, in the early days of Brazilian cinema, possessed the infrastructure to attempt to develop a national film industry preferred the ready profits of exhibiting and distributing foreign films, and even his own production was reduced to a secondary role in film programming.

FOREIGN CINEMAS AND THE END OF THE BELA ÉPOCA

After the relative success of 1908 through 1911, Brazilian production of feature films dropped drastically as the Bela Época gave way to what Paulo Emílio Salles Gomes has called a "decade of penury" for Brazilian cinema (see table 1). Several possible reasons can be ventured for the decline. Film renters appeared in 1911, providing foreign films at a competitive price. Exhibitors found it less attractive to produce their own films than to show the higher-quality foreign films. The distribution sector thus drove a wedge between production and exhibition. Besides, the producers' failure to significantly expand their own markets rendered film production economically unfeasible. A new standard of quality had been imposed by foreign films, and the small local companies could not compete. Many small exhibitors were forced out of business, furthermore, by the rapid expansion of Francisco Serrador's exhibition and distribution chains. The outbreak of World War I no doubt also had an effect, making raw film stock more difficult to come by.

More important, however, by 1912 the American film industry had organized on an international scale, leaving little room on the international scene for less organized concerns. The foreign takeover of the Brazilian market was easily achieved. During the first years of the decade, intense competition for Latin American markets existed between European and North American film industries, whose films were distributed by local companies. When early film "sellers" were replaced by film "renters," that is, distributors who rented films to exhibitors for a percentage of total box-office income, the situation became even more difficult for local production. Foreign films, which had already covered their investment costs in their home market, became less expensive for exhibitors than the locally produced films, which had to recoup their entire investment in the domestic market alone. The somewhat chaotic Brazilian market began to be organized for the commercialization of foreign films, and the incipient Brazilian industry began to lose its market.

World War I virtually eliminated America's European competition in the Brazilian market, and it was not long before Ameri-

Table 1. Brazilian Film Production, 1898–1930

	Documentaries	Fiction	Singing Films	Newsreels[a]	Total
1898	13				13
1899	16				16
1900	20				20
1901	11				11
1902	15				15
1903	6				6
1904	4				4
1905	5				5
1906	12				12
1907	16	3	3		22
1908	107	12	28		147
1909	96	45	64		205
1910	144	21	44	3	209
1911	107	8		2	115
1912	65	8		5	73
1913	66	7		7	73
1914	44	1		2	45
1915	31	7		1	38
1916	9	10		3	19
1917	18	22		8	40
1918	16	8		3	24
1919	24	17			41
1920	25	12		2	37
1921	21	7			28
1922	25	3		1	28
1923	19	10		2	29
1924	30	18		1	48
1925	37	23		3	60
1926	28	19		1	47
1927	64	21		1	85
1928	53	12			65
1929	32	26			58
1930	19	28			47

Source: Paulo Antônio Paranaguá, "Brésil," in Les Cinémas de l'Amerique Latine, ed. Guy Hennebelle and Alfonso Gumucio-Dagrón (Paris: Lherminier, 1981), p. 106. Based on statistics provided in Cronologia Cinematográfica Brasileira (1898–1930) (Rio de Janeiro: Cinemateca do Museu de Arte Moderna, 1979).

Note: Statistics concerning film production in Brazil are notoriously unreliable. Until a definitive filmography of Brazilian cinema is established, all such figures should be seen as approximate.

a. Refers to numbers of series produced, each of which varies with regard to number of films. For this reason they are not included in totals.

can companies, not content with sharing profits with local firms, set up distribution outlets in Brazil. Fox arrived in 1915, Paramount's Companhia Pellículas de Luxo da América do Sul in 1916, Universal in 1921, M-G-M in 1926, Warner Brothers in 1927, First National and Columbia in 1929.

American films occupied over 80 percent of the Brazilian market in the 1920s (table 2). The quantity and value of American exports to Brazil increased consistently during the same period (tables 3 and 4). By the 1920s, neither local nor European producers offered serious competition to the American film industry in the Brazilian market. By 1929, Brazil had become its fourth largest market (in terms of linear feet exported), trailing only Great Britain, Australia, and Argentina (table 5).[27]

Despite the massive presence of American films in the domestic market, Brazilian production figures showed some improvement in the 1920s (see table 1). Between 1921 and 1930, feature film production averaged 16.7 films per year.[28] These films, however, were made by at least eighty-two different production companies, excluding those that started production prior to 1921, making the average number slightly more than two films per company for the ten-year period. The leading production companies of the period were Luis de Barros's Guanabara Filmes (Rio de Janeiro), which produced eight films between 1921 and 1924 and a total of sixteen between 1915 and 1931; Gilberto Rossi (São Paulo),

Table 2. Origin of Films Approved by Brazilian Censors, 1922–1925
(in percent)

	1922	1923	1924	1925
United States	80.0	83.0	83.0	80.3
France	6.0	5.1	8.6	6.6
Germany	8.0	2.7	2.1	1.9
Italy	2.5	4.1	2.6	—
Brazil	—	2.3	1.5	4.0

Source: Paulo Emílio Salles Gomes, Humberto Mauro, Cataquases, Cinearte (São Paulo: Perspectiva, 1974), pp. 299, 357.

Note: Includes all types of films.

Table 3. Brazilian Imports of Motion Pictures, 1913–1927
(in metric tons)

	1913	1915	1920	1924	1925	1926	1927
U.S.	0.6	1.7	18.5	20.2	23.0	32.7	33.6
France	8.5	1.4	1.6	8.3	3.8	2.5	2.3
Germany	0.3	—	2.6	1.4	0.8	1.4	1.5
U. K.	0.2	0.3	0.5	0.6	0.5	0.4	0.4
Italy	8.2	8.3	2.8	—	0.1	0.2	—
Total	18.7	12.9	27.5	31.1	28.6	37.6	37.9

Source: U.S. Department of Commerce, Bureau of Foreign and Domestic Commerce, Motion Pictures in Argentina and Brazil, Trade Information Bulletin, no. 630 (1929).

Note: Totals include imports from other countries not listed in table.

Table 4. U.S. Film Exports to Brazil, 1924–1928

	Linear Feet	Value	% Increase
1924	8,405,094	$295,746	—
1925	10,725,826	337,209	14.02
1926	13,947,118	429,136	27.26
1927	15,921,565	420,215	− 2.08
1928	16,464,410	329,239	− 21.65

Source: U.S. Department of Commerce, Bureau of Foreign and Domestic Commerce, Motion Pictures in Argentina and Brazil, Trade Information Bulletin, no. 630 (1929).

Table 5. Overseas Markets of American Films, 1929 (9 months)

Rank	Country	Linear Feet	Value
1	U.K.	23,111,066	$1,049,760
2	Australia	21,153,317	485,652
3	Argentina	14,829,125	368,344
4	Brazil	12,673,107	303,807
5	Germany	11,532,705	354,501
6	Canada	10,609,548	462,734

Source: Variety, 12 November 1930.

who produced seven films between 1919 and 1927, with five in 1922 alone; Gentil Ruiz's Aurora Filmes (Recife), with five films between 1924 and 1926; Eduardo Abelim's Gaúcha Filmes (Porto Alegre), with four films between 1926 and 1932; Humberto Mauro's Phebo Filmes (Cataguases), with four films between 1926 and 1929; and the del Picchia brothers' Sincrocinex (São Paulo), which produced eleven films from 1929 to 1931.[29]

It should be noted that with shifting economic fortunes, production companies tended to appear and disappear with great rapidity, and that sometimes the same people organized a number of companies under different names in successive years. Although this may indicate more continuity of production than might appear to be the case at first glance, it also indicates the instability of the film industry and the inability of most producers to attain a sufficient return on investments to allow them to develop on a larger scale. The continued production of documentary films during the same period (an average of 32.8 per year), many of which were paid for by commercial organizations, suggests that this type of production actually sustained Brazilian cinema during the 1920s.[30]

As early as 1924 some sectors of Brazilian cinema began to call for state support of the floundering film industry. In the pages of *Para Todos*, for example, Mário Behring suggested that the government should take measures to support a film industry in the country.[31] Behring, however, was not concerned with the production of feature films, and he considered those made in the country to be a "disgrace." Rather, he favored the production of documentaries that would provide propaganda for Brazil abroad. He felt that the government should be concerned with the cinema because of its pedagogical usefulness in the struggle against illiteracy and the attempt to stimulate good work habits and hygiene. In relation to feature films, he called for foreign investment to help create a national film industry. At the same time, he wanted foreign producers to open offices in Brazil to provide competition for local distributors and exhibitors.[32]

Adhemar Gonzaga, on the other hand, was more cautious in asking for government support, suggesting that government-sponsored films usually make things look worse than they really are. In 1925 he joined with Behring in asking the government to revise customs tariffs on raw film stock. Previously, raw stock had entered the country at a price much lower than that of printed film, but importers began claiming that most of their film was stock in order to get it into the country at the lower rate. The government responded by adopting a single rate. This created an unfair burden on national filmmakers, who had to pay the same amount for their stock as importers did for printed film. The struggle lasted for years with no positive result.[33]

Gonzaga also realized that the main problem facing Brazilian cinema was that of exhibition. He felt, correctly, that the industry could survive on the domestic market alone if it could in fact reach that market, which was controlled by "trusts" whose interests were tied to the exhibition of foreign films. In Behring's film magazine Cinearte, Gonzaga idealistically suggested that film programs obligatorily include a Brazilian feature along with each foreign film. He later revised his suggestion to include only the compulsory exhibition of one Brazilian film per month, which, at that time, was almost as unrealistic as his initial suggestion. Gonzaga, and others such as Pedro Lima, made two additional unanswered demands on the government. In industrial terms, they wanted exemption from customs duties for raw film stock, and in commercial terms, the compulsory exhibition of national films. Their campaign on behalf of national cinema was somewhat less than successful. As Gonzaga was to write in 1927: "The interests of foreign film agencies are simply to defend their films' profits, and, as 'owners' of the market, impede in any way possible the entrance of new competitors, even if they are national filmmakers. . . . We need to have our cinema dominating our market. . . . Last year alone we made 14 films. How many were exhibited? None!"[34] The United States government tended to agree with Gonzaga, saying in an official publication in 1929 that the Brazilian industry plays an "insignificant role" in the national market for feature films, although it does note that a number of newsreel producers are active.[35]

In short, by 1930 the Brazilian film industry had been unable to stabilize on a satisfactory scale. Despite the great success of the Bela Época of 1908–1911, it had lost its market to the greater organizational and financial powers of foreign cinemas. The astonishingly rapid growth of the American film industry led quickly to an almost total domination of the Brazilian market. Although Brazilian feature film production never ceased to exist, it was sporadic rather than continuous, artisan rather than industrial. The film industry, as it existed, was largely sustained by the production of documentaries, often paid for by commercial interests. The 1930s, however, would inaugurate a new phase of development for the industry.

2

Sound, Studios, and the State, 1930–1950

THE STATE FIRST turned its attention toward the film industry only after the revolution of 1930 which swept Getúlio Vargas to power. Vargas, who had been finance minister in the government he helped depose and, previously, governor of the state of Rio Grande do Sul, was to dominate Brazilian politics until his suicide in 1954. The revolution which put him in office was the result of a bitter struggle centering most immediately on the presidential election of 1930. Vargas was the candidate of the Liberal Alliance, a loose coalition of opposition groups from Rio Grande do Sul, Minas Gerais, and Paraíba. He lost the election, but won the war, as disgruntled political leaders and army officers moved against and overthrew the government of Washington Luíz.[1]

The revolution was supported by a heterogeneous group that Thomas Skidmore divides into "revolutionary" and "nonrevolutionary" factions.[2] Among the revolutionaries were the "liberal constitutionalists, who wished to implement the classic liberal ideas—free elections, constitutional government, and full civil liberties." Assuming a different revolutionary position were the "semi-authoritarian nationalists," represented largely by young military officers (tenentes) who had participated in a series of unsuccessful revolts in the early twenties. The Prestes column had been an offshoot of these earlier revolts.[3] Concerned mainly with "'national regeneration' and modernization," they were a nationalist group that demanded basic reforms in the direction, structure, and functioning of the Brazilian government, although their programs were only vaguely defined.[4]

Among the nonrevolutionary supporters of the revolution

were high-level military officers who not only disagreed with many of the government's policies, but also felt that the needs of the military had been overlooked, especially since through the twenties they were repeatedly called upon to prop up federal and state governments. Coffee growers also backed the revolution, although they were largely from Washington Luíz's own state of São Paulo. They were angered by his suspension of price supports, a policy whose failure was exacerbated by the Wall Street crash of 1929, which caused coffee prices to drop by 50 percent in a period of less than five months. Other disenchanted political leaders also supported the revolution for their own purposes.[5]

The revolution of 1930, however, was more than just another struggle between rival political groups. It represented, ultimately, a fundamental shift of power from the rural oligarchy to the urban middle sectors and the growing industrial bourgeoisie. The "new" republic witnessed a concentration of power in the hands of the federal government that would have been impossible under the more dispersed federalism of the first republic. It created the conditions, in short, for the transformation of the argicultural-based "oligarchic state" of 1889–1930 into a "bourgeois state."[6]

In 1937, after "seven years of agitated improvisation, including a regionalist revolt in São Paulo, a new Constitution, a popular front movement, a fascist movement, and an attempted Communist coup," Getúlio Vargas initiated an eight-year period of authoritarian rule under the corporatist Estado Novo.[7] Even before the Estado Novo, however, Vargas had begun to take a more aggressive role in the defense of national industry and in the creation or reform of social institutions, political structures, and administrative systems. He created a Ministry of Labor, Industry, and Commerce in 1930, and implemented labor legislation which provided workers with tangible benefits while politically neutralizing them through incorporation in government-sponsored unions.[8]

Among governmental bodies created under Vargas's leadership were the National Coffee Council (1931), the Ministry of Education and Public Health (1932), the Sugar and Alcohol Institute (1933), the Federal Council of Foreign Trade (1934), the National Petroleum Council (1938), the Brazilian Institute of

Geography and Statistics (1938), and the National Steel Company (1941). These organizations, and many others which have not been mentioned, were not the result of a carefully planned program of institutionalization, but should be seen rather as governmental responses to crises and problems that arose in the course of administering the nation's economy and its political system.[9]

The authoritarian Estado Novo lasted from 1937 until 1945, when Vargas was ousted by the military. An interregnum democratic regime under the leadership of General Eurico Dutra ruled the country from 1945 until 1950, when Vargas regained power through electoral politics. The Dutra government represented at least a minor reversal of the interventionist policies of the previous years, which were taken up again when Vargas returned to the presidency. In the midst of a political scandal, Vargas committed suicide in 1954, leaving the Brazilian people a strongly worded, anti-imperialist, quasi-socialist message.[10]

Although state intervention in the film industry did not occur on a large scale, the 1930–1950 period was crucial. During this period, Brazilian cinema witnessed its first serious attempts at large-scale industrialization, initially with the Cinédia Studios (1930), and subsequently with Atlântida (1941) and Vera Cruz (1949). The less-than-satisfactory results of such attempts, especially that of Vera Cruz, led, in the early 1950s, to increased calls for state support and a new mentality regarding models of industrial development. Secondly, despite its limited scope, the principle of state support of the film industry was firmly established in this period. In fact, Carlos Diegues would write in 1975, not without a touch of overstatement, that nothing "essentially new" had occurred in cinema-state relations between this period and 1975.[11] Finally, Vargas laid the groundwork for the institutionalization of a corporative, authoritarian state, the very nature of which goes a long way toward explaining increased intervention in the film industry in the 1960s and 1970s.

SOUND AND THE CREATION OF STUDIOS

The advent of sound in the late twenties brought renewed optimism to those committed to developing a strong national film industry in Brazil. The first sound film exhibited in the country was Ernst Lubitsch's *The Patriot*, which opened in São Paulo's Paramount Theater on 13 April 1929. As had occurred in other countries, the coming of sound frequently provoked bitter debates, which were most intense in the pages of the Chaplin Clube's publication, *O Fan* (Rio de Janeiro), which had been created by Octávio de Faria and Plínio de Sussekind Rocha in 1928. The Chaplin Clube was dedicated to the struggle against sound and to the defense of "true" cinema, that is, black and white silent film. This debate would resurface anachronistically some ten years later in poet Vinícius de Moraes's journalistic film criticism.[12] Opposition to sound also had political implications. A São Paulo politician asked the government to fine exhibitors of English-language talkies to prevent the "corruption" of the Portuguese language and to save the legitimate stage from the degeneration that talkies were sure to bring.[13]

Within the industry itself, however, the arrival of sound was seen primarily in a favorable light. It was felt that foreign talkies would be unintelligible to Brazilian audiences and that local production would finally be able to take hold of the market without serious foreign competition. As a critic of the period wrote:

The appearance of talking cinema brought to each country the unavoidable necessity of nationalizing the cinematographic art.

We will also see ourselves in the situation of creating our own cinema. Movietone was the Waterloo of the American film industry. . . . With Movietone, the North American's commercial intuition has failed. Brazil will have its own cinema.[14]

Based in part on this naive optimism, Adhemar Gonzaga founded the Cinédia Studios in Rio de Janeiro in 1930 and was followed in 1933 by Carmen Santos's Brasil Vita Filmes and in 1936 by Alberto Byington's Sonofilmes, to mention only three of the most significant production companies operative in the 1930s.

Gonzaga's Cinédia was the first attempt at concentrated industrialization in the history of Brazilian cinema. Cinédia was equipped with four sets of sound equipment, a studio large enough to accommodate several simultaneous productions, and two laboratories.[15] Between 1930 and 1945 Cinédia averaged two films a year, with a high of five in 1936. The average cost of producing a Brazilian film in the 1930s was around $7,000, Cinédia's *Bonequinha de Seda (Little Silk Doll,* 1936) costing around $18,000.[16] Brasil Vita and Sonofilmes were less successful, the former producing thirteen films between its founding and 1958, the latter making eleven between 1936 and 1944.[17]

The optimism of those such as Gonzaga was short-lived, and sound actually contributed to a decline in the production levels of Brazilian cinema in the 1930s (table 6). Producers underestimated, on the one hand, the malleability and power of the American film industry and its ability to adapt to the problems caused by sound, and, on the other, the expense of making sound films.

Here again arises the problem implicit in the technology of filmmaking. The Brazilian public soon became accustomed to sound films, even though not spoken in Portuguese, and the technological lag caused Brazilian cinema to fall even further behind American cinema in the domestic market. The equipment for making sound films was of course imported, and the links of dependency were once again strengthened.

Furthermore, the coming of sound caused a decrease in the size of the Brazilian market, since many smaller exhibitors were unable to afford the expensive sound equipment. Attendance levels dropped by 40 percent in the first two years of the decade, and the total number of theaters dropped from 1,650 in 1930 to around 1,370 in 1936.[18] Of this latter number, 1,170 were wired for sound. American imports also temporarily decreased during this period, falling from over 9.5 million linear feet in 1930 to just over 7.5

Table 6. Brazilian Film Production, 1931–1940

1931	17	1936	7
1932	14	1937	6
1933	10	1938	8
1934	7	1939	7
1935	6	1940	13

Source: Alcino Teixeira de Mello, *Legislãço do Cinema Brasileiro* (Rio de Janeiro: Embrafilme, 1978), 2:558.

million in 1933, before rising to over 13 million at the end of the decade.[19] Brazilian filmmakers once again faced the reality of a market dominated by the foreign film, of continued under-capitalization of the industry, and of an increased dependence on European or American technology.

Some enterprising Brazilians tried to capitalize on the novelty. Julian de Moraes, the millionaire president of the prestigious Cruzeiro do Sul society, rented studios in Hollywood to make the first Portuguese-language sound film, The Soul of a Peasant (1929), which was distributed by M-G-M.[20] Paulo Benedetti, who had produced a number of unsuccessful Brazilian films in the 1920s, entered into an agreement with an American company to produce an inexpensive sound system, but the results were some-what less than favorable.[21]

EARLY CINEMATOGRAPHIC LEGISLATION

It was early in the sound era that the state first turned its attention—in ways other than that of traditional censorship—toward the national film industry. On 4 April 1932, President Getúlio Vargas signed into law Decree no. 21,240. This decree centralized all censorship duties which had previously been the prerogative of states or municipalities, created a censorship commission within the Ministry of Education and Public Health (composed of representatives of the chief of police, the juvenile court system, a professor, and a woman educator), and created a "cinematographic tax for popular education" to be levied on all films exhibited in Brazil.

Article 12 of Decree no. 21,240 established that "in each [film] program the inclusion of a film considered educational by the Censorship Commission [would] be obligatory." But more significantly, Article 13 determined that the Ministry of Education and Public Health would establish, based on the quantity and quality of national film production, the proportion of meterage of national films to be included compulsorily in each month's programming. These two articles established the principle of a screen quota for Brazilian films in the domestic market, that is, the principle that the Brazilian government has the power to set aside a portion of screen time for the exhibition of national products. At this point it is a small concession to make to Brazilian producers, albeit certainly not a noncontroversial one.

The government's own justification for the decree, outlined in its introduction, is couched primarily in terms of the educational value of the cinema, which should benefit popular culture, be an instrument of instruction, transmit a proper image of the country, and provide educational benefits for the "masses" of the Brazilian people. It should serve as a means of reaching the nation's illiterates and as an instrument of national unification. Two years later, on 30 June 1934, Vargas reiterated some of these themes in a speech delivered before the newly founded Associação Cinematográfica de Produtores Brasileiros (Brazilian Film Producers Association):

One of the primordial objectives of the Provisional Government has been that of stimulating the intellectual, moral and physical development of the Brazilian people.

Cultivating the land, polishing the intelligence and tempering the character of its citizens, adapting them to the necessities of their "habitat," is the primary duty of the State. Among the most useful factors of instruction the State has at its disposal is the cinema. An element of culture directly influencing thought and imagination, it sharpens qualities of observation, increases scientific knowledge, and broadens general knowledge, without demanding the effort and reserves of erudition that books require and that teachers, in their classrooms, demand . . . .

By supporting the national film industry, the Provisional government has fulfilled an imperious and irrefusable responsiblity. . . .

The role of the cinema can be truly essential. It will bring together, through its incisive vision of facts, the different human nuclei dispersed in the vast territory of the Republic. . . .

We must unite evermore, know each other evermore deeply so that we may evaluate the wealth of our possibilities and study the means to take advantage of them for the benefit of the community.

The cinema will be the book of luminous images in which our coastal and rural populations will learn to love Brazil, increasing confidence in the Fatherland. For the mass of illiterates, it will be the most perfect, the easiest, and the most impressive pedagogical tool.[22]

However, the decree does not fully corroborate Vargas's professed concern with "supporting the national film industry." Only

three of its twenty-four articles, the two mentioned above and
article 17, which reduces by 15 percent customs tariffs on positive
and negative film stock and on educational films, deal with the
cinema *as an industry*. Although the law, however tenuously,
does indeed recognize the right of Brazilian cinema to a guaranteed presence in its own market, it does nothing to hinder the
massive importation of foreign films which have historically glut-
ted that same market; in fact, it makes importation easier by reducing customs tariffs on imports, ostensibly to support the
exhibition sector. The American film industry saw the decree as
an essentially cooperative measure.[23]

Geraldo Santos Pereira suggests that the creation, in Article 18,
of a "Cinematographic Tax for Popular Education" represents a
timid attempt at increasing the cost of importing foreign films and
thus decreasing the number of films entering the country
annually, but in fact the new tax—three hundred *réis* per linear
meter—applied equally to nationally produced films and thus
represented an equal impediment to the development of the national film industry.[24] Film critic and historian Carlos Roberto
Rodrigues de Souza is probably more correct when he observes:

Instead of taking care of *Brazilian cinema*, the law addressed problems
which concerned the *Brazilian cinematographic profession*, meaning, in
a broad sense, all those whose professional activity was linked to the
cinema, that is, first of all, the sector of cinematographic commerce,
totally subordinated to the interests of the American film industry.[25]

In other words, Decree 21,240 addressed problems—tariffs, to be
specific—confronted by those involved in the importation and
exhibition of *foreign* films, and provided only token assistance to
those involved in production of Brazilian films. The tariff reduction took place immediately, but producers had to wage an
arduous struggle for the implementation of the article that provided for the compulsory exhibition of Brazilian "complements."
In short, the law had a little something for everyone—educational
sectors, film importers, and national film producers—but the
development of the national industry clearly took a back seat.

Responding in part to this decree, national producers formed an Associação Cinematográfica de Produtores Brasileiros (ACPB), the first such industry trade group formed among the ranks of Brazilian cinema. A distribution group, the Associação Brasileira Cinematográfica had been formed in 1927 to protect the sector's interests in the domestic market. The ACPB immediately began to organize, in accordance with Article 15, a Congress of Educational Cinema (Convênio Cinematográfico Educativo) under the auspices of the Ministry of Education and Public Health. The Congress, which included the participation of all sectors of the industry (production, distribution, and exhibition) was designed to discuss the general problems of the industry, to develop a program for the production of newsreels of national interest to be included bimonthly in all film programs, to develop film production for children, and to discuss incentives and economic facilities for national producers as well as distributors and exhibitors generally.[26]

After long and drawn-out discussions with distributors and exhibitors, the producers' association reached an agreement on implementing the compulsory exhibition stipulated by Decree 21,240 two years after the law was first enacted. The instructions for compliance with Article 13 were published in the *Diário Oficial* on 26 May 1934. They stipulated that each film session that includes a feature of over 1,000 meters in length must also include a "national film of good quality, synchronized, sonorous or spoken, using the movietone system, filmed in Brazil and developed in national laboratories, with a minimum length of 100 linear meters and approved by censors after the date" the law took effect. The exhibitors, who helped write this, were protected from a lack of quality Brazilian short films by a clause saying that the obligation would be suspended if such a shortage should occur.

Even when finally published the instructions met with virulent opposition from the same distribution and exhibition groups that had helped draft them. Exhibitors, organized into the Sindicato Cinematográfico de Exibidores (Film Exhibitors Syndicate), argued that the fact that they had participated in drafting them did not mean that they agreed with or accepted them. They insisted that the instructions were protectionist, which was in their view particularly unjustified since "the protection precedes *the industry to be protected"* (emphasis in original).[27] In other words, a national film industry did not yet exist, therefore it should not be protected a priori. Exhibitors argued instead for free trade and free enterprise while at the same time asking the government to establish a ceiling on prices they would have to pay for exhibiting national films. They also pointed out that the lowered customs duties for importation of raw film stock had not led to the development of the film industry. "It is not therefore justifiable," they wrote, "to make the exhibition of these films compulsory, that is, to make one businessman obligated [to act] in favor of another."[28] They failed to mention the fact that they received American newsreels free of charge from foreign distributors.[29]

At about the same time, the distributors entered the fray, ostensibly to oppose a proposal then under discussion that would transfer the censorship of films from the Ministry of Education and Public Health to the Ministry of Justice and a newly formed Departamento de Propaganda e Difusão Cultural (Department of Propaganda and Cultural Diffusion). They also opposed a planned 33 percent increase in censorship taxes, arguing that such a measure would eventually make the government lose money, since imports would then decrease, causing corresponding customs duties and import tariffs to decrease as well. The importing distributors, grouped in the Associação Brasileira Cinematográfica (Brazilian Cinematographic Association), furthermore protested the fact that its representatives on the ministry's Censorship Council had been replaced by a representative of the producers' association. The ABC had existed for six years, they observed, and in 1933 alone presented 1,200,000 meters of film for censorship, while national producers had presented only 20,000 meters. Nothing could better represent the almost total domination of the Brazilian market by foreign cinemas than the statistics presented by the importing distributors themselves.[30]

Opposed by such highly organized and economically powerful concerns, producers and other supporters of Brazilian cinema often resorted to ultimately emotional appeals for state and audience support of the still-incipient national industry. Critics in the film magazine *Cinearte*, which dedicated most of its space to American cinema, initiated a campaign in defense of national cinema and invented the slogan "Every Brazilian film should be seen," as if it were a patriotic duty to do so. As Jean-Claude Bernardet and Maria Rita Galvão have written, such expressions attempt to create a "moral imperative" in order to compensate for the absence of a true and profound relationship between national production and the Brazilian public.[31]

Patriotic justifications for supporting Brazilian cinema transcend the country's borders. We have already seen, in the words of Getúlio Vargas himself, the idea that national cinema could be used as an instrument of national unity and integration. During the 1930s and 1940s, arguments concerning the propaganda potential of the cinema were common. As a newspaper of the period wrote, "the day we project the smiles of our people and the splendor of our natural beauties across the screens of the world . . . new horizons will open to our country."[32] The need and importance of the industrial development of Brazilian cinema was thus rarely couched in terms of economics alone. Industrialization was seen, at least rhetorically, as a means to a pedagogical and patriotic end.

The public's apparent preference for foreign, especially American, films is well explained by filmmaker Humberto Mauro:

American superproductions appear regularly throughout the year. Thus the good films are mixed in with more prevalent bad ones, offering a compensatory average of quality so much to the liking of the public.

Brazilian production, however, being so sparse, cannot count on this compensatory element and at the same time has the disadvantage of being compared only to the best films that come from abroad.[33]

Up until the 1940s, the idea was not to protect an already existing Brazilian film industry, but to create one.

The ACPB managed, at least temporarily, to weather the onslaught of exhibitors and distributors, and the instructions for compliance with Article 13 were implemented as planned. Their effect, however, was short-lived, since with the Estado Novo and the creation of the Departamento e Imprensa e Propaganda (DIP; Department of the Press and Propaganda, 1939), the government itself began producing short films that complied with the statutes of compulsory exhibition.[34] In the first three months after the instructions were published, however, some 100 films were produced to fulfill the exigencies of the law. Such production inevitably provided producers with at least a partial income on which to base future production.

The activities of the ACPB are particularly germane to the present discussion for a number of reasons. First, the ACPB was the first industry trade group joining producers in a common cause. Second, its proposals, successful or not, find resonance throughout the subsequent development of the national film industry. Finally, the problems producers encountered in the early 1930s and expressed through the reports of the ACPB are remarkably similar to problems faced by future generations of filmmakers.

The most immediate problem facing the ACPB and its members, and one that has continued to plague the development of Brazilian cinema, was the producer's difficult access to a market dominated by foreign concerns. This is not to say that national films were never exhibited. Oduvaldo Vianna's *Bonequinha de Seda*, produced by Cinédia in 1936, ran for five weeks at Rio de Janeiro's Palácio Theater.[35] Rather, exhibition was sufficiently problematic to impede the stabilization and full-scale development of the industry. The compulsory exhibition of national shorts was an initial step, albeit a timid one, toward the amelioration of this fundamental problem. Other problems can be seen by examining briefly a project for a law protecting the national film industry drawn up by the ACPB in 1934 but never endorsed by the government.[36]

The ACPB project requests, initially, the compulsory exhibition in all programs of one Brazilian film of not less than 300 meters in length, rather than the 100 meters previously stipulated. The ACPB wanted police authorities to enforce the law, fining exhibitors who did not comply with it. A major problem throughout the history of Brazilian cinema has been that, at least until the creation of the Instituto Nacional do Cinema in 1966, such laws had been neither obeyed nor strictly enforced, creating a situation whereby existing laws are theoretically satisfactory for the development of a national film industry, but in practice are virtually useless.

Another major problem faced until today by Brazilian cinema is the lack of a stable capital market for the production of films. Film production is costly and provides a rather slow return on investments. Therefore investors have traditionally been hard to find. To compensate for this lack and to equalize costs and returns, trade organizations have often pressed for governmental subsidies and subventions. ACPB's 1934 proposal requested a subvention in the amount of 30 *milréis* (about $2.10) per linear meter for national fiction films, and 15 *milréis* (about $1.05) per linear meter for "cultural, scientific, or educational films, spoken in Portuguese and produced in Brazil." A commission would be set up to determine which films received such subventions.

The project also proposed a three-year exemption from customs duties on the importation of equipment used in film production, while at the same time requesting a 300 percent increase in duties on imports. They also requested the establishment of financial awards to actors and industry technicians. Finally, the ACPB project stipulated that only those firms which could show that 80 percent of their employees were Brazilian could take advantage of the proposal. Producers were concerned, even at this early date, about the possible internationalization of the Brazilian film industry. On another occasion, the ACPB proposed the creation of a line of bank credit for film production. As mentioned earlier, none of the ACPB proposals were enacted at the time.

In addition to these proposals, the producers associated with the ACPB organized the first distribution cooperative in the history of Brazilian cinema, the DFB (Distribuidores de Filmes Brasileiros), as a means of placing their short films equitably on the market. The idea was for production and distribution to work together to assure a continuity of production, to avoid excessive production (i.e., production with no chance of exhibition), to distribute among all member-producers the advantages and disadvantages of compulsory exhibition, to offer producers the least expensive distribution available, to make possible the financing of future productions, and to create a unity among those actively pursuing the development of Brazilian cinema.[37]

What were the practical results of the Brazilian government's first piece of legislation concerning the film industry? The educational sectors of the government received increased revenue from the "Cinematographic Tax for Popular Education," censorship was centralized, the importation of foreign films was rendered less burdensome by the decreasing of customs tariffs, the national film industry was provided some palliative relief by a reduction of import tariffs on raw film stock and through the implementation of compulsory exhibition of short films. That the new tax was diverted from cinema to education is indicative of the true limits of the concern Vargas's administration had for aiding the film industry in the early 1930s. It was interested less with the development of the industry per se than with the educational ends to which cinema could be put. This becomes even more clear in subsequent legislation.

Vargas's general program of institution building was not limited to economic areas. In 1936 he named a commission, led by anthropologist Edgar Roquette Pinto, then director of the National Museum, to study the possibility of creating a governmental agency designed specifically to use film as an educational or pedagogical instrument. On 13 January 1937, Article 40 of law 378, which reorganized the Ministry of Education and Public Health, created the Instituto Nacional de Cinema Educativo (INCE; National Institute of Educational Cinema). In that same year, not coincidentally, Vargas created the Serviço Nacional do Teatro (National Theater Service) and the Instituto Nacional do Livro (National Book Institute) as a means of incorporating artists and intellectuals into state policy.

The first governmental body designed specifically for the cinema, the INCE had, nevertheless, a strictly pedagogical function, forming part of what has been called Vargas's program of "informal education for the masses."[38] According to the law which gave it birth, INCE was created "to promote and orient the utilization of cinematography especially as an auxiliary process of teaching and as a means of education in general." The INCE existed for almost thirty years until its incorporation, as the Departamento do Filme Educativo (Department of Educational Film), into the Instituto Nacional do Cinema in 1966. During this period it produced or acquired hundreds of educational, scientific, and cultural films and film strips for free circulation to schools and other educational and cultural institutions.

The general guidelines behind its cinematic production were that films be: (1) clear and detailed; (2) unambiguous: (3) logical in sequence development; (4) dynamic; and (5) interesting as an aesthetic whole and in the details of its execution.[39] But the INCE did little to further the development of a national film industry, except perhaps to serve on a very limited scale as a training ground for filmmakers and technicians. According to Geraldo Santos Pereira, the creation of INCE in fact tended to retard the industry's development by giving the false impression that the government was supporting it, when in reality it was merely concerned with education.[40]

In 1939 the Vargas government raised the screen quota for national films to one feature-length film per year in all theaters in the country. The quota was provided in Article 34 of Decree-law 1,494 (30 September 1939), which organized and regulated the activities of the Estado Novo Departamento de Imprensa e Propaganda (DIP). Besides the screen quota, the decree-law outlined general classes and procedures of film censorship, made obligatory the insertion at the beginning or end of all film programs of propaganda messages furnished by the department, and maintained the tax for popular education.

According to this legislation, the DIP, headed by Lourival Fontes, was empowered to determine and pass judgement on the quality of a film eligible for compulsory exhibition, "taking into consideration its sound, synchronization, the correctness of its text, and its technical and artistic level" (Article 36). The law also preserved the compulsory exhibition of short films, considered to be of "good quality," with each cinematic program, but at the same time stipulated that the DIP itself would promote the production of films dealing with current events, public services, governmental initiatives, and historical reconstruction. What it gave with one hand, it thus took away with the other.[41]

This measure also reaffirmed that the importation of printed film and film stock would be taxed by weight and not linear meter. Finally, it included a highly controversial, and futile, item determining a modicum of reciprocity in cinematic trade between nations. Article 50 stipulated that importers of newsreels would be obligated to acquire, for export, nationally produced newsreels in the amount of 10 percent of what they imported. This clause was fought bitterly by foreign concerns, and when it was finally implemented in the 1950s, it temporarily cut off the flow of newsreels to Brazil until the statute was rescinded.

Despite the initiation of a compulsory screen quota for national feature-length films, this decree did not alter in any significant way the state's relationship to the film industry, which it still saw from an educational, moral and censorial perspective. Through the tax for popular education, it continued to drain the industry and divert the revenue to other areas of government. The 1939 law increased the tax to 400 réis per linear meter, an increase of 33 percent over the original rate established in 1932. In an attempt to bolster the development of national laboratories, the law included as well a provision granting an exemption from the above tax for foreign films copied in Brazil, but not for any sector of national production. It also provided the amount of 200 milréis for cash awards to national producers, but the awards were not implemented.

With Decree-law 4,064 (29 January 1942), Vargas created a Conselho Nacional de Cinematografia (National Council of Cinematography) within the DIP. The council, headed by Lourival Fontes, the director general of DIP, was composed of representatives of producers, distributors, exhibitors, and importers.[42] It was empowered "to establish norms for producers, importers, distributors, advertisers, and exhibitors of cinematographic films, regulating the relations between them, and promoting, regulating, and inspecting the production, improvement, circulation, advertisement, and exhibition of Brazilian . . . films throughout the national territory."[43]

The council was the first of a number of governmental bodies designed to study and make recommendations concerning the national film industry, and its creation made some Hollywood ears perk up. A writer in Variety warned that "this modified Hays Office will have absolute power over producers, distributors and exhibitors, whether Brazilian or foreign, operating in this country."[44] In reality, the American industry had little cause for alarm. The arguments of distribution and exhibition groups, traditionally aligned with the interests of foreign cinemas, generally held sway on the council, which did little to improve the situation of Brazilian cinema.[45]

The 1942 law also transferred to the DIP the power to increase the screen quota for Brazilian films in accordance with the development of production and the possibilities of the market. Such a provision reflected the increasing power and ideological nature of the propaganda arm of Vargas's Estado Novo, incorporating instruments of mass communication such as radio and cinema into the corporative policies of the regime.[46] Additionally, the law set, for the first time, the minimum rental paid by exhibitors for Brazilian films at 50 percent of net box-office income, a measure in effect until today. It also set the maximum commission to be charged by distributors of national films at 20 percent in the capital and 30 percent elsewhere. The law thus represented an initial step at regulating the commerce of Brazilian films in the national market.

Renewed Attempts at Industrialization

Despite a war-related scarcity of celluloid, in 1941 producers Moacyr Fenelon, José Carlos Burle, and Alinor Azevedo founded what would turn out to be the most successful attempt at continuous production on an industrial scale in the history of Brazilian cinema, the Atlântida Studios in Rio de Janeiro. Their initial idea was to develop a strong Brazilian cinema through the production of serious, socially conscious films. With this goal in mind, the company produced, in 1943, the films *Moleque Tião (The Boy Tião)*, concerning the life of Sebastião Prata, who is better known as the comic actor Grande Otelo, and *É Prohibido Sonhar (It's Forbidden to Dream)*. These and other films were not as successful as the producers hoped, and in 1944 they changed direction, making the ironically titled *Tristezas Não Pagam Dívidas (Sadness Doesn't Pay Debts)*.

Atlântida become truly successful after its acquisition, in 1947, by Luiz Severiano Riberiro, owner of the largest national distributor (União Cinematográfica Brasileira) and the largest national exhibition circuit. His organization dominated the Rio de Janeiro market, as it does today, as well as markets in the eastern, northern, and northeastern regions of the country.[47] Although his acquisition caused Fenelon and others to leave the company, it provided Atlântida with a vertically integrated system of production, distribution, and exhibition, a system that was responsible not only for the success of Brazilian cinema during the Bela Época, but also for the rapid growth and expansion of the American film industry in the first quarter of the century.

The Ribeiro-controlled Atlântida combined its powerful position in the domestic market with the production in series of relatively inexpensive but immensely popular film genres, notably the *chanchada*, or light musical comedy, often set at Carnival time. Between 1941 and 1977 Atlântida produced some eighty-five films. Its heyday was the period from 1945 to 1962, when it averaged over 3.5 films per year.[48] After that, the *chanchada* began to lose appeal due to the growing influence of television. Atlântida fondly recalled its production of this very popular genre in a 1975 film, *Assim Era Atlântida (That Was Atlântida)*, modeled on the American *That's Entertainment*. Atlântida was successful, in short, not only because of its advantageous position in the domestic market, but also because its production was geared for and based on the commercial potential of that market.[49]

The end of World War II also marked the end of Vargas's Estado Novo and a return to democratic government. The provisional government that preceded the election of General Eurico Dutra (1946–1951) replaced the DIP with a Departamento Nacional de Informações (National Information Department). Regulation 131 of the DNI, published on 18 December 1945, raised the screen quota from one to three films.[50] The new quota was confirmed the following year by Decree 20,493 (24 January 1946), which approved the regulation of the newly organized Service of Censorship of Public Diversions.[51]

Decree 20,493 reaffirmed the government's right to censorship of cinema and other forms of entertainment. It replaced the educators and intellectuals of the ministry of Education and Public Health's Censorship Commission with career police officers under the jurisdiction of the Ministry of Justice. Paradoxically, under the new democratic regime art and culture explicitly became for the first time subjects of national security.

Besides reaffirming, in Article 25, the compulsory exhibition of three national films per year in all theaters throughout the country, the decree maintained the cinematographic tax for popular education at the rate of Cr$0.40 (40 centavos) per linear meter for *all* copies of foreign films to be shown in Brazil: previous legislation had stipulated the payment of the tax per linear meter on *one* copy of a film, the other copies being exempt. National films, on the other hand, would continue to pay for only one copy, regardless of the number of copies in circulation. Foreign films copied in Brazil as well as national educational films would continue to be exempt from the tax. One innovation in the decree was that Cr$200,000 (two hundred thousand cruzeiros) would be set aside for financial awards to producers of Brazilian films. The decree also repeated the unenforced statute of 1939 law which obligated importers of foreign newsreels to acquire and export Brazilian newsreels in the amount of 10 percent of imports. Once again, this measure was not immediately put into effect.[52]

World War II had caused a sharp decrease in imports and a significant increase in exports, leaving Brazil at the end of the war with substantial foreign reserves.[53] From 1945 until 1947 there were virtually no restrictions on imports, foreign exchange was easily available, and the cruzeiro was overvalued at its prewar rate of Cr$18.50 to the dollar. Such a policy led to the rapid depletion of reserves, and in 1947 the government instituted a five-category system of import licensing based on the priorities of the national economy. Essential goods received high priority while consumer goods rated low on the scale. Limits were also placed on profit remittances.

Hollywood was somewhat less than pleased about this new turn of events. With the import licensing system, foreign distributors were limited in the number of films they could bring into the country. Quotas for 1951, for example, were based on the average number of imports during the 1946–1949 period, with little hope of increasing them. There were fears as well that income taxes on distribution profits would be raised considerably. As if that were

not enough, in late 1946 the government placed a ceiling on theater admission tickets (U.S.$.30 in the best theaters, U.S.$.10 in
others), and in 1948 it imposed a limit of 40 percent on distribution rentals. After threatening to quit the Brazilian market due
to "negligible profits," the Motion Pictures Export Association,
formed as an industry cartel under the provisions of the Webb-
Pomerene Export Trade Act of 1918, entered into negotiations
with the Brazilian government and reached an agreement con-
ducive to their continued profitable operation in the country, an
operation which netted the American film industry some $6 mil-
lion in profits in 1947 alone.[54]

Throughout the forties the American industry continued to
dominate virtually unchallenged the Brazilian market. Table 7
refers only to the number of films actually released, not to the
number of films imported, or, in the case of Brazilian cinema, the
number of films produced. Not all films imported are exhibited,
though they do serve as a massive reserve of exhibition potential
against which national films must compete, normally on an unequal basis. Most of the American films imported have covered
their investment in the U.S. market and can thus be sold at a lower
price than Brazilian films. In the Brazilian market one must consider as well that censorship certificates are valid for five years
and that films may be distributed freely throughout this period.
The total number of foreign films on the market at any given time
increases dramatically in such a situation.

After a slump during World War II, Brazilian production increased steadily in the late 1940s (table 8), and this relatively
stable production reflects not only the continued success of Atlântida and, to a lesser extent, Cinédia, but also the appearance of
new production companies such as Cinelândia (1947) and the
renewed activity of producers such as Moacyr Fenelon, who made
six films between 1948 and 1950. Even so, the number of Brazilian
films released during the decade never reached 5 percent of the
total number exhibited (see table 7).

In 1949, in one of the most significant achievements of the
period, the newly founded Sindicato Nacional da Indústria Cinematográfica (SNIC; National Film Industry Syndicate) sought
and attained exemption for a period of five years from customs

Table 7. Origin of Films Released, 1941–1952

	1941	1942	1943	1944	1945	1946	1947	1948	1949	1950	1951	1952
United States	383	363	320	307	310	325	307	313	304	357	441	314
Argentina	9	10	8	16	9	11	9	10	14	10	4	8
Brazil	4	1	6	10	6	7	8	12	12	22	23	34
England	20	17	17	12	8	6	11	19	17	16	25	25
France	12	8	8	5	—	2	14	16	13	14	17	35
Germany	11	—	—	—	—	—	1	2	2	1	—	5
Italy	8	—	—	1	1	1	12	38	54	35	23	46
Mexico	8	5	2	4	1	2	21	20	17	37	22	30
Portugal	1	3	—	—	4	4	2	4	1	3	3	6
Spain	4	2	—	—	1	—	—	1	2	2	1	5
Soviet Union	—	—	—	—	6	4	6	—	—	—	—	—
Other countries	1	—	1	2	—	4	6	3	9	5	15	41
Total	460	409	361	358	347	366	396	438	444	502	573	545

Source: Cine Reporter 19, no. 857 (21 June 1952); ibid. 20, no. 910 (27 June 1953).

Table 8. Brazilian Film Production, 1941–1950

1941	4	1946	10
1942	4	1947	11
1943	8	1948	15
1944	9	1949	21
1945	8	1950	20

Source: Alcino Teixeira de Mello, Legisláço do Cinema Brasileiro (Rio de Janeiro: Embrafilme, 1978), 2:558.

duties and import tariffs on equipment—including cameras, recorders, projectors, copiers, film stock, and other items—to be used in the installation of film studios and laboratories.[55] This was the first piece of legislation designed specifically to meet the developmental needs of the national industry. Although somewhat belated, the exemption is especially important when one remembers that all equipment used in film production in Brazil, including raw film stock, must be imported, and that the national industry is to a great extent dependent on such exemptions for the acquisition of the very expensive equipment needed for sustained and quality production.

Benefiting from the law, and in sharp contrast to the Atlântida Studios, were the Vera Cruz Studios, founded in São Paulo in 1949. Members of São Paulo's industrial bourgeoisie (Franco Zampari and the Matarazzo group) created Vera Cruz and modeled it on the Metro-Goldwyn-Mayer studios in Hollywood. The idea was to create a "quality" cinema, much as the same group had attempted to create a "quality" theater several years earlier by founding the Teatro Brasileiro de Comédia (Brazilian Comedy Theater). "Quality," in both of these cases, meant an elegant form of artistic expression designed to show that Brazilians too know how to make fine films and fine theater. It was to be an art, as Augusto Boal puts it, "made for the rich by the rich."

Vera Cruz imported top-quality equipment, contracted experienced European technicians to guarantee production quality, borrowed directors, scenographers, and actors from the Brazilian Comedy Theater, and invited Brazilian-born Alberto Cavalcânti— then in Europe—to direct the company. Cavalcânti stayed with the organization only until late 1950. Vera Cruz produced eighteen feature films, the most famous of which was Lima Barreto's O Cangaceiro, double prizewinner in Cannes and a worldwide success.[56]

The films of Vera Cruz, and of its "offspring" Maristela (1950) and Multifilmes (1952), improved the technical quality of Brazilian films, increased capital investments in cinema, and incorporated into national cinema the "international cinematic language," with its panoply of conventional devices: sophisticated sets, classical framing, elaborate lighting, fluid cuts and camera movements, scene dissolves, and so on. The actors, the décor, the costumes, and the music often were chosen to evoke a European ambience.

Vera Cruz set up an expensive and luxurious system, but without the economic infrastructure on which to base such a system. Too ambitious, it tried to conquer the world market before consolidating the Brazilian market. To reach the international market, it naively left distribution in the hands of Columbia Pictures, an organization more interested in promoting its own films than in fostering a vital Brazilian industry. In contrast to Atlântida, Vera

Cruz drove production costs far above the lucrative potential of the domestic market and was finally forced to resort to temporary, but ultimately suicidal palliatives to its problem of capital short-ages: short-term, high-interest loans from the Banco do Estado de São Paulo. Unable to recoup its investments in the domestic mar-ket successfully—only one of its films, *O Cangaceiro*, made a profit—and unable to reach the world market, Vera Cruz went bankrupt in 1954.[57] The "dream factory" which was greeted with such enthusiasm in 1949 quickly became a "nightmare factory."[58]

The creation and rapid demise of Vera Cruz sent shock waves through the industry and for many destroyed the perhaps unre-alistic dream of developing an industry based on the large-scale studio model. Such a system has only been successful in the one case of Atlântida, and even this was much more precarious than the extent of its production would seem to indicate. Historically, a small number of groups with large circuits of theaters has controlled exhibition. Their interests, and one must include Atlântida's Luiz Severiano Ribeiro in this group, lie not with the development of Brazilian cinema, but rather with the almost guar-anteed profits of American cinema. With the exception of Atlân-tida's distributor and foreign firms, no nationwide distributor for national films has existed until recently. The possibility of ver-tical integration based on a studio system grew increasingly remote after the failure of Vera Cruz. New strategies had to be formulated, but, as we will see in the next chapter, with the rise and fall of Vera Cruz it became increasingly difficult to reach a consensus within the industry as to what those strategies would comprise. The 1950s saw a marked politicization of discussions concerning the future of Brazilian cinema.[59]

3

Congresses, Conflicts, and State Institutions, 1950–1960

THE CREATION AND subsequent failure of Vera Cruz provoked an increased awareness of the structural problems faced by the film industry and the need for state intervention and support. This awareness was clearly reflected in a series of film industry meetings and congresses held in São Paulo and Rio de Janeiro between 1951 and 1953. A brief discussion of the congresses is essential, for from them would arise some of the principal ideological divisions that would mark the development of Brazilian cinema, and its relation to the state, over the next thirty years.

The general thrust of the congresses was shaped not only by the situation of the film industry, but also, and perhaps more importantly, by the political events and ideological debates that had taken place in the country since the late 1940s. Vargas's authoritarian Estado Novo had been deposed in 1945 to guarantee promised elections, which were won by former Vargas war minister, General Eurico Gaspar Dutra. Before his removal from office, Vargas had taken an ostensible turn to the left in his domestic policy, attacking foreign "trusts" and "cartels" which threatened national security and national sovereignty.[1] He would take up his nationalist, "anti-imperialist" stance again after returning to the presidency in 1951.

Also in 1945, Vargas had decreed a general amnesty which led, among other things, to the legalization of the Brazilian Communist party, which was outlawed again in 1947, and to the release from prison of party leader Luís Carlos Prestes. In the 1945 elections, the Communists won 9 percent of the vote, electing one senator and fourteen congressmen. The process of democratization and the resulting political freedom created a euphoric atmosphere in which national issues were debated with great intensity.

Thomas Skidmore recognizes three principal formulae for economic development as emerging in the late 1940s: the neoliberal formula, which embraced the rules of the marketplace, favored free trade and foreign investment, and essentially opposed large-scale intervention in the economy; the developmentalist-nationalist formula, which was only beginning to be formed at the time and which sought rapid industrialization based on a mixed economy in which the state would offer incentives to the private sector while at the same time pursuing an aggressive policy of state intervention through the creation of public and mixed enterprises designed to overcome bottlenecks and ensure investment in infrastructural sectors that were inattentive to the private sector; and finally, the radical-nationalist formula, espoused by the Brazilian Communist party, among others, which saw Brazil as an exploited victim of the international capitalist system and favored a radical transformation of the country's economy and an end to its dependent relationship with advanced industrial countries.[2] The tension between the developmentalist and the radical-nationalist positions would find repercussions in the Brazilian film industry congresses of the period, as well as in debates in forums such as the journal Fundamentos.

When Vargas returned to office in 1951, the public sector again became more active, although on the whole Vargas followed a moderate developmentalist path. Vargas's appeal was based on "his political philosophy of trabalhismo—a mixture of social welfarism, working-class political activity, and economic nationalism."[3] His program of economic nationalism centered most visibly on his campaign to nationalize the petroleum industry, giving the state a monopoly on drilling and new refineries.[4] The campaign led to the creation of Petrobrás in 1953.

THE CAVALCÂNTI COMMISSION

The first film industry congress took place within the optimistic atmosphere of redemocratization and nationalism. In a sort of prototype for the congresses, the Associação Paulista de

Cinema (São Paulo Film Association) held a series of round-table discussions in August and September of 1951. These round tables were sparked by Alberto Cavalcânti's proposal, then being prepared for consideration by the federal Congress, to create an Instituto Nacional do Cinema (National Film Institute).

Shortly before his inauguration in 1951, Vargas had asked Cavalcânti to form a commission to study the problems of the national film industry and to draw up a proposal for a National Film Institute. The Comissão Nacional do Cinema (National Film Commission), composed largely of filmmakers and critics, including Vinícius de Moraes, Jurandir Noronha, and Diário Carioca critic Décio Vieira Ottoni, drafted what was to be the first in a series of unsuccessful proposals for the establishment of such an institute. In Cavalcânti's words, his task consisted of

a general review of the laws that protect producers, the equitable distribution of raw film stock, the possibilities of penetration in foreign markets, above all in the Portuguese-speaking countries and Latin America.

It foresees as well the establishment of an artistic council for the a priori selection of proposed productions instead of the current a posteriori police censorship.[5]

According to the proposal elaborated by the CNC, which was then revised and sent to Congress by the Vargas administration, the projected Instituto Nacional do Cinema would be empowered to orient the development of Brazilian cinema, to oversee the importation, exportation, distribution, and exhibition of films and the importation and distribution of film stock, to produce documentaries of social and educational interest, to exercise prior film censorship, to establish technical and artistic standards for all films exhibited in the country, to develop protectionist legislation designed to guarantee the industry's stability, and to promote the financing of both short and feature-length national films. In short, Cavalânti proposed a virtual state monopoly of the film industry.[6]

The Cavalcânti Commission, as the CNC has come to be known, also proposed the creation of a film production company of mixed (public and private) ownership in which the government would hold a 51 percent interest.[7] The company, to be called

Filmes do Brasil, would only produce films directed by internationally known figures such as Yves Allegret, Alberto Lattuada, and Luis Buñuel.[8] Cavalcânti, who established his own filmmaking career in Europe with both the French avant-garde and the English documentary movements, had a decidedly internationalist view of the development of the Brazilian film industry, a view that would bring him into conflict with the local producers he claimed his project was designed to protect.

The round-table meetings in São Paulo invited Cavalcânti to discuss his project, but he declined to attend, sending instead commission member Décio Vieira Ottoni. The general thrust of the discussion was an attack on the project, leaving Ottoni little time to respond. The round-table participants opposed the creation of an all-powerful bureaucratic organization such as the proposed institute and favored a National Film Council, in which representatives of the industry would have a larger voice. They felt that the proposal gave too much power to the Institute, allowing it to control the distribution of raw film stock as well as to censor films *before* their production. Prior censorship of films has never existed in Brazil. They were also concerned that the structure of the proposed institute would lead to the domination of Brazilian cinema by foreign capital.[9] After extensive discussion, participants voted their disapproval of the Cavalcânti project as written.

The round tables, guided ideologically by the radical nationalism of the orthodox left, also passed motions defending the use of national themes and rejecting "cosmopolitan" or "denationalizing" themes. Such motions indirectly criticized the films of Vera Cruz, which were said to lack a "national character." Another approved motion set forth a definition of a "Brazilian film," an essential measure since under protectionist legislation such as the screen quota, only Brazilian films qualified. The round table's definition stated that a "national film is produced in Brazil, spoken in Portuguese, produced with at least 60 percent national capital, and has an artistic and technical crew consisting of two-thirds Brazilians."[10]

The points of conflict evident in the round-table discussions were outlined more clearly in the pages of *Fundamentos* by some of the round-table and subsequent congress participants. Debates focused primarily on questions of film content and models of film industry development, topics which are different, yet inevitably closely linked. Those who wrote for *Fundamentos*—Nelson Pereira dos Santos, Alex Viany, Carlos Ortiz, and Rodolfo Nanni, among others—felt that Brazilian cinema should draw from national customs and traditions. They criticized Vera Cruz for transmitting a demoralizing, false and humiliating image of the Brazilian people, a depiction deriving from the bourgeois mentality of Vera Cruz's founders. Opposition to Vera Cruz, and the image it created of the Brazilian people, was based on a recognition of class differences in Brazilian society. As Nelson Pereira dos Santos wrote in relation to the film *Ângela* (Vera Cruz, 1951), "We cannot accept as Brazilians those of classes that live at an advanced material level by exploiting the vast majority of the country's population."[11]

Vera Cruz was seen at different times as a 100 percent Brazilian company and as a tool of North American imperialism. By 1951, *Fundamentos* saw the studios as being compromised by their connection with Universal Pictures, which, along with Columbia, handled the firm's distribution. Universal, wrote dos Santos, "has in its hands a Brazilian Hollywood that produces films in its [Hollywood's] interest, at low cost, and in the country's language, which makes them all the more efficient."[12] He also attacked the company's cosmopolitanism as being characteristic of the national bourgeoisie: "[Cosmopolitanism's] presence in the cinema is the effect of the entire servile policy of the dominant classes in relation to the interests of North American imperialism."[13] The conflict is thus seen not only in foreign/national terms, since the national bourgeoisie is an internal, not an external, factor.

Fundamentos also criticized the industrial mentality of Vera Cruz and its founders, arguing that commercial success alone is not sufficient for the development of Brazilian cinema. The cinema also has an inevitable pedagogical function, and should "educate the people against the bad taste imposed by American cinema and help them struggle against imperialism."[14] Vera Cruz was under attack to the extent that it presented a falsified vision of the Brazilian people. As Mauro de Alencar said at the first Congresso Nacional do Cinema Brasileiro in 1952, Brazil must industrialize in order to develop. Therefore, the industialization of the cinema should be one aspect of the struggle. Industrial cinema, however, is a conventional, cosmopolitan cinema that mystifies the people, and so the struggle must also be against the industrial model then being proposed, in favor of a model that is at one and the same time "industrial" and "independent."[15] These ideas would be taken up again later in the 1950s and, especially, in the 1960s.

Perhaps in response to the founding of Vera Cruz, the work of the Cavalcânti commission, and the heated debates of the São Paulo round tables, the government modified the existing compulsory exhibition law, requiring all theaters in the country to show one feature-length Brazilian film for every eight foreign films exhibited (Decree 30,179, 19 November 1951). Assuming that all foreign films entering the country in, for example, 1950, were exhibited (and they almost certainly were not, at least not immediately), that would mean that Brazilian production that same year would have to be sixty films (it was twenty-two). The new quota, although attacked as being too timid since it did not limit the entrance of foreign films, clearly overstepped the productive capacity of the Brazilian film industry at the time.

Exhibition and distribution groups immediately organized to combat the 8x1 law, as it was called, and succeeded in undercutting it by pressing for and achieving the declaration of another law (Decree 30,700 of 4 February 1952) that revised Decree 30,179, making it refer to film programs and not individual films. This new quota effectively cut in half the maximum screen time for Brazilian films, since most foreign films were at that time exhibited in double features. Under the new law, an exhibitor who consistently programmed double features would have to show only one Brazilian film for every sixteen foreign films.[16] Assuming that each film program, whether single or double, was exhibited for a period of one week (which was not always the case), this new quota amounted to the compulsory exhibition of Brazilian films for at best 42 days per year.

Brazilian filmmakers have always argued that although a

screen quota is important, it is insufficient in that it does nothing to limit the number of foreign films entering the country. It treats the national cinema as the exception in the domestic market instead of resisting unbalanced competition by controlling foreign access to that market. Guback argues convincingly, based on the experience of European countries, that both screen and import quotas are necessary for protectionist policies to be truly effective. The American industry apparently agrees, for the MPEA has stated that the screen quota is the "least undesirable" of possible protectionist measures while it has consistently fought the implementation of import restrictions.[17]

The Cavalcânti proposal was approved in the Federal Chamber of Deputies in late 1952, but it died a slow, anonymous death in the Senate the following year. Opposition to the measure was widespread and often virulent. Cavalcânti himself accused distributors and exhibition "trusts" (read, in the first case, American distributors, and, in the second, Luiz Severiano Ribeiro and the Serrador chain in São Paulo) of attempting to sabotage the plan.[18]

At the time of the INC proposal of 1951–1952, Luiz Severiano Ribeiro controlled over seventy of Rio de Janeiro's movie theaters and was responsible for programming over 400 others throughout the country. His distributor, the União Cinematográfica Brasileira, founded in 1948, had become the largest Brazilian distributor in the country. He also owned a major film laboratory, a print shop for promotional material, and his own advertising agency.[19] While accepting part of the INC proposal, notably the centralization of the government's film activities, he rejected the right of the state to intervene in an economic area that he felt should be ruled by free enterprise and the laws of the market. "How can the state," he said, "dictate norms in an area in which it does not participate, in which is has no financial risk?" He also opposed the fact that exhibitors and distributors would represent a minority on the INC's Deliberative Council. Perhaps paradoxically, Ribeiro favored the 8x1 compulsory exhibition law, although he felt that Brazilian cinema would develop only when it attained a standard of quality equal to that of the foreign film and when the public naturally opted for the national film.[20]

Florentino Llorente, head of Serrador, the largest exhibition network in São Paulo, also opposed the INC project, proposing instead a reduction in the number of films imported. Llorente's argument was that when exhibitors were freed from the block booking that results from the overwhelming number of foreign films in the market, only the best would be imported, leaving ample space of the development of a national cinema. He too, however, opposed state intervention in the relationship between the producer and the exhibitor.[21]

FILM INDUSTRY CONGRESSES

As the Cavalcânti proposal was working its way through the Chamber of Deputies, São Paulo film industry professionals gathered for the I Congresso Paulista de Cinema Brasileiro (I São Paulo Congress of Brazilian Cinema), held from 15 to 17 April, 1952. The Congress was convened to elaborate a definition of "Brazilian film" and to propose measures to guarantee the economic and cultural development of Brazilian cinema.

All sectors of the paulista industry were represented, and thirty-three different theses or papers were discussed. José Inácio de Melo Souza divides the theses into three basic categories: (1) economic, (2) technical, and (3) political-ideological.[22] The economic discussions focused primarily on problems concerning film distribution and the shortage of production capital. Several participants called for the creation of a unified, collective, non-profit distributor for national films. Without such a distributor, producers would continue to be forced to rely on foreign distributors or on Luiz Severiano Riberio's União Cinematográfica Brasileira for nationwide distribution of their films, and it was unlikely that they would receive preferential or even satisfactory treatment from either of these distribution outlets. The idea of a unified distributor would become reality only in the early 1970s when Embrafilme created its distribution sector.

A shortage of finance capital has long been, and continues to be, one of the major problems confronting Brazilian cinema. This shortage historically has led to what is known in the industry as cavação (literally, "digging"), whereby filmmakers raise production capital through any means possible, often from personal contacts in other economic sectors. *Cavação* can include the production of paid documentaries or a process whereby a filmmaker combines small amounts of money from different sources, often in return for a frequently unfulfilled promise of prestige for the investor or the use of all his possessions as collateral on a loan. It has allowed filmmakers to make films sporadically, normally on shoestring budgets, but has not stimulated growth or continuous production in the industry.[23]

As an alternative to the precariousness of *cavação*, some filmmakers and producers have pooled financial resources with those of friends in the industry to form modest production companies. The Atlântida studios, which were so successful in the 1940s and 1950s, were originally created in this manner by Moacyr Fenelon, José Carlos Burle, and Alinor Azevedo. A very few people, among them Adhemar Gonzaga and Carmen Santos, transferred capital from more lucrative activities to the cinema. Most companies based on a share system, such as the Companhia Sul Americana de Filmes, have been dismal failures.[24] None of these options, in fact, have been able to sustain themselves without periodic influxes of capital from scarce outside investors.

For these reasons, participants in the São Paulo Congress saw the state as the "supreme source" of financial resources. They argued, based on a sometimes xenophobic nationalism, that a strong Brazilian cinema was essential to the development and preservation of the "national culture" and that the state had a moral and patriotic duty to defend it. If not, national sovereignty could be threatened. Appeals to morality, civic duty, and patriotism, first used by the film industry in the 1930s, continued in the 1950s. Despite the overstatement, congress participants were keenly aware of the problems facing national cinema and of the most likely source of their solution.

A number of concrete proposals were made in the Congress. Rodolfo Nanni, director of *O Saci (The Saci)* (1953), suggested that lines of credit for film production financing be established in the Banco do Brasil or the Caixa Econômica Federal (Federal Savings Bank). Carl Schell proposed the creation of a film bank, perhaps along the lines of the Mexican Banco Nacional Cinematográfico (formed in 1942) or the National Film Finance Corporation of Great Britain.[25] Others proposed financing programs either through the institutions mentioned above or, on the state level, through the Banco do Estado de São Paulo, which would provide up to 70 percent of total production costs. The Congress's final document, however, was not quite so specific, and simply recommended that the government's attention be called to the problem of film production financing.[26]

Technical theses presented at the Congress concern, on the one hand, the detrimental effect of theatrical acting on Brazilian cinema and the lack of a sufficient number of good scripts, and, on the other, questions relating to film workers and the division of labor in film production. In a scarcely veiled reference to Vera Cruz, participants denounced the "invasion" of Brazilian cinema by foreign technicians who, they argued, took jobs away from national workers. Reflecting the period's *trabalhismo* and the influence of the Brazilian Communist party, congress participants also raised questions concerning the syndicalism of the industry and the protection of workers' rights. Although some argued for the establishment of a minimum number of technicians per film crew, a measure which has had disastrous effects in Mexico, independent producers opposed such an idea since it would inevitably lead to increased production costs.[27] Despite the vocal concern with workers' rights, the Congress's final resolutions do no more than recommend the creation of a film workers' union.[28]

Of most interest, however, are the political-ideological theses presented at the Congress, which José Inácio de Melo Souza divides into four categories, some of which overlap with the larger categories mentioned above: (1) definition of "Brazilian film;" (2) protectionist measures; (3) organization and protection of film workers; and (4) ideological modes of expressing or discussing "Brazilian reality" on film.[29]

According to the Congress's definition, a "Brazilian film" must be produced with 100 percent national capital, be made in Brazilian studios and developed in national laboratories, have a Brazilian story, script, and dialogues, be spoken in Portuguese, be made by a technical and artistic crew composed of at least two-thirds Brazilians, and be directed by a Brazilian or by a foreign national living permanently in Brazil. This definition clearly reflects the strong nationalist sentiments of the postwar period.

Two theses presented concerned protectionist measures. The first, by Joaquim Carlos Nobre, proposed the creation of a National Film Foundation which would support Brazilian cinema at all levels. The Congress soundly rejected his proposal as being an attempt to infringe on the principles of free enterprise.[30] The other thesis, approved unanimously, called for the creation of a Committee for the Defense of Brazilian Cinema that would support the work of independent producers.

The question of the preferred thematics of Brazilian cinema was most forcefully raised by future Cinema Novo leader Nelson Pereira dos Santos in a paper titled "O Problema do Conteúdo no Cinema Brasileiro" ("The Problem of Content in Brazilian Cinema"). Dos Santos saw the question of film content as intimately related to economic and financial matters. Spectators, he suggested, are more interested in content than in technique, although they do know what makes a good film, and Brazilian spectators prefer to see on the screen stories that relate in some way to their own experience and, in a country with a high rate of illiteracy, that are spoken in their own language. They prefer, in short, national to foreign films. By making films on national topics—and dos Santos suggests adaptations of literary works by such writers as Machado de Assis, Aluísio Azevedo, Lima Barreto, José Lins de Rego, and Jorge Amado, along with historical films dealing with the abolition of slavery, the events of Canudos, the *Inconfidência Mineira,* or the *bandeirantes*—directors could attract large numbers of spectators and eventually wrest the domestic market from the hands of foreign distributors. This, consequently, would reduce foreign exchange losses caused by the massive importation of foreign films.[31]

Ironically, the American film industry evidently agreed with dos Santos, as Ray Josephs wrote that the Brazilian industry was making progress and would continue to grow, "particularly if it follows its more recent trend to concentrate on subjects and stories [with] a strong national flavor, rather than . . . trying to compete on a direct basis with the imported variety."[32]

The importance of dos Santos's proposal, made clearly as an alternative to the "cosmopolitanism" of Vera Cruz, is that it outlined a long-term strategy for the development of the Brazilian film industry, a strategy that would become the basis of the Cinema Novo movement in the early 1960s. By emphasizing the national content of films, he de-emphasized or even discarded what he saw as wrong-headed notions about concentrated industrialization. Brazilian cinema, he felt, should find its own industrial model based on simple production techniques—small crews, location shooting, low budgets—and the use of eminently Brazilian themes. Only thus would it break the foreign domination of the internal market and create and "free and independent" national cinema.[33] It was Nelson Pereira dos Santos himself who set the cinematic example, with the neorealist inspired *Rio 40 Graus (Rio 40 Degrees*, 1955), which painted a mural of *carioca* life, focusing on the activities of five peanut vendors from a Rio de Janeiro slum.

Before its conclusion the São Paulo Congress passed a declaration of principles, in which participants assumed a common commitment to struggle for a strong Brazilian cinema, and fourteen resolutions dealing with many of the issues discussed above.[34] In concrete terms, the most important result of the Congress was the recognition of a common unity and purpose among film industry professionals concerning the development of Brazilian cinema.

This unity and common purpose continued on a national scale in the 1 Congresso Nacional de Cinema Brasileiro (First National Congress of Brazilian Cinema), which met in Rio de Janeiro September 22–28, 1952, uniting professionals from all over the country. Although opposed by conservative critics such as Antônio Moniz Vianna, who would later play an important role in the state cinematic apparatus, the CNCB was given an official stamp of approval by the appearance, at the opening session, of the country's vice-president, João Café Filho.[35] The CNCB took up many of the issues discussed in São Paulo. It adopted the earlier congress's definition of "Brazilian film," established a Permanent Commission for the Defense of Brazilian Cinema, called for production financing from the state, and urged the local production of 35mm film stock.[36]

At the same time, the CNCB went farther than the São Paulo

congress. In a clear reference to the Brazilian-American trade treaty of 1935, it urged the government to reject any agreements that give precedence to the importation of films from one foreign country over those of any other. The hope was that American imports would decrease, allowing more space for films from other countries. The congress also requested that block booking by foreign distributors be prohibited by law, and that all foreign films be developed compulsorily in Brazilian laboratories. Block booking, which is in fact prohibited in the United States, ties the exhibition of a box-office success to the subsequent exhibition of a series of lesser films distributed by the same company. The result is the increased occupation of the Brazilian market by films of less than optimal quality, and even less room in the market for the local product. Having all foreign black and white films developed in Brazilian laboratories would cause an increase in import costs, and would thus indirectly limit the number of such films entering the company. The CNCB also requested exemption from all customs duties and import tariffs on the importation of raw film stock and production equipment, recommended that foreign companies be prohibited from distributing Brazilian films in Brazil, and called for the creation of a national film school.[37]

The industry attempted to keep the momentum of the two congresses going by holding the second CNCB in São Paulo from December 12 to 20, 1953. A shadow, however, was hanging over the second congress: the structure of the São Paulo studios (Vera Cruz, Maristela, Multifilmes) was beginning to show signs of weakness. The fear that the structure might indeed collapse was evident in the second CNCB's call to order: "Despite the progress achieved since the 1 CNCB, our film industry is at this moment undergoing a very grave crisis. It does not possess a solid foundation, and it has not yet achieved its hoped-for economic independence. National cinema reflects the crisis of the entire Brazilian economy, struggling against external and internal forces that impede its development."[38] The rhetoric of this call to order ("external and internal forces") finds resonance in that of the Brazilian government during the last months of Vargas's second term in office.

The second CNCB adopted the proposals of the first national

congress and formulated some of its own, recommending: (1) a standard definition of a "Brazilian film" (the same as that of the previous congresses, with the additional proviso that the lead roles in films by played by Brazilian actors); (2) the creation of a film school at the University of Brazil in Rio de Janeiro, and film courses at all public universities; (3) a study of the domestic market and the implementation of import quotas for foreign films; (4) changes in the compulsory exhibition law in accordance with the industry's development; (5) duty-free importation of 35mm film stock; (6) government subsidies for the local manufacture of raw film stock; (7) the institution of a system of credit for production financing using the revenues collected on imports; (8) the diversion of municipal taxes on public entertainment to national producers; (9) the creation of a national network to oversee and inspect box-office receipts and income reporting; and (10) the creation of an official organization, along the lines of Unifrance or Unitalia, to deal with the exportation of Brazilian films.[39]

INTERNAL CONFLICTS AND INCREASED STATE ACTIVITY

One should not presume, however, that the success of the congresses in bringing together film professionals and approving such resolutions eliminated differences and conflicts in the industry. A general consensus existed as to the need to develop a strong film industry, the need for state support, and the many strictly technical measures necessary for the industry's development. Strong divergences existed with regard to the industrial and cultural models to be pursued. On the one hand, some people associated directly or indirectly with Vera Cruz and other studios favored a mode of production based on large studios, a liberal import policy for foreign films, association, if possible, with foreign capital, and the use of cosmopolitan or "universal" themes.[40] This vaguely defined "universalist" group was composed of professionals such as critic-directors Rubem Biáfora and Flávio Tambellini, who was to play a major role in future state organizations such as GEICINE and the Instituto Nacional do Cinema.

On the other hand, independent or "nationalist" producers and directors favored an atomized mode of production based on the use of small crews, low budgets, and location shooting, the implementation of severe import quotas for foreign films, a total rejection of foreign capital participation in the national film industry, and the use of national themes. Nelson Pereira dos Santos and Alex Viany were, in the 1950s, among the leaders of this group.[41] Tension between these two sectors of the film industry, which began to be expressed in the *Fundamentos* discussions mentioned earlier, would in many ways shape its future development as well as the nature of state intervention.

At the same time, one should not overestimate these differences. A certain unity of purpose joined Brazilian filmmakers of all persuasions in a common cause. As Nelson Pereira dos Santos has said of Vera Cruz:

When I say we fought *against* Vera Cruz, there is an important nuance: we did not struggle against Vera Cruz per se, but against its mode of action, against the kind of cinema it was making. But we thought the existence of a production center like Vera Cruz was very important. And whenever we felt that Vera Cruz was threatened, we struggled *for* Vera Cruz. Because in a certain sense it was not merely Franco Zampari's Company, it was an achievement of us all, it was the possibility of making films in São Paulo. So everyone fought for what they thought Vera Cruz should be, not over its existence as such. We did not question whether such a film industry and production center should exist or not. We wanted to preserve what Vera Cruz had, but to do things differently with its resources. Above all, we defended Vera Cruz as Brazilian cinema whenever we felt that it was threatened by the greater enemy, which was foreign cinema. It wasn't simply cinema that we wanted, it was Brazilian cinema.[42]

I will be discussing such divergences and their impact on state policy in this and the remaining chapters of this book, but they should be understood with the qualification outlined by dos Santos: the goal of the groups (a strong national cinema) was the same, despite sometimes intense ideological differences; strategies were not.

The only immediate step taken by the federal government in response to the crisis in and pressure from the film industry was the creation, in 1954, of a Comissão Técnica de Cinema (Technical Film Commission) within the Ministry of Education and Culture.

The CTC was formed at the suggestion of SUMOC (Superintendency of Currency and Credit), which had concluded that national cinema needed financial aid to overcome the economic desequilibrium the industry was experiencing. The CTC was designed to study means of promoting the development of the national film industry, taking into consideration its economic aspects in international terms, since the industry, said the CTC, would achieve stabilization only if competitive internationally.[43] In other words, the foreign film remained the standard by which national films were to be judged, and the international market became the goal to be reached. The influence of Vera Cruz is clear in this formulation. Formed shortly before the suicide of Getúlio Vargas, the CTC had little practical effect.

More concrete action was taken on state and local levels with the formation of state and municipal film commissions in Guanabara and São Paulo. In 1955 the Comissão Municipal de Cinema of São Paulo published a report by Jacques Deheinzelein resulting from a study of the failure of Vera Cruz. The study revealed that of Vera Cruz's eighteen productions, only *O Cangaceiro* paid for itself in the domestic market, bringing in a return of 134 percent of costs. The other films averaged a mere 70 percent of costs, with some returning only 25 percent of initial outlay. To be an attractive investment a film must achieve a return of 140 percent of costs. According to the study there were two ways of achieving this: (1) reduce costs of production, and (2) increase the film's income. Income may be increased by raising the precentage received by the producer (established by law as 50 percent of net box-office receipts minus the distributor's commission, which averaged 20 percent of the producer's share), by raising ticket prices, or by increasing the number of spectators.

The study concluded that it would be difficult to raise the percentage received by the producer since the amount was already high in comparison with that received in other countries. Ticket prices, however, should be raised, since they were 5.5 percent less in 1955 than they had been in 1939. Ticket prices were and are controlled by agencies within the Ministry of Finance. Controlled prices, the study suggested, had resulted in the formation of exhibition "trusts" (read Serrador and Ribeiro) which worked against Brazilian cinema. The number of spectators for national films would increase naturally when producers had a sufficient return on their investment to improve the quality of their films and to maintain an uninterrupted, continuous production which would foster the habit of seeing national films.[44] The first practical result of the commission's work was an important and precedent-setting piece of legislation, municipal law 4854 (30 December 1955).

Law 4854 established financial awards or subsidies for all Brazilian films produced and exhibited in São Paulo. It included films produced in other states so long as programs of reciprocity existed in the home state (i.e., films from Guanabara would be eligible for awards if *paulista* films received equal treatment in Guanabara). The subsidies provided producers an additional income in the amount of 15 percent of the gross profits of their films as well as an additional 10 percent for films of "recognized technical and artistic value." This meant, in the best of terms, that a producer could receive, besides the normal income from exhibition, an additional 25 percent.[45] This law, although on the state level, represents the first governmental subsidy of the national film industry and had far-reaching consequences for its development, since it attempted for the first time to equalize the average cost of a film with the average income (normally below cost) and provided producers with an incentive to accelerate production. The State of Guanabara passed a similar law in the early 1960s, partly to support local production and partly to enable locally produced films to participate, through the reciprocity clause, in the São Paulo program.

São Paulo also set up a program of production financing through the Banco do Estado de São Paulo. This program represented the first direct state support of the production of Brazilian films.[46] The bank financed, through low-interest loans, four films in 1956 and nine in 1957, most of which were produced by Brasil Filmes, a company established in 1956. This helped maintain the vitality of *paulista* production despite the failure of Vera Cruz and other studios.[47] Brasil Filmes, in fact, was in many ways a continuation of Vera Cruz, using its studios and much of its personnel.

Pressure for increased state assistance continued to mount throughout the decade. Antônio A. de Cavalheiro Lima, who worked with Vera Cruz, repeated many of the conclusions of the São Paulo commission in an article, published in 1956, symptomatically titled "Cinema: Problema do Governo" ("Cinema: A Governmental Problem").[48] The author adopted an ideological strategy that would be used by film professionals over the next twenty-five years, arguing that a strong national cinema can be instrumental in the formation of a national identify and, therefore, is properly an area of governmental concern. Cavalheiro Lima argued that the industry, presenting a positive image of the country abroad, could also contribute to the country's economic development by helping to create foreign markets for Brazilian goods. Development of the national industry had been impeded, he suggested, by legislation which dealt with the commercialization of films and not with their production. The nonexistence of import restrictions, low ticket prices, and the lack of state support were seen as key factors in the industry's permanent crisis and current chaos.

In conclusion, Cavalheiro Lima called for a revision of import tariffs so that foreign films would be taxed by linear meter and not by weight, and for governmental use of these tariffs to support the national industry. He also proposed the creation of a fund for production financing in the Banco do Brasil derived from a 15 percent tax on admission tickets. This fund would allow producers to finance up to 70 percent of their production costs. The 15 percent tax on Brazilian films would revert directly to producers rather than going into the fund. Finally, he proposed that the fund also provide a 10 percent exhibition subsidy much like the municipal law in São Paulo.

KUBITSCHEK AND THE PROLIFERATION OF STATE AGENCIES

In 1955, Juscelino Kubitschek was elected president of Brazil. Promising fifty years of development in five, Kubitschek embarked on an ambitious plan of economic expansion and industrial development. He was the only president in the 1930–1964 period to remain in office, legally, throughout his designated

term, partially because of his ability to rally the Brazilian people
around the common ideology of developmentalism.[49] Brasília,
with its ultramodern architecture, is perhaps the most perfect
symbol of Kubitschek's developmentalist ideology. His brand of
developmentalism, however, was fraught with contradiction. Although it was a means of mobilizing support and guaranteeing the
system's stability, it was also an effective tool for controlling
social and political tensions. It toyed with the people's nationalist
sentiments, but based its program of industrialization on foreign
investment.

In response to the events of the previous two years and the
collective force of arguments such as those of Cavalheiro Lima, as
well as to a specific request from the Sindicato Nacional da Indústria Cinematográfica (SNIC), Kubitschek formed a Comissão
Federal de Cinema (Federal Film Commission) on 12 December
1956 to "provide the national film industry adequate means for its
stability and development, taking into consideration the position
of cinema in the cultural and artistic as well as economic fields."[50]
Composed of representatives of all sectors of the film industry,
including Cavalheiro Lima (production), Luiz Severiano Ribeiro
(distribution and exhibition), Paulo Emílio Salles Gomes (from São
Paulo's cinemateca), and Vinícius de Moraes (film criticism), the
CFC existed for only three years before Kubitschek, at the CFC's request, formed the Grupo de Estudos da Indústria Cinematográfica
(GEIC; Film Industry Study Group).

The CFC was divided into five different work groups, each
accounting for a specific area of cinematic activity: (1) the study
and writing of a substitute project for the creation of an Instituto
Nacional do Cinema; (2) legislation, codification, inspection, and
censorship; (3) financing and taxes; (4) exchange rates and
customs duties; (5) cultural and educational aspects of the
cinema.[51]

One of the CFC's principal achievements was the passage of
legislation ending the American film industry's abuse of the Brazilian exchange system. In 1953 the government created a multiple exchange rate system which classified imports into five
categories depending on their "degree of essentiality."[52] The cruzeiro at that time was artificially overvalued at 18.72 to the dollar.

Imports considered essential were purchased at or near the official rate, while inessential or superfluous imports were forced to use the higher free market rate. Although SUMOC's Instruction 118 had placed foreign films in the fourth category, they had been entering the country between 1954 and 1957 without exchange cover; 70 percent of allowable income had been exchanged at the official rate and only 30 percent at the free market rate (see table 9).

This represented, for all intents and purposes, a program of fiscal incentives for foreign cinemas from the Brazilian government. The practice ended with the enactment, due in part to pressure from the CFC, of tariff law no. 3244 (14 August 1957).[53]

The CFC, like the CNC and CTC before it, had no executive power and was limited to making suggestions to the president. Its reports and suggestions primarily concerned technical matters such as exchange rates and, as we have seen, profit remittances, but also dealt with questions such as censorship and the support of cultural institutions. It requested the transferral of censorship to the Ministry of Education and Culture; and it urged the government to provide funds to rebuild São Paulo's *cinemateca*, which had been destroyed by fire. It also revised Cavalcânti's defunct project for the creation of a national film institute.[54] Recognizing the limitations of its organization and powers, the CFC proposed to Kubitschek the creation of the Grupo de Estudos Cinematográficos (GEIC) to further its work.

Table 9. Profit Remittances by Foreign Distributors, 1954–1960
(in U.S. $1,000)

	Total	At Official Exchange Rate	At Free Market Rate
1954	8,962	8,962	—
1955	12,496	10,906	1,590
1956	10,239	8,018	2,221
1957	10,271	8,671	1,600
1958	9,690	490	9,200
1959	5,728	—	5,728
1960	6,085	—	6,085

Source: *Revista do GEICINE* 1 (1961), 14.

Although largely ineffectual, the CFC met with virulent op-position, not only for importers of foreign films, but also from *Correio da Manhã* critic Antônio Moniz Vianna, who renamed it the Comissão Federal do Abacaxi (literally: Federal Pineapple Commission; the term *abacaxi*—pineapple—is often used in Por-tuguese in situations where we might use the word "lemon," especially when referring to less-than-reliable cars). He claimed that the commission was dominated by "swindlers, communists, and useful innocents."[55] An ardent defender of American cinema, Vianna was incensed that the commission would discuss the lim-itation of imports of foreign films. In the sixties, his opposition was neutalized when he was invited to participate in the work of future governmental agencies such as GEICINE.

GEIC was created by executive Decree no. 44,853 on 13 No-vember 1958. Its purpose, much like the CFC's before it, was to study and provide suggestions for incentives to the Brazilian film industry. Also like the CFC, but unlike groups designed to study other economic areas such as the automobile and ship-building industries, GEIC was limited by its lack of executive power. Headed by the minister of Education and Culture, GEIC was com-posed of eight members, most of whom represented what Sérgio Villela and José Mário Ortiz Ramos have called the "universalist" tendency within the film industry:[56] Antônio Augusto de Cav-alheiro Lima, Flávio Tambellini, Jacques Deheinzelein, critic Francisco Luiz de Almeida Salles, Joaquim de Melo Bastos, José Geraldo Santos Pereira, José de Silveira Sampaio, and Luiz Seve-riano Ribeiro.

GEIC proved to be an essentially technical, ostensibly non-ideological organization. It, like its predecessors and the con-gresses earlier in the decade, made recommendations concerning import tariffs, production financing, the proposed Instituto Nacional do Cinema, and the lack of local production of raw film stock. At GEIC's suggestion, Kubitschek signed Decree 47,466 (22 December 1959) revising the compulsory exhibition law. Accord-ing to this revision, all theaters must exhibit Brazilian films at least forty-two days per year, fourteen days in each four-month period, including two Saturdays and two Sundays.[57] Since it depended on the largesse of the federal government, which, despite the rhetoric, still did not consider the cinema an essential activity, GEIC's efforts were largely ineffective.

When asked, in 1959, what was necessary to improve Brazilian cinema, São Paulo producer and director Walter Hugo Khoury responded with an answer very similar to those given since the 1930s: financial aid from the states and the federal government; subsidy programs in other states similar to that in São Paulo; more accessible raw film stock; modification of the system of exhibition and distribution; and a high level of creativity.[58] Critic Francisco Luiz de Almeida Salles, a member of GEIC, responded to the same question by saying that "there is no customs protection, there are no norms to facilitate distribution abroad or at home, there is no program of financing to stimulate production."[59]

Despite these problems, Brazilian film production averaged 31.5 films per year between 1951 and 1960 (see table 10). One should remember when examining table 10 that the 8x1 compulsory exhibition law went into effect in 1951 and was modified in 1952, and that the screen quota was set at forty-two days per year in 1956. The increase over the previous decade (which averaged only eleven films per year) is due not only to the increased screen quota, but also to the appearance of Vera Cruz, Maristela, and Multifilmes early in the decade (they collectively produced thirty-eight films during the period); to the continued production by Atlântida (an average of 3.8 films per year); and to the appearance of new companies such as Brasil Filmes, which produced eight films between 1956 and 1959, Herbert Richers, which was founded in 1956 and averaged over three films per year in the 1950s and more in the 1960s, Oswaldo Massaini's Cinedistri, which was founded in 1957 and produced, among many others, Anselmo Duarte's award-winning *O Pagador de Promessas* (*The Given Word*, 1962), and Amâcio Mazzaropi's P.A.M. Filmes (1959), which produced continuously into the 1980s.[60]

The 1960s would be crucial for the future development of Brazilian cinema, not only in economic terms and in terms of state intervention, but also in cultural and ideological terms with the appearance of Cinema Novo and its new concept of film practice. By 1960 it was widely accepted in the industry that state support was needed, but a consensus did not exist concerning the shape

Table 10. Brazilian Feature Film Production, 1951–1960

1951	22	1956	29
1952	34	1957	36
1953	29	1958	44
1954	25	1959	34
1955	28	1960	34

Source: Alcino Teixeira de Mello, Legislação do Cinema Brasileiro (Rio de Janeiro: Embrafilme, 1978), 2:558.

that support would take. Relations between the state and the industry would deepen in 1961 with the creation, during the fleeting presidency of Jânio Quadros, of the Grupo Executivo da Indústria Cinematográfica (GEICINE; Executive Group of the Film Industry), which finally achieved, after some five years of arduous study, internal struggles, and lobbying, the creation of the Instituto Nacional do Cinema. With GEICINE, the subject of chapter 4, a state policy toward the cinema finally began to take more concrete shape.

4

Cinema Novo and GEICINE, 1960-1966

GEICINE WAS CREATED by Decree 50,278 on 17 February 1961. Jânio Quadros, who had just recently taken office as Brazil's president, chose the head of São Paulo's municipal film commission, Flávio Tambellini, as president of GEICINE. Tambellini's prestige was enhanced by the fact that he was the brother-in-law of former director of the BNDE (National Bank for Economic Development) and future ambassador and finance minister Roberto Campos.[1] GEICINE was the first of the many commissions or groups designed to study problems of the film industry to have executive power, although its power derived not so much from specific legal attributes, as from its greater articulation with key ministries and governmental agencies.

Initially subordinated directly to the president of the republic, and later to the Ministry of Industry and Commerce, GEICINE possessed a degree of autonomy and decision making power unknown to its predecessors.[2] Its executive council was composed of representatives of the president; the Ministries of Justice, Foreign Affairs, and Education and Culture; the BNDE; the Banco do Brasil's departments of Agricultural and Industrial Credit (CREAI), Foreign Trade (CACEX), and Foreign Exchange (Carteira de Câmbio); the Council of Customs Policy (Conselho de Política Aduaneira), and the Superintendency of Money and Credit (SUMOC). The Consultative Council, designed to make recommendations to the executive council, was composed of Tambellini, critic-director Rubem Biáfora, *Correio da Manhã* critic Antônio Moniz Vianna (who, it may be recalled, was so vociferous in his opposition to earlier governmental agencies), producer

87

Manoel Lopes de Oliveira, laboratory representative Desidério Gross, producer Herbert Richers, actress Lola Brah, critic Almeida Salles, exhibitor Florentino Llorente, and distributor Arnaldo Zonari.[3]

The five years of GEICINE's existence—it was incorporated by the Instituto Nacional do Cinema in late 1966—were tumultuous ones in Brazil. After the relative political stability of the Kubitschek administration came a period of chronic instability which led, finally, to the military coup d'état of 1964. In 1960, former São Paulo governor Jânio Quadros was elected to the presidency. In a move which to this day is not totally explained, he resigned in August of 1961, a short seven months after taking office. His vice-president, Vargas protegé João Goulart, was making a state visit to the Republic of China. Some sectors of the military were strongly opposed to Goulart's succession, and as a compromise solution, Congress adopted an amendment establishing a parliamentary system of government.[4]

Goulart returned to Brazil and assumed a weakened presidency. He regained full powers in 1963 after winning a plebiscite rejecting the parliamentary amendment of 1961. But he was unable to gain the confidence of the military at the same time that he alienated much of the country's middle sectors (and the United States) by his apparent political move to the Left. Ideological polarization increased throughout his administration, with both the extreme right and the extreme left calling for undemocratic solutions to Brazil's economic crisis and political unrest. The military, long unhappy with Goulart, moved against him on 31 March 1964, thus initiating a twenty-one-year period of military rule.

The film industry was not exempt from this tumultuous atmosphere, witnessing the appearance of the internationally acclaimed Cinema Novo movement and of the increasingly exacerbated tensions within the industry. Cinema Novo, as part of an ongoing process of cultural transformation, reflects the ideological contradictions of Brazilian society as a whole.[5] The initial phase of Cinema Novo (1960–1964) was informed by a number of historical factors and was influenced to a large degree by the Instituto Superior de Estudos Brasileiros (Higher Institute of Brazilian Studies), which was created by Kubitschek in 1955 with the

express purpose of formulating a national ideology of development. Although it would be simplistic to see Cinema Novo merely
as a reflection of the ideology of ISEB—indeed, at times Cinema
Novo films directly revealed the contradictions of that ideology—
it is nonetheless important to be aware of the kinds of political
and ideological discussions that were taking place and to examine
how Cinema Novo relates to them.[6]

The ISEB was composed of intellectuals of various political
persuasions, including Hélio Jaguaribe, Cândido Mendes, Álvaro
Vieira Pinto, Nelson Werneck Sodré, and Roland Corbisier. Although members of the institute did not always agree on precisely
the concepts used, they did share a number of fundamental ideas.
First of all, they saw autonomous, national, industrial development as an absolute value, as an unquestionable end to be
achieved through a variety of means. And perhaps paradoxically,
given the Institute's makeup, the development they spoke of was
based on a capitalist mode of production. It was only after a stage
of advanced capitalism was achieved that the question of alternative modes of production could be contemplated.

The members of ISEB formulated a nationalist thesis based on
a radical awareness of Brazil's underdevelopment, which was
caused by what they called the country's "colonial situation," its
dependency on advanced industrial powers.[7] They saw the continuation of such relations as an impediment to autonomous
development. They therefore conceived the major contradiction
of Brazilian society as being not capital versus labor, but rather the
"nation" (that which is authentic) versus the "anti-nation" (that
which is alienated from the "nation's" true historical being). The
contradiction was set forth in these terms, rather than, for example, foreign versus national, because they saw imperialism
not as an external determinant but rather as an internal or "inter-
nalized" force in Brazilian society.

The "nation," seen as that part of society which is modern and
progressive, included the industrial bourgeoisie, the urban and
rural proletariat, and the productive sector of the middle class.
The "anti-nation," or that part of society which is traditional,
retrograde, and archaic, including large landowners, export-
import groups, the nonproductive sector of the middle class, and

certain portions of the proletariat; in other words, sectors whose interests lie not with national development but rather with the continued foreign domination of the nation's economy. This dichotomy reflects a dualist vision of society with, on the one hand, a feudal-rural sector dominated by an oligarchy whose interests are tied, through the export economy, to those of industrialized countries, and, on the other, a modern, urban, industrial society led by a supposedly progressive national industrial bourgeoisie dedicated to autonomous national capitalist development. The "nation" / "anti-nation" dichotomy as formulated by ISEB cuts across class lines and thus attempts to efface or ignore questions of class conflict, which, once again, are conveniently postponed until after full capitalist development is achieved.

The intellectuals associated with ISEB felt that for autonomous national development to occur, it was necessary for an enlightened intelligentsia to create an authentic, national, critical consciousness of the country's underdevelopment and its causes, thereby overcoming the country's alienation from its true historical being and leading to a process of social transformation and national liberation. Such a liberation would come through what they called a "bourgeois revolution," that is, a transformation led by enlightened intellectuals such as themselves and by progressive elements of the national bourgeoisie. Although I have merely summarized some of ISEB's positions, which are inevitably more complex than here represented, it can be seen that the contradictions of this developmentalist ideology are immense, to say the least. But it is important to note that many on the Left, including the Brazilian Communist party, shared these views, forming a "populist pact," which Glauber Rocha so brilliantly dissected in *Terra em Transe* (*Land in Anquish*, 1967).[8]

In general terms, Cinema Novo saw itself as part of this process of "de-alienation" through a strategy of *conscientização*, or consciousness-raising. It sought, at least during its initial phase, to show the people the true face of the country's underdevelopment, in the hope that they would gain a critical consciousness and participate in the struggle for national liberation. As Glauber Rocha wrote in "An Aesthetic of Hunger," Cinema Novo *"is not a single film but an evolving complex of films that will ultimately make the public aware of its own misery."*[9]

As did the intellectuals of ISEB, Cinema Novo tended to see the major conflict of Brazilian society as "colonizer" versus "colonized," to use Glauber Rocha's words ("An Aesthetic of Hunger"), rather than to analyze it in terms of class. The movement was engaged in a struggle to create an authentic national culture in opposition to the interests of the colonizer. It also tended to adopt a dualist vision of society, setting a traditional, feudal, backward Brazil tied to imperialist interests in opposition to a progressive, modern Brazil led by sectors of the national bourgeoisie.

Cinema Novo's alliance with supposedly progressive sectors of the national bourgeoisie is revealed not only in its choice of themes, but also in its sources of financing. Many pre-1964 Cinema Novo films, including classics such as Nelson Pereira dos Santos's *Vidas Secas* (*Barren Lives*, 1963), Ruy Guerra's *Os Fuzis* (*The Guns*, 1964), and Glauber Rocha's *Deus e o Diabo na Terra do Sol* (*Black God, White Devil*, 1964), were financed by the National Bank of Minas Gerais, which was owned by the family of politician Magalhães Pinto, one of the civilian conspirators in the coup d'état of 1964.

Closely linked to the central dichotomy set forth by Cinema Novo—colonizer versus colonized—is the movement's attitude toward the development of the film industry. Cinema Novo grew out of the debate concerning film aesthetics and industry development that coincided with the final years of Vera Cruz. At that time, as mentioned in the previous chapter, some producers and directors began to reject the artificiality and expense of the studio system in favor of an independent, artisan mode of production. Influenced by Italian neorealism and aware of the reasons for the failure of Vera Cruz, Cinema Novo determined that the foreign-controlled Brazilian market could not provide an adequate return on expensive studio production and opted instead for an independent and inexpensive mode of production using small crews, location shooting, and nonprofessional actors. This was the first time in the history of Brazilian cinema that such a mode of production was adopted by ideological and aesthetic choice rather than by circumstance.[10]

Glauber Rocha perhaps best expresses Cinema Novo's attitude toward models of film production in his 1963 book *Revisão Crítica do Cinema Brasileiro*. He aligns himself with the French *nouvelle vague* ("new wave"), and its struggle to free itself from the rigidity of industrial cinema and its norms, while at the same time politicizing the *nouvelle vague*'s concept of *auteur*.[11] The *auteur*, according to Rocha, revolts against the mercantile mentality of industrial cinema, which puts profit and easy communication above art. While quoting Truffaut, Bazin, and Godard, Rocha goes a step farther than the initial formula of the *nouvelle vague* and proposes an opposition between "commercial cinema" (illusionistic technique and untruth) and "*auteur* cinema" (freedom of expression and truth). In Rocha's words, "If commercial cinema is the tradition, *auteur* cinema is the revolution. The politics of a modern *auteur* are revolutionary politics: and today it is not even necessary to qualify an *auteur* as revolutionary, because *auteur* is a totalizing noun. . . . The *auteur* is responsible for the truth: his aesthetics are his ethics, his *mise-en-scène* his politics."[12]

The model of neorealism served Cinema Novo well as a production and aesthetic strategy, especially during the first phase of the movement, as filmmakers attempted to portray what they saw as the true face of Brazilian underdevelopment. The critical realism marked by the "aesthetic of hunger" served an important tactical and political function by expressing the radical "otherness" of Brazilian cinema in relation to world cinema.[13] In short, as part of their project of decolonizing Brazilian cinema and attempting to create a critical consciousness in the Brazilian people, in opposition to what they saw as the alienated consciousness fostered by Hollywood, Cinema Novo adopted a new attitude toward the industrial development of Brazilian cinema and a new attitude toward film aesthetics, giving ideas precedence over technical perfection.

It is thus not surprising that those associated with Cinema Novo—Nelson Pereira dos Santos, Glauber Rocha, Carlos Diegues, Luiz Carlos Barreto, and Joaquim Pedro de Andrade, among others—would come into conflict with other areas of the industry, notably the "universalist" sector, based largely in São Paulo (Cinema Novo was primarily a Rio de Janeiro–based movement). Whereas Cinema Novo and the "nationalist" group rejected any foreign participation in the Brazilian film industry, called for effective restrictions on imports, opposed the cloistered artificiality of studio productions, and advocated the use of national themes, the "universalist" group largely favored a studio system, liberal import policies, and association with foreign capital. Directors associated with this group, such as Walter Hugo Khoury, Rubem Biáfora, and Flávio Tambellini, tended to make films with urban settings, dealing with the existential and moral problems of the middle class. The "universalist" group, which had dominated state and municipal film commissions in São Paulo as well as the CFC, GEIC, and now GEICINE, in many respects reflected the general economic and ideological postures of Kubitschek's developmentalism.[14]

While the universalists worked within the state apparatus, pushing for measures that would favor their model of industrialization, the nationalists, joined together by the Cinema Novo movement, created a strong cultural and intellectual presence for Brazilian cinema. Through their widespread international recognition, they brought a prestige value to Brazilian cinema that it had never known before.

José Mário Ortiz Ramos sees the nationalist/universalist conflict as being the key to understanding cinema-state relations from the 1950s to the 1980s.[15] Although there was undeniably a struggle for hegemony between the two groups, such a struggle was essentially concluded by the late 1960s, with a clear victory for the nationalist sector. It is important not to overestimate their differences, first of all because the groups themselves were shifting and unstable, secondly because they represent only two of many tendencies within the industry, and finally because they agreed on most issues confronting the film industry at the time. They disagreed on strategies and tactics and held widely divergent ideological positions, but, as Nelson Pereira dos Santos has said, when Brazilian cinema as a whole was threatened, they managed to display remarkable unity in joining forces.

Both the universalists and the nationalists saw state support for the industry as absolutely essential. Their conception of the state and its role, however, differed considerably. The universalists saw GEICINE, and later the Instituto Nacional do Cinema, as essentially technical, ostensibly neutral, governmental bodies designed solely to aid the development of the industry. The nationalists, especially in the pre-1964 period, perhaps naively saw state intervention as one minor step toward the socialization of the industry and the economy as a whole.

This image of the state is reflected in Maurice Capovilla's 1962 article, " 'GEICINE' e Problemas Econômicos do Cinema Brasileiro," written in response to some of GEICINE's proposals.[16] While praising some of GEICINE's achievements, Capovilla criticized its "typically developmentalist mentality," which favored capitalist forms of development based on free enterprise, equal competition in the market, and collaboration with foreign capital. GEICINE, he suggested, may be a necessary and often useful step, but is condemned to be surpassed "when the cinema, like petroleum in the past, ceases to be a problem of the government to become a product of the government, with both distribution and exhibition nationalized."

The proposals that provoked Capovilla's article, plus a great deal of additional controversy at the time, are exemplary of the universalists' positions. The first proposal would have obligated all distributors of foreign films to distribute Brazilian films at a ratio of ten to one. According to GEICINE, the principal reason for such a proposal was that by not being obligated to distribute national films, both foreign and national distributors automatically became strong competitors of the national product and instruments in a policy of importation rather than in a policy of national film industry development.[17] GEICINE felt that such a measure would result, firstly, in increased competition for national films among distributors, and secondly, in increased participation by distributors in their production, either by producing films themselves, or by co-producing with Brazilian firms or with other foreign producers.[18]

GEICINE's intention in this proposal was to transform foreign film distributors into a group that had an interest in the development of the national film industry, to gear the importation of foreign films to the availability of national films, to create a capital market for film production from within the industry itself, and to improve the enforcement of compulsory exhibition laws, since all distributors would have a direct interest in seeing that the law was obeyed.[19]

In response to GEICINE's proposal, Capovilla noted that at current production levels, the national industry could not supply even 10 percent of the market. At a ten-to-one ratio, Brazilian cinema would have been thirty-seven films short in 1960. More importantly, however, Capovilla criticized the proposal since it could effectively transform foreign distributors into national producers, giving them influence on what should be truly national cultural products. Filmmaking ventures by foreign distributors, furthermore, would inflate production costs. His criticism, rooted in a "radical nationalist" ideology, opposed what he saw here as the potential for the internationalization of the Brazilian film industry.

This potential is seen as well in one of GEICINE's concrete achievements during its tenure: a formal definition of "Brazilian film," necessary to determine which films are eligible for protection under compulsory exhibition legislation. As noted earlier, the film industry had been pressing for such a definition since the film congresses of the early 1950s. The São Paulo Congress and both national congresses adopted similar definitions. According to that of GEICINE, expressed in Decree 51,106 (1 August 1961), a "Brazilian film" is one that is produced by a Brazilian firm and spoken in Portuguese. Its technical crew and cast must be composed of at least two-thirds Brazilians or foreigners residing in the country for more than two years. All studio scenes must be shot in Brazil, and the film must be developed and mixed in the country.

The most significant difference between this and definitions proposed earlier concerns the origin of capital for film production. All of the earlier congresses had approved definitions stating that film production capital must be 100 percent national. GEICINE's definition, which in essence is still in effect today, makes no mention whatsoever of capital. Theoretically, then, Columbia Pictures do Brasil can produce a "Brazilian" film if it meets the other requirements of the law.[20]

Another controversial measure concerned an attempt to increase the capital market for national films through a coproduction program with foreign distributors. GEICINE proposed and achieved a modification of Article 45 of Law 4131 (3 September 1962), a so-called "profit remittance" law. The modification provided that 40 percent of the income tax owed by importers of foreign films would be placed in a special account in the Banco do Brasil for optional use by the distributor in the co-production of national films. Any monies not so used within a specified period of time would revert to the federal government. Film importers and, especially, foreign distributors, were thus allowed under the new law to invest in national films in the amount of up to 50 percent of total production costs. The idea behind the law was that the foreign company would have a vested interest in the film that would lead to its being distributed abroad. As initially formulated—the law was revised in 1966 with the creation of the Instituto Nacional do Cinema and again in 1969 with Embrafilme—the program was somewhat less than successful. Between 1962 and 1966, only seven films, including Nelson Pereira dos Santos's El Justicero (The Enforcer, 1967), were co-produced under the provisions of the law.[21]

Despite the fact that very few foreign distributors chose to use the money for the co-production of Brazilian films, the measure was fought bitterly by many national producers. The law ostensibly increased the amount of capital available for film financing, but, in reality, it provided not so much a stimulus for the national industry as it did a free gift to foreign distributors. The money collected for the purpose of co-production in no way burdened the distributor since it was owed to the government. In effect, the measure provided foreign distributors with the capital necessary to enter national production on a large scale at no cost to them.

Many local observers saw the program as the beginning of the "denationalization" of the Brazilian film industry. Geraldo Veloso, for example, wrote in the Tribuna da Imprensa:

The principal foreign production companies have branches in our country, and when they act on the administrative level they create co-production laws along the lines of those they have with Italy, France, Spain, and Argentina. We are not going to repeat what happened in those countries. The foreign distributors are transformed by law into producers, and they begin massively entering the production sector of the country, with the advantage that they already possess functional structures, since the systems of distribution (the backbone of the film industry) have existed since the first appearance of the cinema.[22]

The co-production program once again reflected the internationalist mentality of the universalist group, firmly entrenched in GEICINE, and their concept of industrialization through foreign investment. As noted earlier, this co-production measure would later (1966) be revised and would become more productive in the period between 1966 and 1969, when it was eliminated under the aegis of Embrafilme.

GEICINE also created a less controversial, but equally ineffective, program of financing for national films. The proposal, which went into effect in 1962, stipulated that producers could receive credit through CREAI (Department of Agricultural and Industrial Credit) of the Banco do Brasil in the amount of up to 60 percent of the total approved budget, not to exceed 30 million cruzeiros. Loan guarantees were to be determined by the bank. The financing would be released in three stages: 50 percent upon approval of the budget, 30 percent upon completion of shooting, and 20 percent when the film was finished. Repayment would commence a maximum of two years from the date of approval, and the producer could receive additional financing when 70 percent of the previous debt had been paid.[23]

Although GEICINE's intention was to provide a source of finance capital for the film industry, the exigencies of CREAI in terms of guarantees and collateral were such that only the largest production companies could possibly take advantage of it. One provision of the loan regulations, for example, stipulated that the producer must deposit in the Banco do Brasil an amount equal to his share of the production costs. That is, in order to receive 60 percent of such costs from CREAI, he would have to deposit an amount equal to the other 40 percent in a separate account. Needless to say, GEICINE's financing program did not have a significant impact on the film industry, and levels of production did not increase during its tenure, averaging 29.5 films per year between 1961 and 1966 as opposed to 31.5 per year the previous decade (see table 11).

Another of GEICINE's priority items was the revision of exchange rates and tariffs for the importation of filmmaking equipment, film stock, and printed foreign films. GEICINE concluded that a revision of current laws should be undertaken due to the

Table 11. Brazilian Feature Film Production, 1961–1966

1961	30	1964	27
1962	27	1965	33
1963	32	1966	28

Source: Alcino Teixeira de Mello, *Legislação do Cinema Brasileiro* (Rio de Janeiro: Embrafilme, 1978), 2:558.

unfavorable conditions national producers faced in relation to importers of foreign films. Tariff Law 3244 (1957) established two categories of imports: a general category to be imported at the free exchange rate and a special category whereby products could be imported without an exchange cover at the official rate.[24]

CACEX (the Banco do Brasil's Department of Foreign Trade) instructions 129 (7 January 1960) and 130 (4 April 1960) permitted distributors to import films in the special category as long as the importation was limited to one master copy. This was done to stimulate and guarantee work for national laboratories, which, theoretically, would benefit by developing the needed copies. According to the 1957 law, however, printed film was taxed at an extremely low rate (one cruzeiro per linear meter for newsreels and negatives; 1.50 cruzeiros for positive copies) while raw film stock was taxed at an ad valorem rate of 10 percent.

Because of inflation, customs duties on foreign films were decreasing considerably in relation to film stock, creating a disadvantageous situation for the national producer. It became less expensive for the foreign distributor to import processed films than for the national producer to import film stock. This situation also undermined the original intention of providing work for national laboratories, because the high cost of film stock and the consequent high cost of developing copies in Brazil led distributors to import all of their copies instead of just a master.

GEICINE therefore proposed (1) that all copies of foreign films, including masters, be imported in the general category at the free exchange rate; (2) that the duties on foreign films be increased to U.S. $4.00 per linear meter; (3) that duties on film stock be reduced to one percent for a period of one year; and (4) that negotiations be reopened with GATT concerning the free international commerce of motion pictures.[25]

Although GEICINE did not achieve all of its objectives, it did achieve a reduction, from 10 to 5 percent, of the customs duties on raw film stock.[26] Its pressure also caused the passage of Law 4546 (10 December 1964), which exempted film equipment from import tariffs and customs duties for a period of twenty-four months, and Law 4662 (3 May 1966), providing similar relief for studios and laboratories.[27]

With the transferral in 1960–1961 of the federal government from Rio de Janeiro to Brasília, censorship of public diversions, which had been centralized by Vargas in 1932, underwent a process of decentralization. This created a serious problem for the film industry, since rather than submitting a film to one official body, distributors would have to submit them to such bodies in all states, that is, to twenty-two different censorship offices. GEICINE estimated, based on the censorship tax proposed by legislators in the State of Guanabara, that the cost to producers to have a single film approved in all twenty-two states would be on the order of 1.5 million cruzeiros, plus the cost of reproducing twenty-two censorship certificates and other expenses.[28]

On the day of its inauguration (13 April 1961) GEICINE received a petition signed by virtually all film industry professional associations (including production, distribution, and exhibition groups as well as critics and cultural entities) urging that censorship once again be centralized as a federal obligation. This is but a minor example of the ability of the industry to unite on issues that affected all of its sectors, regardless of ideological differences. GEICINE immediately established a working group which made a number of recommendations. Since the enforcement of the compulsory exhibition law was a function of the department of censorship, the policing or "fiscalization" of the market intertwined with recommendations specifically concerning the recentralization of censorship activities. The group recommended, in addition, the creation of a single, official theater admission ticket and an improved system of control as well as the revision of the censorship tax, which had been set at Cr$0.40 per linear meter.[29]

GEICINE's activities relative to cultural aspects of cinema were limited. They included an agreement with the ministry of Education and Culture and the Instituto Nacional do Cinema Educativo to publish the magazine *Filme Cultura* (1965), which has undergone various transformations over the years and yet still exists under the aegis of Embrafilme. During its early years, the magazine's editorial policy reflected the internationalism of the members of GEICINE, focusing largely on foreign cinemas and directors. When national filmmakers were discussed, they were normally those who identified with the universalist group in terms of the preferred content of Brazilian films. More recently, especially after 1969, *Filme Cultura* began to focus more on the local industry and now deals almost exclusively with Brazilian cinema.

Under GEICINE's jurisdiction, the screen quota for national films was increased from forty-two to fifty-six days per year of compulsory exhibition (Decree 52,745 of 24 October 1963). It also undertook studies relative to virtually all aspects of the film industry, from the regulation of ticket prices to questions of taxation. One of its studies led to the implementation, in the state of Guanabara, of a law like the 1955 São Paulo statute which provided subsidies to producers based on box-office income in the state.

In late 1963, under GEICINE's influence, Guanabara governor Carlos Lacerda signed into law a decree creating CAIC, the Comissão de Auxílio à Indústria Cinematográfica (Commission for Aid to the Film Industry). CAIC would administer two basic programs of financial assistance to the industry: (1) a system of cash awards or subsidies based on gross exhibition income in the state, and (2) a program of film production financing.[30] Lacerda's decree represented not only an important source of income for *carioca* producers, but also the first attempt by the state to exert ideological control over the film industry. The decree founding CAIC stated that the benefits of the law would be denied to any script or film that advocated, among other things, the use of violence to subvert the political and social order, racial or class prejudice, or propaganda against the democratic system.[31]

In fact, the restrictions of the decree were more flexible than they may at first appear, and CAIC was one of the major sources of funding for Cinema Novo filmmakers. Almost coinciding with the 1964 coup, therefore, was the beginning of a sometimes stormy relationship between the state and Cinema Novo, a relationship that would continue with the federal government's creation of the Instituto Nacional do Cinema in 1966 and Embrafilme in 1969 and that would become formalized in 1973 when Roberto Farias, Cinema Novo's chosen candidate, became head of Embrafilme.

Among Cinema Novo films partially financed by CAIC were Walter Lima, Jr.'s *Menino de Engenho* (*Plantation Boy*, 1965), Roberto Santos's *A Hora e Vez de Augusto Matraga* (*Matraga*, 1965), Joaquim Pedro de Andrade's *O Padre e a Moça*, (*The Priest and the Girl*, 1965), and Arnaldo Jabor's documentary about the middle class, *Opinião Pública* (*Public Opinion*, 1967). CAIC's programs were phased out after the creation of the Instituto Nacional do Cinema in 1966. If the universalist group held power within the state cinematic apparatus (GEICINE), the opposing nationalist group was never far away and was itself actively involved in state policy toward the industry at the time.

If state support was important for the development of Cinema Novo, it was also responsible for its first major rift, a rift which in many ways continues until today. Divisions arose within the movement concerning the position filmmakers should take in relation to CAIC's program of financing, especially given the ideological restrictions written into the law. Ruy Guerra saw such financing as a form of co-optation. Most of the others disagreed, and Guerra soon found himself distanced from the movement as a whole.

Despite Cinema Novo's participation in CAIC's programs, Glauber Rocha, one of the undisputed leaders of Cinema Novo, saw GEICINE's approach to the problems facing the industry as a misguided one resulting in "false" solutions such as bank credits, official awards, co-productions, and the creation of film schools.[32] The true problems are the flood of foreign films in the national market and censorship (and this prior to 1964). Rocha called for severe restrictions on imports by way of heavy customs duties, and legislation reserving 51 percent of the market for Brazilian films. That, combined with reduced import tariffs on film equipment, would, in Rocha's view, solve the basic problem of Brazilian cinema, its inability to command its own market. With regard to censorship, Rocha called for its transfer from the Ministry of Justice (the Federal Police) to the Ministry of Education and Culture:

Once transferred from the hands of ignorant police officials and puritan women to the judgement of intellectuals, critics, professors, and people with proven knowledge of the cultural aspects of the cinema, censorship would not approve half of the poor quality programs represented by B and C American films; nor would it approve French and Italian pornography; nor would it concede the certificate of "good quality" to the immoral chanchadas produced in our studios; nor would it approve commercial documentaries in the service of interests which are anti-educational, distorting, and dishonest in relation to national reality. To the contrary, it would approve the films now habitually prohibited by police censorship.[33]

Rocha's perspective was that by eliminating what he considered to be poor-quality films from the market, there would be plenty of room for Brazilian cinema, which would lead to its stabilization and development, without the need for investing in expensive studio productions. In addition to a reduction in the massive presence of foreign films in the market and the transfer of censorship to MEC, Rocha also called for state assistance in exporting Brazilian films to foreign markets. Despite ideological differences with GEICINE, Glauber Rocha—and Cinema Novo generally— saw continued, indeed increased, state support for the national film industry as absolutely essential.

Early in GEICINE's existence, it recognized its own limitations in effectively performing its designated duties. In the first number of the *Revista do GEICINE*, its president Flávio Tambellini expressed the need to create a governmental body capable of achieving and administering the fundamental designs of the government, and to promote the development and affirmation of the film industry in Brazil. He saw the need for a service within the government with the sole function of enforcing the laws that protect national cinema, for a service of documentation and statistics, for greater control over international co-production agreements, in short, for the administrative execution and control of all these measures.[34]

One of GEICINE's most pressing tasks throughout its tenure was a revision of the earlier projects for the creation of an Instituto Nacional do Cinema. GEICINE first sent a project for the creation of such an institute to the Ministry of Industry and Commerce on 23 August 1963. This specific project, however, became lost in the bureaucratic morass of the soon-to-be-extinct Ministry of Administrative Reform.[35] It would later be revived and, finally, approved in late 1966 despite the opposition of distribution and exhibition groups and of Cinema Novo, which faced a new and difficult political reality in post-1964 Brazil.

5

The Instituto Nacional do Cinema, 1966–1975

W HEN THE MILITARY overthrew the government of João Goulart in 1964, they brought with them an implicit promise to reverse the wave of state interference in the free enterprise system which had characterized the administrations of Quadros and Goulart. President Humberto Castello Branco and his chief economic advisors were convinced of the merits of economic liberalism and free competition as a solution to the profound crisis facing the Brazilian economy. Although the Castello Branco government took some steps in the direction of a greater privatization of the economy, "the disastrous performance of the Brazilian economy from 1964 to 1967 discredited economic liberalism even more thoroughly than the Dutra period [1945–1950] had."[1]

Despite the ideological favoring of economic liberalism and an ever-present laissez-faire rhetoric, the military takeover led not to a decentralization, but rather to an increased centralization of economic decision making.[2] Increased state participation in the economy did not derive, however, from an explicit statist ideology, but rather from the military's concern with national security or from the inability to convince private concerns to invest in areas where prices were held down and the return on investments was slow. As Peter Evans suggests (Dependent Development), the military felt that the ability to produce its own planes was essential to the country's security, so they created the state enterprise Embraer. Embratel (Empresa Brasileira de Telecomunicações) and Telebrás in the field of telecommunications were created for the second reason, since for private firms to be profitable in these areas the government would have had to lift price controls on telephone communications.[3] Through the military's actions, the state became more deeply involved in the national economy than ever before.

Corresponding to expanded public sector activity in the economy under military rule was an increased state intervention in the cultural arena. Support for cultural production also forms part of the ideology of national security. It was felt that programs of development should include not only economic factors, but also psychological, social, and cultural factors. According to this ideology, the state should stimulate cultural production as a means of national integration, but at the same time should maintain that production under the control of the state apparatus. Attempts were made to create what has been called a "National System of Culture," much like the National System of Tourism (consolidated in 1967) or the National System of Telecommunications. The centralization of cultural activities, under the aegis of the state, thus became an implicit goal of the military government.[4]

To that end, in 1966, Flávio Suplicy de Lacerda, head of the Education sector of the Ministry of Education and Culture, created a commission to study and reformulate the country's cultural policy. The commission in turn recommended the creation of a council along the lines of the Federal Education Council, which had been created in 1962. The result of the commission's recommendations was the creation of the Conselho Federal de Cultura (Federal Council of Culture) by Decree-law no. 74 (21 November 1966).[5]

The legal attributes of the Conselho Federal de Cultura included the formulation of a national cultural policy (which resulted in the publication, in 1975, of the *Política Nacional de Cultura*, discussed in Chapter 6); cooperation with federal, state, and local governments as well as educational institutions in the promotion of cultural events; the defense of the national historical and artistic patrimony; the promotion of national campaigns to support cultural and artistic development and so on. The CFC is essentially a normative body designed to provide information and recommendations to the Ministry of Education and Culture with regards to cultural matters. Although it does have limited funding capabilities to sponsor cultural activities (including exhibitions, concerts, and even book publishing), it has no direct authority over any other public or private cultural organizations. Like the Federal Education Council, the CFC is directly subordinated to the Ministry of Education and Culture.

In his *Cultura Brasileira e Identidade Nacional*, Renato Ortiz analyzes the conservative ideology of the CFC, expressed not only in its writings and statements, but also in its very composition. Its members were "traditional intellectuals" drawn from institutes of history and geography and from academies of letters. Their primordial concern was with preserving national traditions and the cultural patrimony. They expressed what Ortiz calls an "ideology of syncretism" (racial, cultural, etc.) which depicts a cultural universe without contradictions, where relationships of power are not revealed.[6]

In his speech inaugurating the CFC (27 February 1967), President Castello Branco expressed his government's concept of culture:

The work of the Revolution [the coup d'état of 1964] in the intellectual field would not be complete if, after such fruitful undertakings in benefit of education, it did not turn to the problems of national culture. Represented by that which has through the years been preserved in libraries, monuments, museums, the theater, the cinema, and in various cultural institutions, culture, in this duality of education and culture, is naturally the most tranquil and least demanding part. One might say that it is the part with grey hair and, perhaps for this reason, is already certain of what it has done and can do for Brazil. We must, however, provide it with the conditions necessary for its preservation, survival, and evolution.[7]

Despite his allowance for some kind of change ("evolution," in his words), Castello Branco expresses an essentially static, conservative, and ultimately class-based conception of culture that includes the cultural artifacts deemed worthy of inclusion in libraries and museums, or consecrated as official monuments. When he speaks of the theater and the cinema he seems to change register, but he is certainly not speaking of anything that could possibly threaten the established values of the military regime.

As we have seen in the last two chapters, Brazilian cinema has not always been characterized as "undemanding" or "tranquil."

Not only has it made specific, often unanswered demands on the federal government, it has also frequently transmitted a political vision diametrically opposed to that of the military and the dominant classes. In purely practical terms, the cinema is demanding because of its unique situation among the arts in Brazil. Its industrial base, dependent on imports, renders it more capital-intensive than other sectors of cultural production, and the fact that it must compete against highly organized and highly capitalized foreign film industries makes its very survival problematic without state assistance. Therefore its stance of economic and cultural nationalism is more pronounced than other areas of cultural production.[8]

The Creation of the Instituto Nacional do Cinema

The long struggle of the film industry to gain government recognition through the creation of a National Film Institute came to fruition on 18 November 1966 when Castello Branco signed Decree-law no. 43. GEICINE's proposal had been submitted to congress on 23 September of that same year and was approved, with some amendments, by the Chamber of Deputies on 4 October.[9] The military government's First and Second Institutional Acts (9 April 1964 and 27 October 1965, respectively) included a provision, known as the *decurso de prazo*, limiting the time congress had to debate and act on the executive-proposed legislation before it automatically became law.[10] The Instituto Nacional do Cinema came into being not by legislative prerogative and approval, for the bill never passed in the Senate, but rather by an executive decree of the Brazilian military government.[11]

The government made a number of changes in GEICINE's initial proposal before finally approving the Institute. GEICINE had proposed that the Institute, a "legal entity" with technical autonomy, be subordinated to the Ministry of Industry and Commerce and have the power, among other things, to exercise film censorship. In its other attributes, the Institute would have been rather meek, having the power to undertake studies and make recommendations to proper government officials concerning the development of the film industry. It did, however, include the right to establish norms for the compulsory exhibition of national films and their compulsory distribution by foreign companies as well as the right to determine policy with regards to theater admission prices.[12]

As it finally came into being, the Instituto Nacional do Cinema, hereafter referred to as INC, was a federal *autarquia* (a semi-autonomous organization) subordinated not to the Ministry of Industry and Commerce but rather to the Ministry of Education and Culture. It was not given power of censorship, which was retained by the Ministry of Justice, but it was empowered to formulate and execute governmental policy relative to the development of the film industry (Decree-law no. 43, Article 4, I) and to regulate, in conjunction with the Banco Central, the importation of foreign films for exhibition both in theaters and on television (4, II). It was further empowered to regulate the production, distribution, and exhibition of Brazilian films, setting rental prices as well as terms and conditions of payments (4, III), to regulate the rental of foreign films (4, V), and to concede production financing and awards to national producers (4, VI). It was also to carry out the educational and cultural activities of the Instituto Nacional de Cinema Educativo (INCE) as well as the normative activities of GEICINE, both of which it incorporated (Article 31). In many ways, the institute described by Decree-law no. 43 theoretically had considerably more power than that originally proposed by GEICINE.

As might be expected, the proposed INC had a mixed reception in the film industry and on occasion provoked virulent and even vituperative responses. It was a question, fundamentally, of who wielded power within the industry, as different groups, reflecting different political and industrial ideologies, struggled for dominance and hegemony. Opinion vis-à-vis the INC generally broke down along the lines of the nationalist/universalist dichotomy outlined in the previous chapter, with the universalists favoring its approval (they, after all, had been active in GEICINE) and the nationalists opposing it, although one must recognize the fact that such an opposition represents an oversimplification. Geraldo Santos Pereira summarized the opposition to INC concisely (and it should be noted that he himself was a member of GEICINE):

there are positions of antagonism characterized by ideological, political, professional, and personal conviction. There are those who want to avoid financial losses from aspects of the project that would go against their professional interests; there are those who hold an inalterable and predominantly ideological suspicion of the government that elaborated the bill and that will, for some time, direct the Institute; there are those who reject any intervention whatsoever of the public sector in an activity they consider to be an exclusively private domain . . . ; and there are those, finally, who follow a radical line of political opposition and who include the cinema among the forces that . . . struggle against the current government.[13]

Opposition to the proposed INC thus brought about an unlikely alliance of mainstream Cinema Novo participants such as Glauber Rocha and Nelson Pereira dos Santos, exhibition and distribution groups, and conservative newspapers, although their opposition was often for different reasons.

Although it had favored and accepted state aid as provided by CAIC, itself a creation of GEICINE, the Cinema Novo group opposed the INC on political grounds, fearing that it would result in a "totalitarian 'statizing' of art" and that it represented an attempt by the universalist group, and the military regime, to eliminate Cinema Novo. Nelson Pereira do Santos denounced the institute as "fascist" and "paternalist" and suggested that its result would be political and ideological pressure on producers and directors to create a "well-behaved" national cinema run by people like GEICINE's president Flávio Tambellini. In short, dos Santos and others feared that the INC would lead to a loss of freedom of expression as well as of economic freedom, since it would tend to monopolize finance capital for national film production.[14]

Distribution and exhibition groups, predictably, opposed the INC as an infringement on the free enterprise system. They compared it to a governmental body "typical of the Iron Curtain."[15] So whereas Cinema Novo attacked INC as "fascist," other groups denounced it as communistic. Newspapers such as the *Jornal do Brasil* and the *Jornal do Commércio* published editorials against the Institute. The *Jornal do Brasil* wrote that the national film industry obviously needed financial aid, but not an institute based so clearly on protectionist, statist, and quasi-totalitarian philosophical conceptions. "Sterile officialism will do little more than suffocate the achievements of the film industry over the last few years," it suggested. Besides, with the then upcoming elections, the existence of the *decurso de prazo*, and the general political situation, the timing of the proposed INC could not have been worse.[16]

The *Jornal do Commércio* was more direct and vituperative. It called the law a "monstrosity" and recommended psychiatric treatment for those who proposed it. "While the government is considering freeing capital goods from statism, while it contemplates the reprivatization of sectors invaded by the interventionist wave of the communizing period of João Goulart . . . there arises from governmental convolutions a prime example of state totalitarianism." It went on to refer to the law as undemocratic, and, shifting to biological images, called it a "birth control pill of cinematic creativity that will transform one of our most promising manufactured goods into a condemned fetus."[17]

The two major aspects of state policy toward the film industry—cultural and economic—are revealed in the opposition to the INC. On the one hand, filmmakers with a strong sense of the cultural and even political importance of the cinema feared limitations on, or repression of, freedom of expression and creativity. On the other, those who tended to see the industry in purely economic terms opposed the Institute on the grounds that it represented unjustifiable government interference in the free enterprise system. This ultimately ideological bind has accompanied state cinematic policy until today, as it has been forced to reconcile the two sides of its assumed responsibility toward the industry.

While the project was working its way through congress, the National Film Industry Syndicate (SNIC) sent a memorandum to Castello Branco asking him to withdaw the project, not because of any specific opposition to its attributes, but rather because it had apparently been elaborated without the active participation of large sectors of the industry (an accusation vehemently denied by Tambellini and by SNIC's president Ronaldo Lupo, who refused to sign the document). The memorandum, signed by professionals throughout the industry, including Cinema Novo participants, defended the spirit of free enterprise as indispensable to the development of the industry, but suggested that the project as formulated did not attend to the interests of the industry. The memorandum was delivered to the president's representatives by São Paulo producer Oswaldo Massaini, Rio producer Herbert Richers, newsreel producer Carlos Niemeyer, and Cinema Novo leader Nelson Pereira dos Santos.[18]

At the same time, a group of São Paulo professionals organized within the Film Workers Union of São Paulo, sent a message of support for INC. Included in this larger number of supporters were Maurice Capovilla, who had earlier denounced some of GEICINE's proposals, SNIC president Lupo, and Cinema Novo participants Gustavo Dahl and Paulo César Saraceni.[19]

Although the nationalist/universalist dichotomy did in fact exist and held divergent opinions with regards to the creation of INC, the division is not quite as clear as José Mário Ortiz Ramos makes it sound in his *Cinema, Estado, e Lutas Culturais*.[20] The nationalists paradoxically held the same position vis-à-vis the INC as those distributors and exhibitors whose interests were tied to the continued foreign domination of the domestic film industry and who defended private enterprise. The universalists, on the other hand, had widespread support for their stance of economic nationalism (despite the existence of some measures that would permit foreign investment in the national industry).

Both sides were ultimately pragmatic. As we saw in the previous chapter, Nelson Pereira dos Santos had participated in GEICINE's co-production program with *El Justicero* and would continue to do so under the aegis of INC. Shortly after INC became law, industry professionals met in the Primeira Conferência Nacional do Cinema Brasileiro (First National Conference of Brazilian Cinema). The conference's final declaration, signed by nationalists and universalists alike, called INC an "indispensable instrument for the reformulation, codification, and stimulus of sectors that make up the structure of the Brazilian film industry" and called on all industry professionals to join forces, "without prejudices or partisanship," to allow INC to function normally. The declaration was signed, among others, by producer Luiz Carlos Barreto, who, like Nelson Pereira dos Santos, had been extremely vocal in his opposition to INC.[21] Since INC was a reality, there was no longer any reason for such vocal opposition, and most film-makers, regardless of their political persuasion, attempted to take advantage of its potential benefits.

ORGANIZATION AND ACTIVITIES OF INC

The organization of the INC, as determined by Decree-law no. 43, comprised a three-level structure: (1) a president, named by the president of the Republic with the advice and recommendations of the minister of education and culture; (2) a Deliberative Council, composed of representatives of the Ministry of Education and Culture, the Ministry of Justice, the Ministry of Industry and Commerce, the Ministry of Foreign Affairs, the Extraordinary Ministry for Planning and Economic Coordination, and the Banco Central; the members of this Council were designated by the president of the Republic after being nominated by their respective agencies; (3) a Consultative Council, composed of one representative each of: film producers, distributors, exhibitors, critics, and directors; these were chosen by the minister of education and culture from lists of three names provided by each of the various sectors of the industry. The Consultative Council, which by law was to meet once a month, made recommendations to the Deliberative Council, whose decisions took the form of resolutions with executive power. In its nine years of existence (1966–1975), the INC passed 112 resolutions dealing with all aspects of the film industry in Brazil.[22]

The Institute's budget derived essentially from four sources: (1) a tax known as a "contribution" for the development of the film industry calculated and collected from foreign and national producers and distributors according to the linear meterage of all films destined for exhibition in theaters or on television; (2) the sale of standardized tickets and income reporting sheets (bordereaux) to exhibitors: (3) a deposit of a percentage of income tax owed by foreign distributors (see chapter 4); and (4) fines collected for the violation of laws and regulations concerning the industry.[23] The INC also received minimal amounts from the Ministry of Education and Culture.

By its very nature as an autarquia, the INC was not intended as a profit-making organization. The *autarquia* is designed to undertake indirect or "decentralized" administrative duties, that is, its function is to engage in activities typical of public administration which require greater financial and administrative autonomy than direct administration by a government ministry would allow. By definition *autarquias* do not engage in entrepreneurial activities. Within the Brazilian government, most *autarquias* are found in the areas of education, health, and social services, but others do exist, with normative and regulatory functions, in areas connected with economic development or national security.[24]

A great majority of the 112 resolutions of the INC deal with support for the production sector of the industry and fall into four basic categories: (1) financing of imported production equipment, (2) financial awards and subsidies, (3) production financing, and (4) compulsory exhibition of national films. This last item represents an important means of economic support to producers, but at the same time is seen by exhibitors as an unfair onus and as an example of unwanted (and, in their mind, unwarranted) state intervention in the free enterprise system.

INC Resolution 14 (21 September 1967) provided credit of up to 60 percent of the total cost of equipment importation (cameras and accessories, lighting and accessories, editing tables, recording equipment), in an amount not to exceed Cr$50,000. The equipment itself was to be used as collateral, and the repayment terms were liberal: six payments starting thirteen months after signing the contract, at 12 percent interest per annum (inflation, at the time, was running well over 20 percent) and a 6 percent "service tax." A second resolution (Res. 83 of 17 April 1973) conceded further credit for such imports: 70 percent of contracted costs not to exceed Cr$140,000, and to be repaid in thirty-six monthly payments beginning twelve months after signing at an interest rate of only four percent per annum. Such support was and is essential to the development of the industry.

The INC provided economic assistance to film professionals by granting several kinds of awards and subsidies. INC Resolution 19 (26 December 1967), for example, established the INC Award, the name of which was later changed to the Coruja de Ouro (Res. 43, 11 September 1970). This award, similar to the American Oscar, gave financial prizes to film artists and technicians. Awards were given for best director, script, photography, actor, actress, editor, supporting actor and actress, musical score, scenography, and wardrobe. Three additional awards were given to directors of short subjects.

José Mário Ortiz Ramos suggests that the hegemonic struggle taking place within the Brazilian film industry and the state cinematic apparatus is reflected in the INC's choice of films to be awarded such prizes. Although he recognizes that the awards committees attempted to "efface their own position" behind one of neutrality, he says that preferences for the universalist or nationalist tendencies can be traced by the awards given. Between 1966 and 1970, for example, he sees a "certain predominance" of the universalists, which would be a natural reflection of their power within INC.[25] The idea that the universalists dominated the awards supports his argument, but unfortunately does not correspond to reality (see table 12). In fact, between 1966 and 1970, awards for best director were evenly distributed between the two groups, with Walter Hugo Khoury representing the universalists and Glauber Rocha and David Neves the nationalists. Ozualdo Candeias, who won in 1968, was independent of both groups, and more closely represented the underground or experimental cinema then arising in São Paulo.

A closer examination of individual years further undercuts

Table 12. INC's Best Director Awards, 1966–1975

1966	Walter Hugo Khoury (Corpo Ardente)
1967	Ozualdo R. Candeias (A Margem)
1968	Walter Hugo Khoury (As Amorosas)
1969	Glauber Rocha (O Dragão da Maldade Contra o Santo Guerreiro)
1970	David Neves (Memória de Helena)
1971	Domingos de Oliveira (A Culpa)
1972	Walter Hugo Khoury (As Deusas)
1973	Leon Hirszman (São Bernardo)
1974	Nelson Pereira dos Santos (O Amuleto de Ogum)
1975	Eduardo Escorel (Lição de Amor)

Source: Araken Campos Pereira, Jr., Cinema Brasileiro, 1908–1978 (Santos: Editora Casa do Cinema, 1980).

Ramos's assertion (see table 13). Of the nine major awards given in 1966, five (best actor, actress, screenplay, editing, and music) went to films by directors connected to Cinema Novo and therefore to the nationalists, while four awards went to Khoury's *Corpo Ardente*.

In 1967 *no* awards went to the universalist group, while *eight* went to directors associated with Cinema Novo: four for Domingos de Oliveira's *Todas as Mulheres do Mundo (All the Women in the World)*, three for Luiz Sérgio Person's *Caso dos Irmãos Naves (The Case of the Naves Brothers)*, and one for Rocha's *Terra em Transe (Land in Anguish)*. In 1968, three awards, for best director, actor, and supporting actress, went to films of the universalist group, and two to Cinema Novo films: best actress to Irene Stefânia in Nelson Pereira dos Santo's *Fome de Amor (Hunger for Love)*; best scenographer to Anísio Medeiros for Paulo César Saraceni's *Capitu*; and, perhaps surprisingly, four to Rogério Sganzerla's strikingly original underground film, *Bandido da Luz Vermelha (The Red Light Bandit)*.

In 1969, Cinema Novo once again swept the INC awards, with films such as Rocha's *O Dragão da Maldade Contra o Santo Guerreiro (Antônio das Mortes)*, best director; Joaquim Pedro de Andrade's *Macunaíma*, actor, scenography; Antônio Carlos Fontoura's *Copacabana me Engana (Copacabana Deceives Me)*, actress, supporting actress, screenplay; and Gustavo Dahl's *O Bravo Guerreiro (The Brave Warrior)*, cinematography. The fact of

Table 13. INC Awards, 1966

Best Director	Walter Hugo Khoury *(Corpo Ardente)*
Best Actor	Leonardo Vilar (R. Santos, *Matraga*)
Best Actress	Anecy Rocha (C. Diegues, *A Grande Cidade*)
Best Supporting Actor	Sérgio Hingst *(Corpo Ardente)*
Best Supporting Actress	Lillian Lemmertz *(Corpo Ardente)*
Best Screenplay	Walter Lima, Jr. (Lima, *Menino de Engenho*)
Best Cinematography	Rodolfo Icsey *(Corpo Ardente)*
Best Editing	Gustavo Dahl *(A Grande Cidade)*
Best Music	Carlos Lyra (J. P. Andrade, *O Padre e a Moça*)

Source: Araken Campos Pereira, Jr., *Cinema Brasileiro, 1908–1978* (Santos: Editora Casa do Cinema, 1980).

the matter is that although the universalist group may have controlled the INC in its initial years, Cinema Novo filmmakers were responsible for the best that Brazilian cinema had to offer at the time, and there is no evidence that they were in any way discriminated against in the INC awards process by the universalist group led by Flávio Tambellini. At the same time, the fact that Cinema Novo films were chosen for the INC awards, and that the awards were accepted by the Cinema Novo group in no way implies its support for all of the Institute's policies nor for the military regime of which INC was a part.

The INC also established production subsidies based on the box-office income of films (Res. 15, 28 September 1967). The subsidy program was the first direct federal aid to the national film industry and was modeled on the program initiated by the government of São Paulo in 1955, and of CAIC's subsidy initiated in the state of Guanabara in the mid-1960s. The program, like those on the state level, attempted to equate the average cost of a film with its average income and to provide producers with an incentive to accelerate production.

The subsidies were initially in the amount of 10 percent of a film's net income calculated during the first twenty-four months of exhibition, with the award corresponding to the second twelve-month period being half that of the first. The films that were most successful at the box office thus received the most money from INC. The subsidy was designed to benefit production as a whole, with no discrimination as to genre, social or cultural relevance, or even technical quality. This often put the state in the awkward position of supporting films of which it might not ordinarily approve. In 1968, for example, the films receiving the most money under this program were Alcino Diniz's *Jovens Pra Frente* (*Onward Youth!*), Mozael Silveria's *Maria Bonita, Rainha do Cangaço* (*Maria Bonita, Queen of the Outlaws*), Roberto Farias's *Roberto Carlos em Ritmo de Adventura* (*Roberto Carlos in the Rhythm of Adventure*), Carlos Alberto de Souza Barros's *Dois na Lona* (*Two on the Canvas*), and *As Libertinas* (*The Libertine Women*), a three-episode film directed by São Paulo filmmakers Carlos Reichenbach Filho, Antônio Lima, and João Callegaro. None of these films is likely to be considered a classic of Brazilian cinema.

It was illogical for the INC to provide the largest subsidies for the films that least needed it, so in 1970 (Res. 39, 30 June 1970) it altered the subsidy program, providing lower subsidies to those at the high and low ends of the scale. The rationale for this change was that highly successful films did not need an additional subsidy, and those which failed at the box office did not deserve one.

The revised subsidy continued to be paid according to box-office income, calculated according to the monthly minimum wage. It was divided into four categories: films with a net income of (1) up to 1,000 times the monthly minimum wage received a 5 percent subsidy; (2) between 1,000 and 4,500 times received a 20 percent subsidy; (3) between 4,500 and 6,000 received a 5 percent subsidy; and (4) over 6,000 times the monthly minimum wage received no additional subsidy. This measure indicates a change in the orientation of the state cinema apparatus from an apparently neutral policy (neutral in the sense that all films, regardless of success, received an equal percentage) to a policy supporting average success in the marketplace. It also implies the recognition that certain films will make a profit without state support and that others may have cultural value and yet lack a strong commercial potential. The measure attempted to make success in the marketplace at least a partial goal of culturally oriented filmmakers.

In 1973, the INC initiated another change in the subsidy program, this time in an attempt to stimulate the production of children's films, historical films, and films based on literary works of "undeniable value" (Res. 81, 20 March 1973). This new resolution provided, for films in these three categories, a 10 percent subsidy for those in the 0 to 500 monthly minimum wage range, 50 percent for those drawing between 500 and 2,500, 10 percent for those earning between 2,500 and 3,000 times the monthly minimum wage, and no subsidy for those earning more than 3,000 times the monthly minimum wage. This resolution represented the first time the state had attempted to stimulate the production of specific kinds of films, although there is little evidence to suggest that the resolution had any real effect on the nature of Brazilian film production, where both historical films and, especially, children's films have, until more recently, been few and far between. Literary adaptations have long been a mainstay of Brazilian cinema, and while many films continued to be based on literary works, and thus participated in the program, no discernible increase in such adaptations occurred as a result of the subsidy.

INC Resolution 15, which first established the subsidy program, also created an "additional award for quality" in the amount of up to 15 percent of net income, to selected films with an "elevated technical, artistic, or cultural level." Initially these additional awards were to be made with funds remaining from the subsidy program. The quality award was modified by Resolution 39 (30 June 1970) and set at the fixed rate of 300 times the monthly minimum wage. Whereas Resolution 15 had not stipulated the number of quality awards to be conceded, Resolution 39 determined that twelve films per year would be chosen for the additional awards. The films in this category were chosen by a panel of representatives from different sectors of the industry, including critics. Since the amount of the award, after 1970, was based on the monthly minimum wage, it was free from the dictates of the marketplace. In the nine years of its existence, the INC paid out some 47 million cruzeiros (unadjusted) in general subsidies and an additional 6 million to the so-called quality films (see table 14).

If Cinema Novo, as we suggested earlier, dominated the INC's professional awards, so too did it dominate its additional awards

Table 14. INC Production Subsidies, 1966–1975
(in cruzeiros)

	General Subsidies	Additional Awards
1967	345,271.18	—
1968	621,610.05	113,141.43
1969	1,997,706.27	98,604.15
1970	3,809,123.90	302,362.23
1971	3,571,046.06	673,920.00
1972	5,008,008.47	812,160.00
1973	6,648,854.00	967,680.00
1974	8,683,530.00	1,356,480.00
1975	16,461,732.85	1,803,600.00

Source: Instituto Nacional do Cinema, *Informativo SIP* (1973), pp. 25–26; *Informativo SIP* (1974), pp. 23–24; Embrafilme, *Informações sobre a Indústria Cinematográfica Brasileira* (1975), pp. 24–25.

for quality (see table 15). In the first four years of these awards, the universalist group had only five films selected, whereas filmmakers associated with Cinema Novo had seventeen. The universalists may have maintained hegemony within the INC, but certainly not within the industry, and even within the INC they were more objective than Ramos would have us believe. What was important about the quality awards was that, between 1969 and 1975, they provided additional income for, on average, 15 percent of total Brazilian film production.

Table 15. INC Additional Awards for Quality, 1967–1975

	Film	*Director*
1967	*Todas as Mulheres do Mundo*	Domingos de Oliveira
	O Caso dos Irmãos Naves	Luiz Sérgio Person
	O Menino e o Vento	Carlos Hugo Christensen
1968	*Antes o Verão*	Gerson Tavares
	As Amorosas	Walter Hugo Khoury
	A Margem	Ozualdo Candeias
	Fome de Amor	Nelson Pereira dos Santos
1969	*Macunaíma*	Joaquim Pedro de Andrade
	Copacabana me Engana	Antônio Carlos Fontoura
	O Dragão da Maldade	Glauber Rocha
	Brasil Ano 2000	Walter Lima, Jr.
	O Quarto	Rubem Biáfora
	O Bandido da Luz Vermelha	Rogério Sganzerla
	A Compadecida	George Jonas
	Viagem ao Fim do Mundo	Fernando C. Campos
1970	*Quelé do Pajeú*	Anselmo Duarte
	Palácio dos Anjos	Walter Hugo Khoury
	A Moreninha	Glauco M. Laurelli
	Memória de Helena	David Neves
	Juliana do Amor Perdido	Sérgio Ricardo
	Um Uísque Antes, Um Cigarro Depois	F. Tambellini
	Marcelo Zona Sul	Xavier de Oliveira
	Vingança dos Doze	Marcos Farias
	Profeta da Fome	Maurice Capovilla
	Sanque Quente em Tarde Fria	Fernando C. Campos
	Os Deuses e os Mortos	Ruy Guerra
	Os Herdeiros	Carlos Diegues

Table 15—Continued

Film	Director
1971 Ana Terra	Durval Gomes Garcia
A Casa Assassinada	Paula César Saraceni
A Culpa	Domingos de Oliveria
O Donzelo	Stefan Wohl
Em Família	Paulo Porto
As 4 Chaves Mágicas	Alberto Salvá
Um Certo Capitão Rodrigo	Anselmo Duarte
Um Homem sem Importância	Alberto Salvá
A Guerra dos Pelados	Sílvio Back
O Barão Otelo no Barato dos Bilhões	M. Borges
Pra Quem Fica, Tchau	Reginaldo Farias
Cordélia, Cordélia	Rodolfo Nanni
1972 Fora das Grades	Astolfo Araújo
Como Era Gostoso o meu Francês	N. P. dos Santos
A Viúva Virgem	Pedro Rovai
Cassy Jones, o Magnífico Sedutor	L. S. Person
Independência ou Morte	Carlos Coimbra
Roleta Russa, o Jogo da Vida	Bráulio Pedroso
Toda Nudez Será Castigada	Arnaldo Jabor
Um Anjo Mau	Roberto Santos
As Deusas	Walter Hugo Khoury
Piconzé	Ypê Nakashima
Os Sóis da Ilha da Pascoa	Pierre Kast
Viver de Morrer	Jorge Ileli
1973 Compasso de Espera	Antunes Filho
O Descarte	Anselmo Duarte
O Fabuloso Fittipaldi	Roberto Farias
A Faca e o Rio	George Sluizer
Joana Francesa	Carlos Diegues
Obessão	Jece Valadão
Os Primeiros Momentos	Pedro Camargo
Sagarana: O Duelo	Paulo Thiago
São Bernardo	Leon Hirszman
Tati, a Garota	Bruno Barreto
O Último Êxtase	Walter Hugo Khoury
Vai Trabalhar, Vagabundo	Hugo Carvana
1974 O Comprador de Frazendas	Alberto Pieralisi
Uirá—Um Índio em Busca de Deus	Gustavo Dahl
O Marginal	Carlos Manga
O Anjo da Noite	Walter Hugo Khoury

Table 15—Continued

Film	Director
Pureza Prohibida	Alfredo Sternheim
A Noite do Espantalho	Sérgio Ricardo
Sedução	Fauzi Mansur
Ainda Agarro Esta Vizinha	Pedro Rovai
O Amuleto de Ogum	Nelson Pereira dos Santos
Os Condenados	Zelito Viana
A Rainha Diaba	Antônio Carlos Fontoura
A Estrela Sobe	Bruno Barreto
1975 *A Lenda de Ubirajara*	André L. Oliveira
A Ovelha Negra	Haroldo Marinho Barbosa
Guerra Conjugal	Joaquim Pedro de Andrade
O Caçador de Fantasmas	Flávio Migliaccio
O Casal	Daniel Filho
O Desejo	Walter Hugo Khoury
O Pistoleiro	Oscar Santana
O Predileto	Roberto Palmari
O Rei da Noite	Hector Babenco
Passe Livre	Oswaldo Caldeira
Pecado na Sacristia	Miguel Borges

Source: 1967–1972: Dieter Goebel and Carlos Rodrigues de Souza, *A Economia Cinematográfica Brasileira,* unpublished, 1975; 1973: *Filme Cultura* 8, no. 26 (September 1974), 55: 1974: Instituto Nacional do Cinema, *Boletim Informativo SIP* (1975), p. 15; 1975: Embrafilme, *Informações sobre a Indústria Cinematográfica Brasileira, Anuário de 1975,* p. 15.

What one does notice about the awards is the virtual absence of explicitly political films between 1970, when *Os Deuses e os Mortos (The Gods and the Dead)*, a film about the process of capital accumulation in the cacao region of southern Bahia, and *Os Herdeiros (The Heirs)*, a panorama of forty years of Brazilian politics, were selected, and 1973, when *São Bernardo*, Leon Hirszman's brilliant adaptation of Graciliano Ramo's classic novel, was chosen. This absence is of course owing to the larger political situation of the country at the time, the most repressive period of military rule in Brazil.

Like GEICINE before it, the INC set up a program of film production financing based on the 1962 profit remittance law (discussed in chapter 4) that had determined that 40 percent of a foreign distributor's income tax on profit derived from the exhibition of foreign films should be deposited, optionally, in the Banco do Brasil for possible use by the distributor in the co-production of national films. Prior to the creation of INC, only seven films had been co-produced under this system. The deposit, originally established as an option to allow foreign distributors to participate financially in the co-production of Brazilian films, represented the internationalist mentality of the group that headed INC in its first year of existence.

The 1966 decree-law that founded INC reaffirmed the deposit and made it mandatory, while at the same time stipulating that if the distributor chose not to co-produce national films, the money would become part of INC's budget rather than simply reverting to the federal government as had previously been the case (Decree-law no 43, Art. 28, items 1 and 2). The prospect of involuntarily aiding the development of Brazilian cinema apparently changed the mind of some distributors, for between 1966 and 1969, when Embrafilme was founded and the co-production option was eliminated, thirty-eight films were financed under this program (see Appendix B for a complete listing). In 1969, the deposit became part of Embrafilme's budget with no possibility of co-production using these funds.[26]

Although many producers took advantage of this financing program (twenty-seven different production companies, in fact), opposition to it, as noted in chapter 4, was widespread, since it represented a potential bonus for foreign distributors that could result in the internationalization of the industry. One might expect, given its internationalist predilections, that the universalist group would have a greater propensity to participate in the co-production program than filmmakers and producers aligned with the "nationalist" group. In fact, in 1968, Walter Hugo Khoury, Rubem Biáfora, Flávio Tambellini, and Carlos Hugo Christensen, the four directors most closely associated with the universalist group, did receive co-production financing. But so did directors associated with Cinema Novo such as Carlos Diegues (Os Herdeiros), Joaquim Pedro de Andrade (Macunaíma), Roberto Santos (O Homem Nu; The Nude Man), Eduardo Coutinho (O Homem que Comprou o Mundo; The Man Who Bought the World), and Carlos Alberto

Prates Correia *(Os Marginais; The Outlaws)*. The program led to seemingly strange associations, as Walter Hugo Khoury's Kâmera Filmes joined with Screen Gems and Columbia Pictures to produce Cinema Novo director Arnaldo Jabor's hermetic *Pindorama*. The co-production program, in fact, became an important source of financing for Cinema Novo directors in a period when production capital was increasingly difficult to come by.

The decree-law founding INC explicitly gave it the power to set the screen quota for Brazilian films. The precise dimensions of the quota vary according to the size of the city and the number of days per week a theater operates. When INC was founded, the quota, it may be recalled, was set at fifty-six days per year of compulsory exhibition. When it was absorbed by Embrafilme in 1975, the quota had risen to 112 days per year, a 100 percent increase in nine years (see table 32, on p. 185).

INC Resolution 3 (11 May 1967) provisionally confirmed the quota at fifty-six days until criteria concerning the market potential of national films could be established. In late 1969, the Institute conceded an additional seven days for the exhibition of Brazilian films, effectively raising the quota for that year to sixty-three days (Res. 31, 18 September 1969). It repeated this action during the first half of 1970 (Res. 35, 23 April 1970), before finally raising the quota for the second half of 1970 to the equivalent of eighty-four days per year, making the effective quota for 1970 seventy-seven days of compulsory exhibition (thirty-five days in the first half, forty-two during the second half; Res. 38, 30 June 1970). This same resolution set the quota for 1971 onward at twenty-eight days of compulsory exhibition per quarter, or 112 days per year. Since the previous increases had been provisional, or had applied to one year alone, this increase in fact *doubled* the screen quota from the fifty-six days reaffirmed by INC Resolution 3.

As might be expected, Resolution 38 was fought bitterly by exhibition and distribution groups who claimed to be losing money even with the quota of fifty-six days per year. It was of course heartily supported by producers, who felt that production itself could double under the measure. Because of pressure from exhibition and distribution groups, a new resolution was passed before the new quota went into effect, reducing it to ninety-eight days per year or forty-nine days per semester (Res. 49, 29 December 1970). Exhibition groups continued their pressure, however, and succeeded in having the screen quota lowered even further, to eighty-four days per year (Res. 60, 16 September 1971). INC president Ricardo Cravo Albin was adamantly opposed to this second reduction, as he had been to the first, and submitted his resignation rather than sign the resolution. He was replaced by Brigadier Armando Troia, who signed the reduction to eighty-four days per year.[27] The quota did not reach 112 days again until mid-1975, shortly before INC was absorbed by Embrafilme (Res. 106, 30 June 1975).

Although Ricardo Cravo Albin was president of INC for only a year and a half (from March 1970 until September 1971), his administration seems to be indicative of a new mentality arising within the state cinematic apparatus that would come to the fore much more evidently with the reorientation and restructuring of Embrafilme in 1973 and 1975. Ramos suggests that it was under Albin's administration that the universalists began to lose power to the nationalists, although we have seen that such a dichotomy ceased to have much significance after the creation of INC.[28]

Albin was the third of INC's six presidents, having been preceded by Flávio Tambellini (who held the post provisionally upon INC's creation) and Durval Gomes Garcia (1967–1970). He was followed by Armando Troia (1971–1972), Carlos Guimarães de Matos, Jr. (1972–1974), who left INC to assume a lucrative position as an executive with the Cinema International Corporation, and Alcino Teixeira de Mello (1974–1975).

A lawyer by training, Albin took office after having been nominated by Minister of Education and Culture Jarbas Passarinho, and confirmed by Brazil's president, Emílio Garrastazu Médici. Prior to that time, he had had little experience in, or knowledge of, the technicalities of film production. He had, however, been active in the cultural field as president of the film council of Rio de Janeiro's Museu de Imagem e Som. When told by Passarinho of his nomination, Albin responded that he did not understand anything about the cinema, to which the minister replied, "So what? When I took over the Ministry of Education and Culture I didn't know anything about education. Now I know more than a lot of people."[29] Albin's confirmation was opposed by people such as INC's executive secretary Antônio Moniz Vianna, who saw his selection as a victory of the "festive Left" (read Cinema Novo).[30]

When Albin took office, he had neither a clear idea of the possibilities of the INC, nor a program for the development of the film industry. He recognized three basic types of films: commercial, artistic, and cultural or didactic films. It was his feeling that INC should be dedicated primarily to the encouragement of commercial films, but that the ideal would be to promote films of high artistic quality that were also popular with broad sectors of the Brazilian public. He told filmmakers that to reach this ideal, they should follow the example of Joaquim Pedro de Andrade (one of the founding fathers of Cinema Novo) and make films like *Macunaíma*.[31] Cinema Novo was indeed gaining dominance within the state cinema apparatus.

In its continued support and expansion of the screen quota, and its establishment of the subsidy program, the INC can be seen as essentially neutral, in that all national films could potentially benefit from the reserve market through a process of competition with other Brazilian films. Furthermore, all films with box-office incomes falling between established boundaries were qualified to participate in the subsidy program. Its programs of quality awards and co-productions supported films across the entire spectrum of the industry, with no apparent ideological or political orientation.

This in no way implies that the Brazilian state itself was neutral. The Institute was in many ways a reflection of the regime that created it and was designed to foster capital accumulation in the private sector of the industry. Its model, as already noted, was based not only on subsidies and other awards, but also on collaboration with foreign capital. Within these parameters, INC did not exercise direct ideological control. That duty was fulfilled by the government's censorship agency in the Ministry of Justice's federal police.

Cinema Novo and the Instituto Nacional do Cinema

It is important to recognize that the period of INC's existence, 1966–1975, was, especially between 1969 and 1973, one of the most repressive periods of military rule in Brazil. Many films, including Andrade's *Macunaíma* and dos Santos's *Como era gostoso o meu francês (How Tasty Was My Little Frenchman)*, both of which were co-produced under the INC program, had problems with censorship, while a number of directors, including Glauber Rocha and Ruy Guerra, were forced to film abroad, or at least search elsewhere for production financing. Other filmmakers and film professionals were arrested during the period for "ideological offenses." The coercive state apparatus maintained strict control even while the Instituto Nacional do Cinema served a technical function in the industry.

Although the INC did not exercise direct ideological control, it would be simplistic to asume that it did not have a profound indirect ideological and political influence on the industry. The Institute did not exist in isolation. It was part of an often repressive state apparatus that attempted to silence opposition, while at the same time imposing an economic model that has frequently been referred to in the press and elsewhere as "savage capitalism." To understand fully the impact of state policy on the industry during this period, it will perhaps be useful to trace the evolution of Cinema Novo from 1964 to around 1973, when state policy underwent a process of reorientation that clearly favored the Cinema Novo group.[32]

As mentioned in the previous chapter, in its initial phase (1960–1964) Cinema Novo had a fairly well-defined political purpose, tied to the process of *conscientização* (consciousness raising) in the hope that the Brazilian people would gain a critical awareness of the country's underdevelopment and "colonial situation," and join in the struggle for national liberation. The films of the period, often about the country's lumpen, sought out the dark corners of Brazilian society—urban slums, the impoverished Northeast—where its contradictions were most apparent. Films like *Vidas Secas* (Nelson Pereira dos Santos, 1963), *Os Fuzis* (Ruy Guerra, 1964), and *Deus e o Diabo na Terra do Sol* (Glauber Rocha, 1964) best exemplify this tendency.

The coup d'état of 1964 caught Cinema Novo, and the Left generally, off guard, and initiated a second phase, which continued until about 1968. Despite repression and censorship, there was still room for cultural and political discussion, although any effective link between leftist intellectuals and the potentially revolutionary classes was prohibited. During this period, the focus of Cinema Novo shifted from rural to urban Brazil, as film-makers turned their cameras on themselves, so to speak, in an attempt to understand the failure of the Left in 1964. Paulo César Saraceni's *O Desafio* (*The Challenge*, 1965) deals with a young, anguished, and impotent journalist in post-1964 Brazil. Rocha's *Terra em Transe* portrays the vacillation of a poet between the Left and the Right, and his final, suicidal option for individual armed struggle. Gustavo Dahl's *O Bravo Guerreiro* focuses on the struggle of an idealistic young congressman, and ends with a shot of him looking into a mirror while pointing a gun into his mouth, unable even to pull the trigger. In Nelson Pereira dos Santos's *Fome de Amor* (1968) the revolutionary leader is deaf, dumb, and blind. These films and others express the disillusion and despair of intellectuals after 1964.

The 1964 coup cut short the initial political course of Cinema Novo. This does not mean that its participants ceased making political films after that date, nor that the movement abandoned its critical vision of Brazilian society. Rather, the terms of the discussion were radically altered. As Ruy Guerra puts it:

Cinema Novo had very little time to develop. We began making our first films in 1962, and in 1964 there was the coup d'état. So we had only two years. From 1964 to 1968 there was a limited political and economic space for a certain kind of production, but it became increasingly difficult to make films. In truth, the birth, apogee, and decline of Cinema Novo came in a very short period of time. Furthermore, the economic conditions that permitted the financing of Cinema Novo ceased to exist after 1964.[33]

The economic conditions Guerra refers to include the financing provided to a number of early Cinema Novo films, including his own, by José Luiz de Magalhães Lins of the Banco Nacional de Minas Gerais.

But a paradox in Cinema Novo's initial strategies of political action contributed to a change in tactics in the post-1964 period. Although the movement had opposed traditional modes of cinematic production and the aesthetic forms accompanying them, its participants had made no real attempt to create alternative or parallel exhibition circuits. Rather, they released their films in established commercial circuits that had been built primarily for the exhibition of foreign films. The Brazilian public, long conditioned by Hollywood, was generally unreceptive to the "aesthetics of hunger" of early Cinema Novo films, which became in many ways a group of films made by and for an enlightened, intellectual elite, and not for broad sectors of the film-going public, much less for Brazil's impoverished masses.

Cinema Novo's low-cost production methods soon began to show their limitations. Like Vera Cruz before it, Cinema Novo made the mistake of assuming that simply making a film was enough to assure its success on the market. Directors and producers came to depend on distributors, and even exhibitors, for postproduction financing, which put them in the disadvantageous position of having to pay a larger percentage than usual for the distribution and exhibition of their films.[34] The problem of a return on investments became critical at a time that the movement was feeling intense ideological pressure in a less than favorable political situation.

Exhibitors argued that Cinema Novo films were too intellectual for success in the market, and so the production of more popular films became imperative if Cinema Novo was to continue to exist. The struggle for the market thus became a priority, and with that struggle came a number of aesthetic and ideological concessions. Namely, Cinema Novo largely abandoned its attempt to use film as a political tool in the struggle for national liberation (at least in the terms proposed prior to 1964) and made more of an effort to please the public. As Jean-Claude Bernardet and Maria Rita Galvão have put it, Cinema Novo abandoned the *povo* (the common people), which was theoretically the object of its first films, for the public, which was and is largely middle-class.[35]

Cinema Novo took a number of steps to solve the problem of reaching a broad audience. First, producers and directors formed a distribution cooperative (Difilme) as a strategy for placing their films more easily in the multinational-controlled market. Second, they began to make films with a more popular appeal, by turning toward literary classics: Joaquim Pedro de Andrade's O Padre e a Moça (1965) is based on a poem by Carlos Drummond de Andrade; Walter Lima, Jr.'s Menino de Engenho (1965) on a novel by José Lins do Rego; Roberto Santo's A Hora e Vez de Augusto Matraga (1966) on a short story by João Guimarães Rosa; and Paulo César Saraceni's Capitu (1968) is based on Machado de Assis's masterpiece, Dom Casmurro. Comedy also became an acceptable mode of discourse, in such films as Nelson Pereira dos Santos's El Justicero (1967), Domingos de Oliveira's Todas as Mulheres do Mundo (1967), and Roberto Farias's Toda Donzela Tem um Pai que é uma Fera (Every Maiden Has a Father Who Is a Beast, 1967).

These circumstances—restrictions created by the political situation, economic difficulties, and the necessity to woo the market—dovetailed precisely with the INC's vision of its responsibilities. As Renato Ortiz points out, the Institute's leaders attempted to dissociate the cultural product itself from its conditions of production and consumption, and to focus primarily on the question of the market and the public. The INC therefore tended to support, at least in its leaders' public statements, a cinema conceived as a form of entertainment based on the public's supposed likes and dislikes. "The INC thus tries to combat two postures which opposed its market-oriented propositions: aestheticism and ideological cinema" (Renato Ortiz, Cultura Brasileira). "Aestheticism," in this case, refers to Cinema Novo's attempts to find a new cinematic language to transmit its ideas to a public conditioned by Hollywood, and "ideological cinema" to the movement's political inclination.[36] When Ricardo Cravo Albin urged filmmakers to make films like Macunaíma, it was thus not because he approved of its politics, but rather because it was based on a national literary classic, and because it was a great success in the marketplace.

Cinema Novo came under political pressure because of the new political reality. The state's coercive apparatus, in the form of censorship, limited the themes that could be treated in films, and a number of filmmakers had to seek financing outside Brazil. The reality of the marketplace had an equally coercive effect, as directors were forced to make concessions to the public's taste. Ruy Guerra sees such "economic censorship," as he calls it, as more serious than political censorship:

Official, political censorship forms only a small part of a whole process of restriction within the broader context of an economic project that makes a certain kind of cinema viable. A certain economic control, exercised by distributors, producers, and exhibitors, constitutes a repressive scheme within the overall colonial situation of Brazilian cinema. The financing of certain kinds of films is impossible, even without censorship, because the structures that would give access to popular sectors do not exist. So one cannot develop political projects, but merely commercial ones. This context does not allow a truly critical cinema, for even if its films got by the censors, they would not be viable as commercial productions. Official censorship is less harmful than the extremely violent economic censorship that results from a structure completely dominated by the foreign film, by large distributors, [and] by exhibition networks.[37]

The emphasis on the market would become even greater in the 1970s as Embrafilme became the major source of financing for Cinema Novo directors. In the movement's only collective manifesto, written paradoxically after it was deemed moribund, they rejected the "public at all cost" philosophy of the state cinematic apparatus and the "bureaucratic cinema of statistics and pseudointellectual myths."[38] They rejected, and continue to reject, low-level commercialism at the expense of serious cultural expression.

INC's programs were not met with unanimity of support from any social sector. The co-production program, for example, came under fire not from the Left, as one might expect, but rather from the Right. INC was criticized not for being biased in favor of any specific filmmaker or group of filmmakers, but rather for apparently lacking criteria for determining what films it would finance. Exemplary of this sort of criticism is a series of articles published in the influential O Estado de São Paulo under the general title "O MEC e o cinema nacional" ("The Ministry of Education and Culture and National Cinema"). Although couched in a tone of exaggerated moralism, these articles, written by Rubens Rodrigues dos

Santos, are in many ways indicative of reigning conceptions about what state aid to the film industry should comprise.[39]

Dos Santos wrote that the government's responsibility vis-à-vis the film industry was to "stimulate good cinema, the kind of cinema that helps build healthy young people, that preserves moral standards and the values of [our] nationality." But what had occurred, suggested the writer, was that INC has used public funds in the production and subvention of "mediocre" films charged with violence, eroticism, and low-level slapstick. He quickly added that he was not opposed to the production of violent, erotic, or idiotic films per se, merely to their being produced with government support. He felt that it was inexcusable for the government to provide "certificates of exhibition" and exhibition subsidies to films such as Gamal, o Delírio do Sexo (Gamal, The Delirium of Sex, João Batista de Andrade, 1970), Caveira My Friend (Skull, My Friend, Álvaro Guimarães, 1970), O Pornógrafo (The Pornographer, João Callegaro, 1971), and Nenê Bandalho (Emílio Fontana, 1971), four films representing the experimental or "underground" tendency of Brazilian cinema.

He continued by noting that since 1967 INC had distributed some 10 million cruzeiros to finance twenty-five films (plus others which had not yet been completed when he wrote the articles) under the compulsory deposit co-production program. Censors had declared seventeen of these films inappropriate for those under the age of eighteen, four inappropriate for those under the age of fourteen, one inappropriate for those under the age of ten, and only three as appropriate to the general public. Dos Santos's conclusion was that the INC's policy was misdirected, since 70 percent of the films it was involved with were judged to be damaging in one way or another to Brazil's youth.

It never occurred to Dos Santos that the problem might rest with the arbitrary criteria of Brazil's police censors rather than with those of the Instituto Nacional do Cinema. The type of accusation made by dos Santos has reappeared with some frequency over the years, most recently in 1980 when a federal senator made headlines by denouncing Embrafilme for producing pornographic films. His denunciation led President João Figueiredo to make an uninformed statement against such practices, which in reality never existed.[40] More often than not, such accusations are based on hearsay, on a cursory glance at the titles of some films, or on a lack of concrete information concerning the true activities of the state cinematic apparatus.

Table 16. Brazilian Feature Film Production, 1965–1975

1965	33	1971	94
1966	28	1972	70
1967	44	1973	58
1968	54	1974	77
1969	53	1975	85
1970	83		

Source: Alcino Teixeira de Mello, *Legislação do Cinema Brasileiro* (Rio de Janeiro: Embrafilme, 1978), 2:558.

Under the programs established by the Instituto Nacional do Cinema, production increased from thirty-three films in 1965, the year prior to INC's creation, to eighty-five films in 1975, the final year of its existence, an increase of 157 percent (see table 16). The sharpest increase came in 1970 (56 percent), when many of the films co-produced under the compulsory deposit program were completed. Production during the INC period reached a high of ninety-four in 1971, which can in part be accounted for by the completion of the remainder of the projects under the same program. After 1971–1972 it becomes increasingly difficult to credit the INC with increases in production since, although its subsidy programs continued, its single co-production program terminated with the creation of Embrafilme in 1969. In the early 1970s, Embrafilme replaced INC as the major state agency involved in film production financing. One reason for the decline in production in 1972 and 1973 is that official production programs were in a period of transition, and no financing was released between the end of the INC program (1969) and the beginning of Embrafilme's loan program (1971).

EXHIBITION AND DISTRIBUTION

A perusal of INC's resolutions concerning exhibition reveals that the Institute was not always aware of, or concerned with, the problems faced by this sector of the Brazilian film industry. Resolutions were often conceived of in terms of subsidies to producers *at the expense of* exhibitors. Some exhibition groups, both foreign and domestically owned, have fought bitterly the increasing screen quota for Brazilian films. In addition to the quota, legislation also determined that the exhibitor must pay the national producer 50 percent of net box-office income (Res. 3, 11 May 1967, which reaffirmed a statute of Decree-law 4,064, 29 January 1942; see chapter 2), whereas they were permitted to negotiate the percentage paid for the exhibition of foreign films.

Besides being obligated to show Brazilian features a certain number of days per year, exhibitors were also forced to comply with legislation providing compulsory exhibition of short subjects deemed by INC as deserving "Special Classification" (Res. 4, 12 May 1967). Compulsory exhibition of so-qualified short documentaries had the following evolution during INC's existence: in 1967, 28 days per year (Res. 4); 1971, 28 days confirmed (Res. 64, 1 October 1971); 1973, 35 days per year (Res. 87, 4 May 1973); and in 1975, 56 days per year (Res. 107, 30 June 1975). To fulfill the requirements of the law, short films were to be included in a program with foreign features rather than national films. The rental price of these films was fixed by INC as the equivalent value of 0.8 percent of the number of seats available in each theater, in each session exhibited, calculated according to the highest admission price in effect (Res. 4). If, for example, a theater had 1,000 seats at an admission price of $2 per ticket, the short film would be entitled to 0.8 percent times 2,000, or $16 per session, independent of the number of patrons actually attending.

As a means of policing the market and assuring proper return to producers, the INC established the obligatory use by exhibitors of standardized tickets and income-reporting sheets, printed and sold by INC (Res. 23, 6 August 1968; Res. 36, 27 May 1970; Res. 51, 14 January 1971; Res. 58, 14 May 1971; Res. 93, 19 February 1974).

Legislation also established the obligatory use of cash registers and entrance gates sold by INC that registered the number of spectators entering individual theaters (Res. 94, 20 May 1974). Once again, this represented an increase in costs for exhibitors. Numerous court orders, largely unsuccessful, have been obtained by exhibition groups against the use of these machines and especially against the obligatory purchase from INC of rolls of paper (tickets) to be used in the cash register, sold at over ten times the market price. The sale of these items was a major source of INC's, and later Embrafilme's, income.[41]

The action of INC relative to the distribution sector is limited to three basic areas: (1) regulation of income for the distribution of Brazilian films; (2) the compulsory deposit of a portion of income tax (for foreign distributors); and (3) the compulsory copying of films in Brazil. Resolution 7 (9 June 1967) stipulated that distributors of Brazilian films may charge the producer no more than 20 percent of his share for distribution in cities of over 2 million people and no more than 25 percent in cities under 2 million. The producer's share of the film's net income—gross income minus expenses for advertising, box office inspection, and other general expenses—was, as we have seen, set by the INC at 50 percent. No restrictions were placed on the amount charged for the distribution of foreign films.

Resolution 20 (8 January 1968) regulates the remission of profits in accordance with previous laws stipulating that 40 percent of income tax due must be deposited in an account, in the name of INC, for possible use in the co-production of national films.

Resolution 74 (5 September 1972) had far-reaching effects, for it established the obligatory copying of all foreign films in Brazilian laboratories, a measure to take effect gradually until full copying began in January 1976. This resolution was intended to have two basic effects: (1) to support the development of a vital sector of the film industry (laboratories) and (2) to make the importation of foreign films more expensive, thus providing an incentive for exhibitors to show more Brazilian films.

Despite increased costs for operating in the country, the American film industry continued to hold a wide advantage in the Brazilian market. Table 17 shows that gross billings of MPEA com-

Table 17. Gross Billings of MPEA Affiliates in Brazil, 1963–1973

	In Actual Dollars	% Change from Previous Year	In 1963 Dollars	% Change from Previous Year
1963	7,171,588	—	7,171,588	—
1964	7,246,749	+ 1.0%	7,152,541	− 0.3%
1965	7,822,209	+ 7.9%	7,587,543	+ 6.1%
1966	10,285,422	+31.5%	9,700,096	+27.8%
1967	14,577,804	+41.7%	13,857,887	+37.8%
1968	13,571,300	− 6.9%	11,942,744	−10.7%
1969	16,986,484	+24.8%	14,141,947	+18.4%
1970	17,382,947	+ 2.6%	13,697,762	− 3.1%
1971	15,603,941	−10.2%	11,800,859	−13.9%
1972	15,328,671	− 1.8%	11,221,319	− 4.9%
1973	16,048,423	+ 4.7%	11,057,363	− 1.5%

Source: Variety, 14 August 1974.

Note: Net market growth, 1963 to 1973 (actual dollars): −123.8%. Net market growth, 1963 to 1973 (constant dollars): −54.2%.

Table 18. Top Foreign Markets for Major U.S. Film Companies, 1963–1973, by 1973 Rankings

	1963	1964	1965	1966	1967	1968	1969	1970	1971	1972	1973
Italy	2	2	2	2	2	2	2	2	1	2	1
Canada	6	5	4	3	3	3	3	4	3	3	2
West Germany	3	3	3	4	5	6	6	5	5	6	3
United Kingdom	1	1	1	1	1	1	1	1	2	1	4
France	4	4	5	5	4	4	4	3	4	4	5
Japan	5	6	6	6	6	5	5	6	6	5	6
Australia	8	8	7	8	8	7	8	7	7	7	7
South Africa	11	11	10	9	10	10	11	10	11	11	8
BRAZIL	10	10	11	10	9	9	7	8	8	9	9
Spain	7	7	8	7	7	8	9	9	9	8	10
Mexico	9	9	9	11	11	11	10	11	10	10	11
Sweden	15	13	13	13	12	13	12	13	13	13	12
Switzerland	17	16	15	16	16	17	16	15	16	15	13
Venezuela	14	15	16	15	17	16	15	14	12	12	14
Argentina	12	12	12	12	13	12	13	12	14	17	15

Source: Variety, 15 May 1974.

Note: Countries are listed in order of 1973 rankings. Gaps are accounted for by countries that ranked in the top fifteen in previous years but not in 1973.

panies operating in Brazil increased from slightly over $7 million in 1963 to over $16 million in 1973, in actual dollars, and from $7 million to over $11.5 million in constant 1963 dollars. Table 18 reveals that throughout the INC period Brazil continued to be an important market for the American film industry, and never ranked lower than tenth among all that industry's foreign markets. The U.S. industry, through its distributors and the local representative of the MPEA, Harry Stone, vigorously fought measures that would in any way limit its access to the Brazilian market.

6

Embrafilme, CONCINE, and a New Direction in State Policy, 1969–1980

On 13 DECEMBER 1968, sparked by an impasse in its constitutional relationship with congress, the Brazilian executive, under the leadership of President Artur da Costa e Silva and a hard-line minister of justice, Luis Antônio da Gama e Silva, decreed the Fifth Institutional Act. The act, which initiated the most repressive period of military rule in Brazil, "granted the president authority to recess legislative bodies, to intervene in the states without limit, to cancel elective mandates and suspend political rights, to suspend constitutional guarantees with regard to civil service tenure, etc., to confiscate property acquired by illicit means, issue complementary acts, and set aside the right of habeas corpus."[1] It led to the imposition of the strongest censorship yet known in Brazil, and eventually forced a number of political leaders, artists, and intellectuals, including Glauber Rocha, Chico Buarque de Hollanda, Caetano Veloso, and Gilberto Gil, into exile. The appearance of armed movements in opposition to the regime led, in turn, to the institutionalization of torture, and a national campaign by the military against "subversion."

It was within this political context that Embrafilme (the Empresa Brasileira de Filmes) was created by Decree-law 862 (9 September 1969), promulgated by the provisional military junta ruling Brazil during the illness of President Costa e Silva under the powers of the First and Fifth Institutional Acts.[2] And it was within a context of political repression that state policy toward the film industry changed direction in the early 1970s, moving away from the relatively neutral, technical solutions of the 1960s toward a form of state capitalism in which the government be-

137

came an active agent and productive force in the industry. This chapter will examine the creation of Embrafilme, the redirection and consolidation of a state policy toward the industry, the results and implications of the reorientation, and finally the contradictions of state policy toward the industry, which led, eventually, to the most severe crisis in the history of Brazilian cinema.

State enterprises, of either public or mixed ownership, have been created in many economic sectors in Brazil to guarantee national security (Petrobrás, for example), to organize a sector that cannot develop adequately in a competitive, free market system, or to provide supplementary economic support to private enterprises.[3] Mixed-ownership enterprises are organized according to the same principle followed by private enterprises, with the exception that the state retains, by law, a majority interest. Such enterprises are by definition designed to engage in economic activities, theoretically generating profit for the state, and stimulating capital accumulation in related private-sector firms. Desite its initially limited rationale and attributes, the creation of Embrafilme marks a considerable change in government policy toward the film industry, with state taking a more direct role in the industry's affairs.

THE CREATION OF EMBRAFILME

A mixed-ownership enterprise subordinated to the Ministry of Education and Culture, Embrafilme was created initially to promote and distribute Brazilian films abroad.[4] Its initial social capital was to be 6 million cruzeiros, divided into 600,000 shares of common stock worth ten cruzeiros each. In reality, Embrafilme was (and continues to be) a mixed-ownership enterprise in name and organization only, for upon its creation 70 percent of its stock belonged to the federal government, 29.4 percent to the Instituto Nacional do Cinema (itself a federal autarquia), and only 0.6 percent to private shareholders.[5]

In 1975 Embrafilme was reorganized, and the enterprise officially absorbed the executive functions of the INC. At that time its capital was increased from 6 million to 80 million cruzeiros (slightly under U.S.$10 million), with the state holding a 99.9

percent share. In 1976 a new policy-making body, the Conselho Nacional do Cinema (National Film Council; CONCINE), was created to assume the legislative functions of the now-defunct Instituto Nacional do Cinema. CONCINE determines policy that is executed by Embrafilme.[6]

Embrafilme was the brainchild of INC president Durval Gomes Garcia, and, like INC before it, it was created in an authoritarian manner, without the participation or even knowledge of broad sectors of the film industry. Not even the National Film Industry Syndicate (SNIC) was consulted prior to its creation.[7] Embrafilme therefore naturally had a somewhat less than cordial reception in the industry and other areas of Brazilian society. In an editorial, the *Jornal do Brasil* questioned the need for a new governmental film agency, especially one designed to promote Brazilian cinema abroad, since it had not yet consolidated its place in the domestic market.[8]

Along the same lines, participants in an industry Symposium on the Cinema and Its Market, held during the Fifth Brasília Film Festival, sent a statement to Minister of Education and Culture Jarbas Passarinho, a portion of which reads as follows:

The recent creation of Embrafilme . . . has not and will not alter the current situation [of the Brazilian film industry] if the legislation that created it is maintained in its present form. Designed for the distribution of Brazilian films abroad, Embrafilme ignores the fundamental necessity of first occupying the domestic market. The Brazilian film industry receives only 11 percent of the gross income of its own market, while foreign films receive 89 percent.

It seems to us that the penetration of Brazilian films in the international market is very difficult at the present moment, despite the prestige some directors have achieved. We are fully aware that highly developed nations such as Japan have only a restricted foreign market for their films.

It is our view that the strengthening of the domestic market is the indispensable prerequisite for a correct policy of expansion for our cinema. Through well-conceived state planning, Brazilian cinema's progress in the internal market could be so great that it could lead, as a consequences to the placing of national films in the international market.[9]

It was thus felt that, like the Vera Cruz experiment in the 1950s, the state, in creating Embrafilme, was putting the cart before the horse by focusing on the international market, and was at best premature since Brazilian cinema had not yet solidified its position in the domestic market.

Initially Embrafilme was not particularly successful in its primary function of foreign distribution. In its first nine years, Embrafilme had negotiated sales of only U.S.$300,000. More recently, however, its attempts at exporting have begun to bear fruit, reaching the figure of U.S.$4 million in 1982 (see table 19). The figure was expected to rise to over $5,000,000 in 1984. It is important to note, however, that as film industry professionals had predicted, Brazilian cinema penetrated foreign markets after it had attained considerable success in its own market, not before. Embrafilme has in recent years opened small offices in the United States and France as well as in several Latin American countries. Packages of Brazilian films have been sold recently to both the Republic of China and the Soviet Union. Emphasis, however, remains focused on Latin American markets, where Brazilian films have been highly competitive with films from all nations.[10]

Even as initially formulated, Embrafilme's attributes went far beyond the distribution of Brazilian films abroad. According to Article 2 of Decree-law 862, Embrafilme's objective was to distribute and promote films abroad (including participating in festivals and foreign showings) and "to engage in commercial or industrial activities related to the principal object of its ac-

Table 19. Brazilian Film Exports, 1978–1983
(in U.S. dollars)

1978	165,000
1979	900,000
1980	1,400,000
1981	990,500
1982	4,000,000
1983	2,000,000

Sources: Embrafilme, Annual Report 1981; Gazeta Mercantil, 27 April 1981; Variety, 13 April 1983, 21 March 1984.

tivity."[11] The key to Embrafilme's rapid expansion into areas other than the foreign distribution of Brazilian films lies in the final clause of its definition of attributes. It quickly replaced the Instituto Nacional do Cinema as the primary government source of film production financing.[12]

Embrafilme's income for its diverse activities, according to the legislation that give it birth, was to derive from (1) loans and donations from unspecified sources; (2) profit from the distribution of films, credit operations, bank deposits, and the sale of patrimonial bonds; (3) interest and service taxes on financing programs; (4) the fund deriving from a portion of the income tax on foreign films, which had previously reverted to INC; (5) subsidies and other monies from the federal or state governments; (6) other unspecified sources.[13] With the creation of Embrafilme, the foreign distributor's option to co-produce national films with the portion of income tax retained in a special fund was eliminated, and the deposit became a permanent part of the enterprise's budget.

Since its creation, Embrafilme has been responsible for many different kinds of activities, commercial and noncommercial. It produces and distributes cultural and educational films to schools and other nonprofit organizations throughout the country. It supports the production of short subjects and documentaries. It is involved in the preservation of Brazil's cinematic memory through the restoration of films that were thought to be lost, or that are in an advanced stage of deterioration. It cooperates with the efforts of the *cinematecas* (film archives) of both Rio de Janeiro and São Paulo and is responsible for the 1980 renovation of the *cinemateca* in Rio de Janeiro's Museum of Modern Art. It organizes film courses for industry technicians and, in coordination with CAPES (Coordenação do Aperfeiçoamento de Pessoal de Nível Superior—Coordinator for Training Higher Education Personnel), it has provided scholarships for study abroad in the area of film production. It gathers and publishes statistics concerning the film industry as a whole and, in coordination with CONCINE, it serves as an industry watchdog to assure that all theaters comply with existing cinematic legislation. It publishes books on cinema and the magazine *Filme Cultura* and has recently organized complete retrospectives of the films of Humberto Mauro (1984) and Glauber Rocha (1985).[14]

This chapter will discuss Embrafilme's commercial activities, since they have a more direct bearing on the development of the film industry, and will bring in noncommercial activities only to the extent that they effect or alter the performance of the enterprise as a whole. In many ways, as we shall see, Embrafilme is unique as a mixed-ownership enterprise in Brazil, precisely because of its legal obligation to engage in noncommercial, nonprofit cultural activities.

SUPPORTIVE STATE POLICY UNDER EMBRAFILME

In 1970, its first full year of operation, Embrafilme began granting producers low-interest (10 percent) loans for film production financing. The amount available varied according to the size and experience of the production company. Until mid-1974 producers wanting production financing under this program were divided into three categories according to the number of films they had been producing annually. Sixty percent of available resources were reserved for those who had produced an average of two to three films per year, 20 percent for those averaging one to two films per year, and the final 20 percent for beginning producers. Since few production companies averaged over two films per year, the program was clearly designed to support well-established, presumably successful firms.

In 1974, under the directorship of Roberto Farias, the program was altered to further benefit stable (in terms of the Brazilian industry) production companies. Only those firms with a social capital of over 100,000 cruzeiros (which, at the time, was under U.S.$15,000) were eligible for financing, and beginning producers were eliminated from consideration. This alteration attempted to benefit and stimulate capital accumulation in at least minimally established firms.[15] Because the enterprise decided to concentrate its resources in the co-production program which had been initiated in 1973, the loan program was phased out after 1979.

Between 1970 and 1979, eighty-two films by fifty-six different production companies were financed under this program (see table 20).[16] Brazilian production for the 1970–1974 period, when this program was at its strongest, was 382 films, or an average of 76.4 films per year (see table 16 and Appendix A). Although many of the films financed were not completed in the year contracts were signed, it is safe to say that during this period Embrafilme financed over 25 percent of national film production under the program (see Appendix C for partial listing).[17]

Decisions to grant film production financing were made on purely technical grounds, taking into consideration the size of the company, its production history, the number of national and international awards it had won, and its experience. Embrafilme did not analyze scripts, but merely required that a ten-page synopsis be submitted with the application. It was, in fact, financing production companies, and not making qualitative or ideological judgments about the films in question. When asked about its apparent lack of cultural criteria for granting financing, Embrafilme's director at the time, José Osvaldo Meira Pena, is quoted as having said: "When El Greco was asked to paint the churches of Toledo, the Inquisition judged the paintings after they were finished, and approved or disapproved. When the BNH [Banco

Table 20. Films Financed by Embrafilme's Loan Program, 1970–1979

	Number	Amount In Cruzieros	Amount (in U.S. dollars)
1970	12	2,400,000	522,875
1971	13	1,978,000	373,913
1972	30	6,494,000	1,095,109
1973	27	5,221,000	851,712
1974	23	6,320,000	930,780
1975	6	1,800,000	221,402
1976	4	1,640,000	153,701
1977	3	1,525,000	107,850
1978	3	2,055,000	113,724
1979	3	1,096,585	40,689

Sources: 1970: *O Estado de São Paulo*, 7 February 1971; 1971–1979: Embrafilme, Annual Reports.

Note: Different publications, even those issued by Embrafilme, give different figures for some years. Nevertheless, the general pattern remains the same.

Nacional de Habitação; National Housing Bank] finances projects, it does not demand that they all be drawn up by Lúcio Costa or [Oscar] Niemeyer."[18] In other words, he saw Embrafilme's duties in quantitative, industrial terms rather than in qualitative or cultural terms.

Such an attitude may seem reasonable for most industries, but the film industry is different in that its product transmits cultural, social, and ideological values, and such "neutrality" was seen as unacceptable by many segments of Brazilian society. The influential *O Estado de São Paulo* editorialized that Embrafilme should *not* be a merely technical agency, but rather should finance only films of high quality which contribute to the "moral foundation of Brazilian society."[19] Once again we see a conflict between the cultural and the economic responsibilites of the state cinematic apparatus.

Internationally acclaimed director and Cinema Novo veteran Nelson Pereira dos Santos was more direct, speaking of the major contradiction within Embrafilme. "We had," he said, " 'the Ministry of Education and Culture presents *The Virgin Widow* or *The Woman Who Does I Don't Know What . . .*' This was a violent contradiction within the moralism of the Brazilian military, with the government financing shit."[20] In fact, among the films financed by the state under the loan program were titles like *A Infidelidade ao Alcance de Todos (Infidelity Within Everyone's Reach*, Aníbal Massaini Neto and Olivier Perroy, 1972), *Os Mansos (The Lenient Husbands*, Pedro Rovai and others, 1972), *Quando as Mulheres Querem Provas (When Women Want Proof*, Cláudio MacDowell, 1975), and *Um Varão entre as Mulheres (A Macho Among Women*, Victor di Mello, 1975). Such a contradiction, which had the military government producing erotic comedies *(pornochanchadas)*, led inevitably to the reformulation of Embrafilme's policy of production financing.

Different kinds of possible reformulation were discussed in a film industry congress sponsored by the INC in October 1972. As suggested earlier, such congresses are important since they provide rare occasions on which representatives of different sectors of the industry join together to discuss the major problems confronting each of them. This in no way implies a unity of vision or purpose; proposals of one sector frequently contradict those of another. In this sense, such congresses also provide an opportunity to measure the conflicts existing within the industry and the progress (or lack thereof) made toward industrial development.

As was consistent with the period, the 1 Congresso da Indústria Cinematográfica (First Film Industry Congress) was organized and conducted in a rather authoritarian manner. The industry itself did not participate in its conception, organization, or composition. The INC chose the participants from each sector and developed a set of regulations that left little room for debate, especially from those not specifically invited to speak.[21] Nevertheless, the congress marked a turning point in the development of state policy toward the industry. As José Mário Ortiz Ramos puts it, it served "as the moment of political confluence between the interest of producers and the state."[22] It was during this congress that producers put forth a "Projeto Brasileiro de Cinema" (Brazilian Project for the Cinema) which resulted in the restructuring of Embrafilme, the creation of CONCINE, and the phasing out of the Instituto Nacional do Cinema.

Discussions at the congress were broad and wide-ranging, and the producers' proposals should be seen within the context of those made by other sectors. One of the weaknesses of state policy, as we shall see, has been that the government has tended to support production without meeting the needs of other sectors, a policy that can only cause problems in the long run. Sectors represented in the congress included, besides the traditionally antagonistic production and exhibition sectors, technicians, sound studios, laboratories, distributors, directors, directors of short films, critics, and actors.[23]

Both actors and technicians appealed to the INC that their respective professions be officially recognized, regulated, and covered by existing labor legislation and protection. The forceful presence of technicians, represented by director of photography José de Almeida, revealed the poor work conditions faced by the sector, and the precariousness of an industry that had not developed even minimum guidelines for relations between workers to producers.[24] Implicit in the statements of both technicians and actors was a recognition of the corporative nature of the Brazilian state. Their professions did not legally exist and were not covered by labor legislation until recognized and regulated by the federal government.[25]

Representatives of sound studios called for obligatory dubbing of all foreign films (a proposal critics unanimously rejected on aesthetic grounds), and for financing for re-equipping studios and theaters. They argued that the frequent complaints about the sound quality of Brazilian films were due not to the studios but rather to the antiquated and poorly maintained equipment of theaters themselves, whence the need for financial assistance to the exhibition sector. Representatives of laboratories expressed concern over the taxes paid by distributors, and suggested that censorship taxes be paid per film, regardless of the number of copies reproduced, rather than by linear meter of each copy, which simply added expense to the distribution of films in the country.

Film directors, represented by Anselmo Duarte, Sílvio Back, and Carlos Alberto de Souza Barros, certainly not the most militant of Brazilian directors—Duarte and Barros had started with Vera Cruz, Back is a regional filmmaker from Paraná, Cinema Novo directors were not represented—called for direct financing from Embrafilme to directors, thus guaranteeing them authorial control over the final product. They also requested limitations on imports of foreign films, and the implementation of a Law of Similars for Brazilian films.

The Law of Similars, designed to protect developing national industries such as the automobile industry, imposes heavy import duties and restrictions on foreign products when "similar" products are manufactured in the country. The argument in favor of this has recurred within the Brazilian film industry since at least the 1960s, although it is essentially fallacious. Besides being a commodity, a manufactured product, a film is also a form of artistic and cultural expression and is thus difficult to quantify (see the discussion of the concept of "aesthetic labor" in the introduction of this book). No one would call for limitations on imports of paintings or novels, although they too are produced in Brazil. The imposition of a Law of Similars on the film industry would result in a form, however attenuated, of cultural isolation. This is not to say that the presence of foreign films in the market has not been an impediment to the development of the Brazilian film industry, but merely that there are better ways of resolving the problem. Without some sort of restrictions on imports, Brazilian cinema would not have made the great strides it has over the last two decades.

Among other proposals issued by directors were the classification of foreign films into different categories according to their technical quality and cultural importance (presumably, films of lesser quality would either not be imported or would suffer restrictions of some kind, and this would amount to a form of censorship), the revitalization of the Vera Cruz studios (Duarte and Barros, again, began their careers with Vera Cruz), the resolution of the question of royalties for directors (they wanted 10 percent of a film's income), a compulsory exhibition law for television, and respect for the integrity of the director's work (that is, they wanted laws guaranteeing them the final cut in the film production process). The directors' presentation was not without its moments of humor, such as when they proposed a law demanding eight positive reviews for each negative one.

Distributors, as might be expected, opposed any forced limitation on imports, arguing that the market itself is selective and establishes its own limits. They also argued that not all films imported are actually exhibited, so the exhibition figure is the more important one. What they failed to mention is that the high number of films imported creates a vast reserve of films that could take the place of the Brazilian product in theaters or on television.

The most important proposals of the congress, however, were presented by the antagonistic sectors of exhibition and production. Exhibitors, represented by José Borba Vita, president of the National Committee of Film Exhibitors, an umbrella organization of exhibition syndicates and associations throughout the country, presented a twenty-one-point proposal, none of which was put into effect, revealing the divorce not only between producers and exhibitors, but also between exhibitors and the state, a situation that would have extremely adverse consequences for the development of Brazilian cinema. (See chapter 7 for a discussion of the historical relationship between producers, exhibitors, and the state).

Most of the items in the exhibitors' list of proposals fall into three categories: financial incentives, standardized tickets and income reporting devices, and the compulsory exhibition of Brazilian films. They requested long-term financing from the INC or Embrafilme to allow them to re-equip their theaters with new sound and projection equipment and asked for the Institute's help in reducing some of the onerous taxes they were forced to pay, specifically the tax on services, which consumed some 5 percent of the theaters' gross income.[26]

Speaking for all exhibitors, José Borba Vita also requested that standardized tickets (implemented by INC Res. 23, 6 August 1968) be sold to them at cost. The sale of standardized tickets and box-office reporting sheets represented a major portion of INC's income. He also requested that theaters in cities with no sales agent for such tickets be exempt from the regulation, and that any new systems implemented by INC or Embrafilme to oversee box-office reporting be at no additional cost to exhibitors. These proposals, seemingly quite logical in their attempt to reduce operational costs, especially in major urban centers where real estate values had been skyrocketing, causing rents and leases to go up accordingly, were not well received by the Congress, and exhibitors received no relief in any of the areas discussed.

The most controversial of the exhibitors' proposals concerned the compulsory exhibition of Brazilian films, proposals that led producer-director Jece Valadão to suggest sarcastically that as a twenty-second item on their agenda exhibitors should include the prohibition of Brazilian film production. The compulsory exhibition of national films has long been the backbone of state policy toward the industry and has been essential for the industry's development. Yet exhibitors have traditionally seen the screen quota as an unwanted and unfair imposition by the state on the free enterprise system. They have argued continuously, and unsuccessfully, that the average income of Brazilian films is lower than that of foreign films and that with the national film they do not make enough profit to pay even the maintenance costs of their theaters. Early in 1972, the failure of exhibitors to obey the compulsory exhibition law had led INC to close twenty-eight first-run theaters in São Paulo.[27]

Exhibitors have argued that they are not opposed to Brazilian films as long as they are of a technical and cultural quality sufficient to attract the public, but they are opposed to being forced by law to show films of poor quality that no one wants to see simply because they are Brazilian. In a logic that parallels that of the Motion Pictures Association of America and the Motion Pictures Export Association of America, exhibitors declare that the laws of the marketplace should be respected and that the government, through the INC and Embrafilme, cannot force anyone to see a specific film. Producers, on the other hand, have countered that without a screen quota they would have no chance at all to show their product, given the historically close ties between exhibitors and distributors of foreign films. Both producers and exhibitors are obviously correct in their assessments of the situation, and the resulting impasse exists until this day, with ultimately disastrous effects on the industry's development.[28]

Among the exhibitors' proposals at the 1 Congresso da Indústria Cinematográfica, (1 CICB) were the revision of INC Res. 60, which had lowered the screen quota from ninety-eight to eighty-four days per year (this after INC had raised it to 112). Although the proposal gives no specifics, exhibitors presumably wanted it lowered even further on the grounds that there existed an insufficient number of quality national films to fulfill the quota. They also wanted films classified into three categories ("A," "B," and "C") according to quality and commercial potential, with a sliding scale applied to the amount they would have to pay for films in each category (by law exhibitors must pay 50 percent of net box-office income to the producer of national films; the exhibition of foreign films is negotiable).

The exhibitors also wanted to modify the terms of the compulsory exhibition law, so that no theater would be obliged to show a national film that had already been exhibited in another theater within a one kilometer radius, and so that theaters equipped to show films in Cinerama would not be forced to show Brazilian films not produced under the same system. Exhibitors also felt that they should not be forced to pay freight charges for films exhibited under the compulsory exhibition law. As a response, perhaps, to the temporary closing of twenty-eight theaters in São Paulo, José Borba Vita suggested that the system of fines be modified to take into consideration the average income of each theater (rather than across-the-board rates), and that INC should declare an amnesty for all exhibitors who were behind in their obligation to show national films.

In a proposal that should have met with a degree of receptivity on the part of producers, Borba Vita suggested that the transmission of imported "canned" television programs be prohibited during prime time and that a compulsory exhibition law also be applied to television networks. As already noted, the exhibitors' suggestions were not met with a great degree of cordiality by producers, who have traditionally seen exhibitors as inimical to the development of Brazilian cinema. However, closer examination of their proposals should have been in order, for, to state the obvious, a production sector without an exhibition sector in which to release its films is destined to obsolescence.

The 1 CICB marks a turning point in the relationship between Brazilian cinema and the state, as well as the beginning of the clear hegemony of the Cinema Novo group in the state cinematic apparatus. This hegemony would be formalized in 1974 with the selection of producer-director Roberto Farias, Cinema Novo's chosen candidate, to head Embrafilme.

Represented by Farias, Luiz Carlos Barreto, Walter Hugo Khouri, Oswaldo Massaini, and Alfredo Palácios, the producers presented, and subsequently sent to Minister of Education and Culture Jarbas Passarinho, a "Brazilian Project for the Cinema," summarized in a five-point program (the placement of the adjective of nationality is significant, attempting to couch the project, not the cinema, in patriotic and nationalistic terms): (1) the administrative and operational reformulation of the INC and Embrafilme; (2) limitations on imports; (3) the improvement of the exhibition market; (4) the inclusion of Brazilian cinema in the broader context of the country's economic and cultural development; and (5) exemption from state and municipal taxes for all sectors of the industry (production, distribution, and exhibition).[29] The reformulation mentioned in the first item included the transformation of the INC into a National Film Council and the transformation of Embrafilme from a mixed-ownership enterprise to a public enterprise.[30]

In response to the producers' request for the reformulation of the state cinematic apparatus, the minister of education and culture named a commission, composed of the president of INC and the director of Embrafilme, among others, to study and make recommendations concerning the proposed reformulation.

THE REORIENTATION OF STATE POLICY

In 1975 Embrafilme was reorganized by Law 6281 (9 December), signed by president Ernesto Geisel (1974–1979) after approval by the Brazilian congress. At that time Embrafilme formally absorbed the executive functions of the Instituto Nacional do Cinema, but it remained, at least in name and in its administrative capacity, a mixed-ownership enterprise.[31] Law 6281 also stipulated the creation of a normative body with legislative functions to establish state policy in relation to the film industry. This "body to be named" was created in 1976 as the Conselho Nacional do Cinema (CONCINE; Decree-law 77,299, 16 March 1976).

According to the 1975 law, Embrafilme was empowered to execute national film policy, observing all pertinent laws as well as the norms and resolutions of the soon-to-be-created CONCINE. The shares of Embrafilme belonging to INC (29.4 percent) reverted to the federal government, leaving the state with a 99.9 percent interest. At the time of the reorganization, private capital comprised only 0.0528 percent of the total.[32]

Under its expanded powers, Embrafilme was authorized to include in its activities: (1) the co-production, acquisition, exportation and importation of films; (2) the financing of the film industry; (3) the distribution, exhibition, and commercialization of films in Brazil and abroad; (4) the promotion of national film festivals and Brazil's participation in international festivals; (5) the creation, when and where necessary, of subsidiaries to act in any area of cinematic activity; and (6) the concession of prizes and incentives for national films, including the continuation of the subsidy program created by the INC. In short, Embrafilme was legally provided with a virtual monopoly on cinematic activity in the country, although it has never acted in true monopolistic fashion.

In cultural terms, Embrafilme was authorized to participate in the following activities: (1) research, restoration, and conservation of films; (2) production, co-production, and dissemination of educational, scientific, technical and cultural films; (3) training of professionals; (4) documentation and publication of film-related books and magazines; and (5) other culturally oriented film programs. These activities were to be carried out, when possible, in conjunction with film schools, cinematecas, film societies (cineclubes), and other nonprofit organizations.

I mention the range of Embrafilme's mandated cultural activities since they make it a virtually unique among mixed-ownership enterprises in Brazil. Such noncommercial activities have consistently consumed up to 15 percent of Embrafilme's total budget, making it that much more difficult to operate profitably under the logic of capitalist enterprises. Embrafilme's situation is unique in that it has a dual role, industrial and cultural, reflecting the nature of the product manufactured by the film industry.

After reorganization, Embrafilme's budget consisted of distribution income, the sale of standardized tickets and box-office reporting sheets, interest on film-financing loans, a tax ("contribution") paid by foreign and domestic producers for the development of the industry, plus a percentage of the income tax owned by foreign distributors for the commercialization of films in the country. Up to 15 percent of its annual budget has come, in individual years, directly from the Ministry of Education and Culture, and it has taken out loans from the National Development Bank to finance film projects, but by and large its budget derives from the industry itself.

As organized by Decree-law 77,299, CONCINE was to have a president, named by the president of the Republic and based on the recommendations of the minister of education and culture, and it was to be composed of representatives of the president's Secretariat of Planning and of each of the following ministries: Education and Culture, Justice, Industry and Commerce, Foreign Affairs, Finance, and Communications, each to be chosen by the respective minister of state. Its members, furthermore, would include the director general of Embrafilme, the director of the Department of Cultural Affairs of MEC, and representatives of three major sectors of the film industry (production, distribution and exhibition, and direction). Decisions of CONCINE are, by law, taken by majority vote.

CONCINE was empowered to advise the minister of education and culture, to whom it was subordinated, in the formulation of a policy for the development of the film industry, to establish norms regulating the import and export of films for theatrical circuits, television, and any other means of communication, to establish regulations for the commercialization of national and foreign films (prices and means of payment), to formulate a national policy of ticket prices (in reality, CONCINE can only make recommendations as to ticket prices, which are set by SUNAB), to regulate the services of laboratories and sound studios, to establish norms for co-production with other countries, to regulate the production of foreign films in Brazil, to regulate programs of film industry financing, and, among many other attributes, to set the screen quota for Brazilian films.[33] In short, CONCINE was created as a policy-making body, setting policies to be carried out by Embrafilme.

The reformulation of Embrafilme and the creation of CONCINE coincided with an expansion of state intervention in the cultural arena, by the creation of the Fundação Nacional de Arte (National Art Foundation; FUNARTE), and the crystallization of its cultural policy with the formulation in 1975 and publication in 1976 of the document "Política Nacional de Culture" ("National Policy of Culture"). This document, the major official statement concerning the government's cultural role, was written by the Conselho Federal de Cultura (created in 1966; see chapter 5).

According to this document, the cultural policy of the Brazilian government is founded on a number of basic principles that reflect the historical, social, and spiritual values of the Brazilian people. The document says explicitly that the state role includes support of the spontaneous cultural production of the Brazilian people and in no way implies that the state has the right to direct such production or to in any way impede freedom of cultural or artistic creation. The state's responsibility, in other words, is ostensibly to support and stimulate cultural production, not control it. With specific reference to the cinema, the policy statement merely asserts that the state's role is to support national cinematic production, making it more competitive and providing it with an "artistic base." [34]

The "Política Nacional de Cultura" is infused with a nationalist sentiment that is broad enough to include virtually all Brazilian cinematic production. It formulates a desire to construct a harmonious "national identity" on a symbolic level based on respect for regional and cultural diversity and the preservation of the nation's cultural and historical patrimony. In ideological terms, it attempts to efface class conflict and support class harmony. It represents an attempt by the state to create a consensus regarding the goals of Brazilian culture and to establish its own hegemony over cultural sectors which have in the past been controlled only through coercive measures such as censorship. This attempt to establish hegemony and, simultaneously, increased legitimacy, led the state to centralize cultural production under its authority.

José Mário Ortiz Ramos makes much of the policy's ability to co-opt or otherwise influence those active in cultural production, using *Bye Bye Brasil* (Carlos Diegues, 1980) as an example of a film infused with its attempt to create a national identity through the preservation of regional diversity. [35] Although there may be points of contact between Diegues's film and the "Política Nacional de Cultura," the policy statement hardly represents a plan for action or a specific model of preferred cultural production. To say that Diegues was in any way influenced by the document, or the policy it represents, is to overstate the case and to lend the statement more importance than it deserves. This is not to say that there was no ideological pressure involved in the reorientation of state policy toward the industry in the early 1970s, merely that the document to which Ramos gives so much credit is relatively unimportant when viewed in terms of the practical, concrete effects it had on the film industry.

The 1975 reorganization formalized Embrafilme's power to engage in a number of programs that it had initiated prior to the restructuring. In 1973 the enterprise began its activity as a distributor, thus taking up and expanding on the idea of a producer/director-owned distributor which Luiz Carlos Barreto and others had developed in the mid-1960s with the creation of Difilme. Embrafilme's distributor was set up with headquarters in Rio de Janeiro and a second office in São Paulo. In 1974 it expanded into other areas of the country (Botucatu in the state of São Paulo, Salvador, Porto Alegre, Belo Horizonte, and Recife). To expand into the last three sites, Embrafilme purchased the distribution offices of Ipanema Filmes, a private distributor owned by future Embrafilme director Roberto Farias.[36] Embrafilme thus became the first central distributor for Brazilian films to be established on a national, rather than regional, basis.

Since 1973 Embrafilme's distributor has grown into the second-largest distributor in Brazil, trailing only the Cinema International Corporation, which includes Metro, Paramount, Buena Vista (Disney), and Universal.[37] By 1981, Embrafilme's distribution income was on the order of 800 million cruzeiros, while CIC's was around 1.1 billion cruzeiros (see table 21).[38] Embrafilme's commission for films distributed averaged some 12 percent of the gross income. The distributor accounts for some 30 to 35 percent of all national films distributed in Brazil. It is a purely commercial operation, functioning as do most other distributors in the country, handling films it has financed or co-produced as well as independently produced features (See Appendix D).[39]

Table 21. Gross Income of Embrafilme's Distribution Sector, 1974–1981

	Cruzeiros	U.S. Dollars
1974	3,962,102	583,520
1975	11,630,977	1,430,624
1976	30,013,585	2,812,894
1977	67,000,000	4,738,330
1978	121,000,000	6,696,181
1979	183,300,000	6,801,482
1980	524,000,000	9,941,187
1981	800,000,000	8,591,065

Source: Embrafilme, annual reports.

The activity of the state in the distribution of national films is not, however, with out its paradoxes. The first film Embrafilme picked up for distribution in 1973–1974 was Leon Hirszman's *São Bernardo*, a fairly literal adaptation of Graciliano Ramos's homonymous 1934 novel. The film, produced in 1971–1972 by Hirszman's own Saga Filmes, had been held up by federal censors for seven months, causing the bankruptcy of the production company. The kind of tension mentioned in the previous chapter—the state supporting a film with one hand and attempting to repress it with the other—thus continued into the seventies, not only with *São Bernardo*, but also with films such as Wladimir Carvalho's documentary *O País de São Saruê* (*The Country of Saint Saruê*, banned from 1971 until 1979) and Jorge Bodansky and Orlando Senna's *Iracema* (1975). The *Pra Frente Brasil* (*Onward Brazil*, 1982) affair is perhaps the most notorious of such episodes. More recently, in 1984, Embrafilme declined to distribute Sílvio Tendler's documentary *Jango*, fearing political consequences. Such episodes further underline the fact that the Brazilian state is not monolithic and should be seen as a site of contradiction.

Advances to producers on the distribution of their films became available with Embrafilme's creation of its own distributor, thus providing another form of financial assistance to undercapitalized production companies. The amount provided varies according to the film's stage of production and to its relationship to the enterprise; that is, if a film is co-produced by Embrafilme it may receive up to a certain amount, if not, it falls into another category and receives a different amount. The advance on distribution may be paid at the project stage, at the postproduction stage, or when the film is completed and ready for distribution. The amount invested in distribution per se varies according to what is judged to be the commercial potential and the marketing needs of the individual film.[40]

Also in 1973, under the directorship of former Social Security (INPS) chief Walter Graciosa and during the Médici regime (1969–1974), Embrafilme initiated a program of co-production financing. As originally formulated, the enterprise participated in selected film projects with up to 30 percent of total production costs and received in return a 30 percent share of profits. With an advance on distribution of another 30 percent, the state covered up to 60 percent of a film's production costs. In 1973 and 1974 Graciosa's Embrafilme signed contracts for the co-production of eight feature films, including Nelson Pereira dos Santos's *O Amuleto de Ogum* (*Ogum's Amulet*, 1974). One of the eight films contracted was never completed (see Appendix E for a complete listing of films co-produced under this program).

The co-production program expanded rapidly after Roberto Farias, himself an experienced producer and director, was named by President Ernesto Geisel to replace Graciosa in 1974. Farias's tenure as Embrafilme's director represented the first time that an industry professional was chosen to head the state film enterprise. Under his leadership from 1974 to 1979, Embrafilme signed contracts for the co-production of 108 feature films plus nineteen pilots for television series (Appendix E). These films were made (or proposed, in the case of the few that remain uncompleted) by eighty-seven different production companies and over ninety different directors. Under Farias, the 30 percent limit was suspended, and Embrafilme provided up to 100 percent of a film's financing in some cases—for example, Glauber Rocha's *A Idade da Terra* (*The Age of the Earth*, 1980) and Leon Hirszman's *Eles Não Usam Black-Tie* (*They Don't Wear Black Tie*, 1981).

Embrafilme's decision to co-produce a film with independent producers or to grant other forms of financing is made by the enterprise's directorate (the director general, the administrative director, and the director of noncommercial operations) based on a point system that considers the producer's or director's prior experience and activity in the film industry. The first three items on Embrafilme's list of priorities for co-production and other forms of financing concern the number of prizes won in national and international festivals, including the INC's awards for quality. Such guidelines naturally favored producers and directors connected with the Cinema Novo group, which had attained international prestige through its many awards in film festivals throughout the world and in Brazil. Although it has financed beginning directors who have worked with other directors (for example, Tizuka Yamaski who, before making *Gaijin* [1980], had worked as a scenographer with Nelson Pereira dos Santos and as an assistant director with Glauber Rocha).

Decisions to co-produce are made at the script or story level; Embrafilme interferes on no other level of film production unless asked to render technical assistance. Intervention in the content of films does not occur. In a speech before the Federal Chamber of Deputies on 30 May 1979, Embrafilme's then director general, career diplomat Celso Amorim (1979–1982) affirmed that Embrafilme does not "exercise any function or activity directly related to censorship . . . to such an extent that it has co-produced two films that are currently interdicted by censors." He goes on to say that Embrafilme per se does not produce films, but rather makes film projects by independent producers viable:

Embrafilme does not create projects, it does not have a department that elaborates film scripts, that prepares films. With respect to the projects that are submitted for consideration, Embrafilme is limited to, and should be limited to, verifying the technical and professional capacity of its director and producer, . . . but in no way does Embrafilme pass judgment on thematic or formal content.[41]

Discussions I have had with many different people in the Brazilian film industry unanimously confirm Amorim's statement that Embrafilme does not exert direct ideological control over filmmakers or film projects.

CONTRADICTIONS AND CONFLICTS

There have been, however, isolated cases in which the state cinematic apparatus has taken actions that amount to a form of censorship. In 1975 Jorge Bodansky and Orlando Senna co-directed the film *Iracema*. The film was shot in 16mm using Kodak 7247 stock, which Brazilian laboratories evidently were not equipped to develop successfully. Consequently, the directors had the film developed in West Germany, where it had been picked up for distribution on German television. Since it was not developed in Brazil, the film did not technically conform to the legal definition of "Brazilian film," and therefore the Instituto Nacional de Cinema, and subsequently CONCINE, denied it the necessary certificate classifying it as a national film. *Iracema* thus entered a sort of catch-22 situation; it could not be exhibited as a Brazilian film and enjoy the protected rights thereof, nor could it be submitted to censors as a foreign film, since it was obviously a Brazilian film.

This bureaucratic interdiction lasted until 1980 when the film was finally released as a Brazilian film. In that year it won top honors in the Embrafilme-sponsored Brasília Film Festival and was picked up for distribution by Embrafilme itself. Although bureaucrats argued that the film's interdiction was a technical, legal matter, there is no doubt that the film's controversial nature —comparing the prostitution of a young Indian girl to the rape of the Amazon region by the military government and its multinational counterparts—had something to do with the film's problems. Bruno Barreto's *Amor Bandido* (*Bandit Love*, 1978), was mixed in Europe but had no problem under the same law.

In the wake of the *Pra Frente Brasil* affair, furthermore, Embrafilme's director Roberto Parreira was quoted as having said, "Everyone has the right to make the film they want, but not necessarily with Embrafilme's money," implying that the enterprise would consider the political repercussions of a film before agreeing to co-produce. The enterprise's refusal to distribute Tendler's *Jango* tends to confirm that political considerations do exist in Embrafilme's decision-making process, although no clear-cut pattern can be delineated.[42]

The indirect constraints placed on filmmakers are perhaps more important than direct constraints. In the previous chapter it was shown that under the INC the marketplace became central to state policy. What Ruy Guerra said about economic censorship being more violent than political censorship certainly applies throughout the seventies and into the eighties. It would have been unthinkable for a director to make a film about police torture of political prisoners in, say, 1975, not only because censorship would be certain, but also because, knowing that fact, no producer would be willng to invest the necessary capital. When Hector Babenco was planning *Lúcio Flávio, O Passageiro da Agonia*

(*Lúcio Flávio, the Passenger of Agony*, 1977), which deals with death squads and the torture of common criminals, he consulted police censors *prior* to filming. They granted their tentative approval on the condition that no uniformed policemen be shown as participating in the scenes involving the death squads, that no participants in the death squads be seen in police vans or squad cars, and that a text appear at the end of the film saying that the police officials involved in the case had since been arrested and punished.[43]

The co-production program marks a fundamental redirection in state policy toward the film industry. In the late 1960s, it may be recalled, the primary form of assistance to the production sector was a subsidy program based on the box-office income of all national films exhibited in the country. It was a relatively neutral subsidy which benefited all national production. Even INC's program of co-productions with foreign distributors was an essentially neutral program in which the Institute merely administered funds. Decisions as to film projects undertaken in this program were made by the foreign distributor and the local producer. Under the current co-production program, the granting of production financing became much more selective. When the state decides to finance a limited number of films, it must inevitably choose *which* Brazilian cinema it will support. This causes the state, on the one hand, to enter into competition with nonfavored sectors of the industry and, on the other, to become a site of contention for competing groups.

One result of the reorientation of state policy has been to make "independent" filmmakers (i.e., filmmakers who do not own their own production company or who do not have a solid financial base) dependent on the state for production financing. It has created structures which could potentially allow the state to control all significant film production in Brazil. Although the state claims that the goal of its policy is to make the cinema more competitive in its own market, the screen quota and the various forms of financial assistance it provides have in fact suspended the rules of the market for national films. Brazilian films no longer compete against foreign films in the domestic market. Rather, they compete against each other in the reserve market. Since Embrafilme is the major if not sole source for much production financing, it has itself become a marketplace where filmmakers compete against each other for the right to make films. Add to this the frequently arbitrary nature of film censorship, and we have a situation in which the independent filmmaker is faced with uncertainty about what is permissible both politically and economically.

The dominance of the Cinema Novo group became clear with the reorientation of state policy. The first film Embrafilme picked up for distribution was Leon Hirszman's *São Bernardo*. Hirszman was one of the founders of Cinema Novo. The first film contracted for co-production was Cinema Novo veteran Nelson Pereira dos Santos's *O Amuleto de Ogum*. Since that time, almost all films by Cinema Novo participants have been co-produced by Embrafilme, and those that were not co-produced—dos Santos's *Estrada da Vida* (*Road of Life*, 1980), Guerra's *A Queda* (*The Fall*, 1978), Jabor's *Eu te Amo* (*I Love You*, 1981)—were distributed by the enterprise and received distribution advances that facilitated their completion.

Despite ideological differences, it is in fact not surprising that Cinema Novo would participate in, and come to dominate, state programs of assistance to the film industry. As suggested in chapter 4, the relationship between Cinema Novo and the state began to be outlined as early as 1964 with the creation of CAIC and its financing of a number of early Cinema Novo films. The relationship continued into the INC period, as Cinema Novo directors not only received a predominance of the Institute's awards for quality but also participated in the INC-administered co-production program. Cinema Novo directors have always had a pragmatic attitude toward film production financing, accepting funds from many sources while at the same time rejecting outside interference and retaining authorial control over their films. Unlike some of their critics, they have also revealed an awareness of the complexity of the state, often arguing that accepting money from the state in no way implies support of other policies of the federal government.[44]

The question might then be asked why the military government would want to support the Cinema Novo filmmakers who had often revealed attitudes harshly critical of the regime, its policies, and the economic model it imposed? In his frequently virulent *Tribuna de Imprensa*, Hélio Fernandes suggests that by financing Cinema Novo, Embrafilme was supposedly following orders from Golbery do Couto e Silva to buy off its most vocal participants, although he offers no evidence to support his claim.[45] We have seen that the combination of market constraints and censorship had effectively depoliticized Brazilian cinema even prior to the reorientation, but the idea of state support as "preemptive co-optation" appears frequently in analyses of the state role.[46]

Cinema-state relations are too complex to be simplistically explained away as part of a policy of co-optation. After all, with increased state support, the industry finally achieved what it had sought since the 1930s. Renato Ortiz, citing Carlos Lessa, sees increased state investments in the area of culture during the 1973–1975 period as one result of the economic optimism produced by the "miracle" of 1967–1973 as reflected in the Second Plano Nacional de Desenvolvimento (PND; National Plan of Development, formulated for the period 1974–1976). Previous governments had focused primarily on economic aspects of development, although they had given lip service to the need for the "humanization of development" or for "psychosocial development" to accompany economic development. The Geisel regime, according to this theory, attempted to put such ideas into action and thus gave more attention to the area of culture.[47]

In another vein, Jorge Schnitman suggests that, on the one hand, by supporting Cinema Novo directors the government was attempting "to present an image of a more enlightened authoritarianism taking concrete steps in the cultural arena, of which [the] cinema had high national and international visibility," and, on the other, it wanted to "present a cultural image different from the *chanchada*, and Cinema Novo directors were the only directors that could do it.[48]

Despite his confusion between the *chanchada* (a form of musical comedy produced from the mid-1930s until the early 1960s) and the *pornochanchada* (the *chanchada's* debased offspring— usually a poorly made film featuring a very vulgar sort of eroticism), Schnitman's remarks are to the point. The reorientation of state policy began in 1972–1973 during the Médici regime, the harshest period of military rule. Increased governmental support for cultural activity was a response to the authoritarian regime's crisis of legitimacy. By granting increased funding to filmmakers, especially those who had previously shown strong oppositional stances, the government was clearly attempting to establish a level of cultural hegemony that it was otherwise unable to attain.

At the same time, the state cinematic apparatus had come under severe criticism from diverse sectors of civil society because of its financing of poor-quality, frequently erotic films. The only filmmakers to achieve both national and international cultural and intellectual prestige were precisely those associated with Cinema Novo. So what occurred was a convergence of interests and a marriage of convenience. The state financed films of Cinema Novo participants, among others, while they in turn lent state policy a certain amount of prestige and helped it develop, at least on one front, a liberal image contradicted by its more violent and coercive activities.

In the words of former planning minister João Paulo dos Reis Velloso, himself an avid film fan and friend of Nelson Pereira dos Santos and other Cinema Novo participants (who, he says, sought him out to request state support), the regime's idea was to have fifteen or twenty filmmakers producing continuously with government support:

Our objective was not to make an experimental, formally sophisticated and hermetic type of cinema. Not that that was excluded, but it wasn't our primary objective. We had to make a kind of cinema that really reached the people, a culturally dignified cinema. . . . From the beginning [1972–1973] there was an understanding that the government would not culturally constrain anyone. The filmmaker would have artistic freedom to make his film, but at the same time I warned them that although political cinema is certainly legitimate, they should not make a doctrinaire, propagandistic cinema.[49]

Reis Velloso's statement reflects the market mentality of the state apparatus, a concern with the cultural validity of the film production (supposedly in contrast to the lack thereof of the *pornochan-*

chada), and a recognition of the political limits to be observed. A tacit agreement thus existed between the authoritarian state and filmmakers that certain boundaries would not be crossed. With few exceptions, Cinema Novo was never a propagandistic cinema, so its participants were largely able to work within the limits set forth. When films happened to cross the boundaries of permissibility, the censorship of federal police was waiting.

The reorientation of the state's financial assistance to the industry gave rise to conflicting positions among those who favored continued state intervention. New dichotomies arose replacing the nationalist/universalist dichotomy which to a great extent had shaped state policy in the 1960s. The major points of conflict concern cultural versus commercial views of the state role, and independent versus concentrationist views of the proper industrial model the state should support. These dichotomies are of course closely related.

On the cultural side are filmmakers who feel that the state should support films based on their cultural importance, with no regard to commercial potential. In Brazilian film circles, this kind of film is known as a miúra. At the extreme of this position are documentarists such as Sílvio Tendler (Os Anos JK [The JK Years] and Jango) and some state bureaucrats who would like to see Embrafilme limited to the production of cultural and educational films, much like its forerunner, the Instituto Nacional do Cinema Educativo, founded by Getúlio Vargas in 1937.

In his master's thesis, "Cinema e Estado: Em Defesa do Miúra" ("Cinema and State: In Defense of the Miúra"), filmmaker and professor Tendler argues that in a market economy the production of cultural and experimental films is more directly related to the state than is that of feature, commercial films:

Forming opinions and, in the case of countries with a market economy, correcting the distortions inherent in a circuit oriented toward easy profit, cultural cinema is one of the foundations for the sedimentation of national cultural values. On the other hand, experimental cinema is the great innovator of aesthetic and cultural standards and is the major source for the formation of new cadres who will feed into the industry. Without support of cultural and experimental cinema, no country can possess a quality cinematography nor a technically and artistically competent industry.[50]

Although Tendler frequently overstates his case and almost totally ignores the industrial dimensions of Brazilian cinema, his views are reflective of those of an important segment of the industry.

At the other extreme of the cultural/commercial dichotomy are filmmakers and producers such as Pedro Rovai and Jece Valadão, who think that commercial potential should be the only thing that concerns the state enterprise in its attempts to support the industry's development. Rovai, known as a producer and director of *pornochanchadas (A Viúva Virgem [The Virgin Widow]*, 1972, often said to be the first *pornochanchada*), feels that Embrafilme should finance production companies, much as the state does in other economic sectors, and not individual film projects. "It's necessary to make films that are competitive with foreign films. We cannot accept the idea of each filmmaker doing his own thing. Embrafilme is apparently beneficial, but as poorly organized as it is, it has a negative impact . . . . Films that don't make a cent in the name of culture? That's culture? It's an elite, bourgeois culture."[51] Rovai sees the cultural/commercial division as a false dichotomy and feels that once a film is projected on the screen it transmits cultural values. He is of course correct, but given the extreme distance that separates films like Hirszman's *São Bernardo*, for example, from Mozael Silveira's *Com a Cama na Cabeça (Bed Maniacs* [INC's translation], 1973), the dichotomy is a very real one.

Other directors, such as Cinema Novo veterans Nelson Periera dos Santos, Carlos Diegues, and Arnaldo Jabor, attempt to combine the cultural and the commercial, making films that speak to the Brazilian people in culturally relevant terms and are also successful at the box office. But, as is symptomatic of the divisions within the film industry, they are often bitterly attacked for favoring "superproductions" (an absurd concept within the context of Brazilian cinema) at the expense of "independent," more authentically authorial productions. Embrafilme has attempted to please both camps. It has set up programs for the production of cultural films and documentaries and has financed beginning directors and others such as Glauber Rocha and Júlio Bressane, whose films have limited commercial appeal, although the majority of its funding has gone to films with a more commercial appeal.

The independent/concentrationist dichotomy grows out of the cultural/commercial dichotomy and in a sense repeats the division of the early 1950s between studio-based models and independent modes of production. Independent filmmakers have no firm commercial structure and few sources of production financing other than the state, and yet they have contributed decisively to the critical success of Brazilian cinema over the last twenty years. Their production companies often consist of little more than a small office, a desk, and a file cabinet. They normally do not own complete filmmaking equipment, yet they constitute the vast majority of Brazilian cinematic activity.[52] Since 1978 many of them have joined together in a cooperative that lends technical assistance to the projects of its members.[53] Although they are obviously not opposed to making successful films, they see commercial success as secondary to cultural or social relevance. By financing individual films rather than production companies, Embrafilme has tended to support these independent filmmakers, reinforcing an atomized model of production rather than turning , as did Mexico, to a production model based on large studios.

In recent years the concentrationist group, and I use the term "group" very loosely, has gained considerable strength and power within Embrafilme. Headed by producers such as Luiz Carlos Barreto, Jarbas Barbosa, and Jece Valadão, the "group" is composed of medium-sized production companies which have complete filmmaking equipment and fairly large and permanent staffs. Unlike the independents, they normally produce several films a year (sometimes directed by independents), often in partnership with private investors, both national and foreign. They call on Embrafilme to adopt a more entrepreneurial attitude leading to increased capital accumulation in the industry. As a means to that end, they favor the concentration of Embrafilme's resources in a few films with strong commercial potential. Some of them would like to see Embrafilme, or at least its profitable sectors, sold to private firms (preferably their own). Although they exert a tre-

mendous amount of pressure on the state enterprise, lists of Embrafilme's co-productions in recent years tend to indicate that they
do not yet have the upper hand, and that the independents held
sway throughout the 1970s and into the 1980s (See Appendix E).

All of these positions are debated within an enterprise belonging to a state that is itself subject to various kinds of pressures and
tensions. The state, through its various cultural entities, espouses
strong nationalism on the level of the production of symbolic
goods, while its economic policy is decidedly internationalist.[54]
Although it has implemented protectionist policies favorable to
the film industry, it has been careful not to offend directly the
interests of the American industry by imposing import quotas.
Another form of tension lies in the hegemonic versus the coercive
aspects of state policy mentioned earlier. Its cultural policy espouses complete freedom of expression, yet the *Pra Frente Brasil*
affair, among others, reveals the limits of tolerance of the state's
coercive apparatus.

By the end of the 1970s, Embrafilme and state policy toward
the Brazilian film industry seemed to be on the right track. It had
been at least partially responsible for the best that Brazilian cinema had to offer, including such highly acclaimed films as *O
Amuleto de Ogum* (Nelson Pereira dos Santos, 1974), *Lição de
Amor (Lesson of Love*, Eduardo Escorel, 1976), *Xica da Silva* (Car-
los Diegues, 1976), *Mar de Rosas (Sea of Roses*, Ana Carolina,
1978), *Chuvas de Verão (Summer Showers*, Carlos Diegues, 1978),
Coronel Delmiro Gouveia (Colonel Delmiro Gouveia, Geraldo
Sarno, 1978), *Tudo Bem (All's Well*, Arnaldo Jabor, 1978), *Gaijin*
(Tizuka Yamasaki, 1980), *Bye Bye Brasil* (Carlos Diegues, 1980),
Pixote (Hector Babenco, 1980), and *Eles Não Usam Black-Tie*
(Leon Hirszman, 1981), among many others. It accounts for some
35 percent of all national films distributed in the country, and
most films that would be considered "quality" products are linked
to Embrafilme in some way, either through financing, co-production, or distribution.[55]

In industrial terms, state policy toward the film industry
seemed to be equally successful. Between 1974 and 1978 the
screen quota for Brazilian films increased from 84 to 133 days per
year, an increase of 58 percent. During the same period, the total

Table 22. Film Spectators in Brazil, 1971–1978

	Brazilian Films	Foreign Films	Total
1971	28,082,358	174,937,981	203,020,339
1972	30,967,603	160,521,647	191,489,250
1973	30,815,445	162,562,206	193,377,651
1974	30,665,515	170,625,487	201,291,002
1975	48,859,308	226,521,138	275,380,446
1976	52,046,653	198,484,198	250,530,851
1977	50,937,897	157,398,185	208,336,002
1978	61,854,842	149,802,182	211,657,024

Source: Embrafilme, Cinejornal 1 (July 1980), 3.

Table 23. Box-Office Income, 1971–1978
(in U.S. dollars)

	Brazilian Films	Foreign Films	Total
1971	10,139,678	61,813,402	71,953,080
1972	12,523,102	65,666,104	78,189,206
1973	13,257,911	75,588,678	88,846,589
1974	13,223,446	67,530,206	80,753,652
1975	21,505,116	97,235,984	118,741,100
1976	23,700,309	86,658,884	110,359,193
1977	32,059,766	100,437,040	132,496,806
1978	42,929,252	101,567,570	144,496,822

Source: Based on data from Embrafilme, Cinejornal 1 (July 1980), 4.

number of spectators for Brazilian films doubled from 30 to 60 million (see table 22). Total income of Brazilian films went from around U.S. $13 million in 1974 to over $42 million in 1978, an increase of well over 200 percent (see table 23). During the same period, the gross income of foreign films increased only 19 percent.[56] The production average continued to increase throughout the decade (see table 24), and Brazilian cinema's share of its own market increased from around 15 percent in 1974 to over 30 percent in 1980 (see table 25).

While these statistics are impressive, one must be careful not to give Embrafilme sole credit for Brazilian cinema's expansion in

Table 24. Brazilian Feature Film Production, 1976–1984

1976	84
1977	72
1978	101
1979	96
1980	102
1981	80
1982	86
1983	84
1984	90

Source: Alcino Teixeira de Mello, *Legislação do Cinema Brasileiro* (Rio de Janeiro: Embrafilme, 1978), 2:558; Embrafilme, annual reports, 1978, 1979, 1980; *Variety*, 17 March 1982, 4 May 1983, 21 March 1984, 20 March 1985.

Table 25. Market Division Between Brazilian and Foreign Films, 1971–1980
(percent of total spectators)

	Brazilian	Foreign
1971	13.8	86.2
1972	16.2	83.8
1973	15.9	84.1
1974	15.2	84.8
1975	17.7	82.3
1976	20.8	79.2
1977	24.5	75.5
1978	29.2	70.8
1979	29.1	70.9
1980	30.8	69.2

Source: Embrafilme, *Cinejornal* 4 (September 1982), 5–6.

its own market during the 1970s. Of the twenty top-drawing films between 1970 and 1980, only four—*Dona Flor e Seus Dois Maridos (Dona Flor and Her Two Husbands)*, *A Dama do Lotação (Lady on the Bus)*, *Lúcio Flávio*, and *Xica da Silva*—had financial backing from the enterprise. There is a significant sector of the industry that is opposed to state intervention all together, or that has achieved success in the market without state assistance other than the reserve market and the various subsidy programs.[57]

Despite the statistical indications of success and the high quality of many films produced by Embrafilme, by the late 1970s Brazilian cinema was in a state of crisis, torn by internal conflicts and dissension, and the direction of state policy was being severely questioned in many areas of the industry, the government and the press. Chapter 7 will outline some of the factors contributing to the crisis of 1983–1984, the most severe in the history of Brazilian cinema.

7

Moving Toward Crisis, 1980–1984

IN HIS EXCELLENT book on the Mexican film industry, Alberto Ruy Sánchez writes that the words "crisis" and "Mexican cinema" are often synonymous. Although all national cinemas have cyclical periods of growth and decline, in Mexico "the frequency of crises is such that it seems like a permanent feature of the industry, and the successive 'restructurings' have done little more than rearrange the conditions of its depression."[1] The state, Sánchez suggests, has intervened in the industry by keeping in rhythm with its crises. Crisis has been the justification for certain state economic measures, and the "monster of red-numbers has been, on another level, the personage that sustains all of the national fictions that Mexican cinema prescribes us. Mexican films, with its genres and subgenres, formed in moments of counter-crisis, are like insects that fly around the irritated eyes of the monster."

The same may not apply in every respect to the Brazilian situation, but one crisis succeeded another in Brazilian cinema from the mid to late 1970s until the mid-1980s, when it reached the most severe point in the recent history of the industry. After the rise in the number of spectators, in production figures, and in the income of national films in the 1970s, subsequent years witnessed a downturn that virtually reversed the economic progress of the previous decade. The market drastically diminished in size, making the industrial viability of Brazilian cinema dubious at best.

In this case, statistics are more eloquent than words. (see table 26). The number of registered 35 millimeter theaters declined from a high of 3,276 in 1975 to a mere 1,553 in 1984, a decline of

Table 26. Brazilian Film Market, 1975–August 1984

	Theaters	Attendance (in thousands)	% Change	Attendance per Capita
1975	3,276	275,382	—	2.6
1976	3,161	250,532	− 9.0	2.3
1977	3,156	208,532	− 16.8	1.9
1978	2,973	211,658	+ 1.6	1.9
1979	2,937	191,908	− 9.3	1.6
1980	2,410	164,774	− 14.1	1.4
1981	2,244	138,892	− 15.7	1.1
1982	1,988	117,800	− 15.8	0.9
1983	1,882	106,536	− 9.6	0.8
1984	1,553	89,939	− 15.6	n.a.

Sources: Variety, 8 August 1984; 1984 figures from Embrafilme.

Note: Other sources reveal slightly different figures for the number of registered theaters, but the basic pattern remains the same.

over 52 percent. From 1975 to 1983 the number of seats offered (in all sessions) decreased from 1.2 billion to 828 million, a drop of 32 percent. Per capita attendance went from 2.6 times a year in 1975 to 0.8 times per year in 1983. The number of spectators for Brazilian films dropped from 50,688,000 in 1980 (after a high of 61,800,000 in 1978) to a mere 30,637,544 in 1984, a decline of almost 40 percent. Income of national films went from around U.S. $34 million (1.8 billion cruzeiros) in 1980 to around $25.8 million (14.9 billion cruzeiros) in 1983. National film production, in turn, declined from 102 films in 1980 to 86 in 1982 and 84 in 1983. But the crisis is less apparent in the number of films produced than in their quality. Between 1981 and 1985, pornographic films accounted for an average of almost 73 percent of total production.[2]

The crisis of Brazilian cinema in the 1980s is part of the larger crisis of the national economy in a period when the economic "miracle" of the 1967–1973 period, characterized by high growth rates and relatively low inflation, has been replaced by an economic nightmare with a 100-billion-dollar debt and inflation rates of well over 200 percent. The economic crisis forced the government to impose severe restrictions on imports, making film production costs rise dramatically. The cycle of decline is clear: film production costs increased rapidly at a time when the market was shrinking. Ticket prices have not kept pace with inflation, thus reducing even further the income for producers and exhibitors alike. Brazilian cinema has entered a downward spiral whose end is not yet in sight.

There are of course many reasons for the decline of the Brazilian film industry in the first half of the 1980s. High inflation rates have made filmgoing a luxury for much of the Brazilian population; in addition, high crime rates in large cities make many people think twice about going out at night. In this chapter I will attempt to put the crisis in perspective, discussing, among other things, the relationship of the film industry to television, increased production costs, the role of foreign cinema, and most importantly, the relationship between the state and exhibitors, which is clearly the key to any sustained growth in the industry as a whole.

TELEVISION

Television has had a negative effect on Brazilian cinema in two ways. First, it provides vast numbers of the population with easily accessible, inexpensive, yet generally high-quality entertainment, causing many to prefer to watch *novelas*, variety programs, or dubbed foreign films in the comfort of their homes, rather than go out to face parking problems, long lines on weekend nights, and frequently uncomfortable theaters. Second, it has not provided the film industry with additional income to compensate for the decline of theatrical revenues.

Historically there has been little integration between the film industry and television in Brazil. When television was inaugurated in São Paulo in 1950, other entrepreneurs from this industrial city were engaged in the creation of the ill-fated Vera Cruz studios (see chapter 3).[3] Since the cinema had not yet been able to establish itself with the country's potential audience as a strong audiovisual tradition—with the obvious exception of the *chanchada*, which was disdained by most intellectual circles—television had to depend on its own resources and on certain forms of presentation that it borrowed not from cinema but from radio. In the 1960s Brazilian cinema, led ideologically by Cinema Novo, did not take television particularly seriously and made no attempt to reach a modus vivendi that would allow for more integration between the two media.

After 1964, successive military regimes saw television as a prime instrument of national integration and consequently, following a doctrine of "security and development," established such institutions as Embratel (Brazilian Telecommunications Enterprise, 1965), Dentel (National Department of Telecommunications, 1965), and the Ministry of Communications (1967), all of which were designed to support, regulate, or in some cases create a national telecommunications network and to participate in the international telecommunications system.[4] Such organizations provided the infrastructure on which private television networks could develop.

In part because of government support, the television industry expanded rapidly in the 1960s and 1970s (see table 27). The number of television sets in use rose from 1.2 million in 1962 to over 18 million in 1980, reaching an estimated potential audience of 80 million.[5] In other words, television can reach more Brazilians in a single evening than the national cinema does in an entire year.

The lack of integration of television and Brazilian cinema is

Table 27. Television Sets in Use in Brazil, 1962–1980

1962	1,275,000	1972	6,746,000
1963	1,553,000	1973	7,950,000
1964	1,867,000	1974	8,979,000
1965	2,202,000	1975	10,185,000
1966	2,583,000	1976	11,603,000
1967	2,985,000	1977	13,196,000
1968	3,579,000	1978	14,818,000
1969	4,225,000	1979	16,737,000
1970	4,931,000	1980	18,300,000
1971	5,809,000		

Source: Sérgio Caparelli, Televisão e Capitalismo no Brasil (Porto Alegre: L&PM, 1982), p. 88. Based on data from the Associação Brasileira da Indústria Elétrica e Eletrônica (ABINEE).

evident in the scant presence of national films on the country's television screens (see table 28). In 1980, only 2 percent of all feature films shown on Brazilian television were Brazilian. The figures in the chart refer only to feature-length theatrical films and do not include foreign "canned" programs. Foreign films, which have already covered their costs of production in other markets, can be negotiated at lower prices than can the national product, giving them an advantageous position for television sales. At the same time, many of the best Brazilian films are prohibited for viewers under the age of eighteen, making their exhibition on television problematic except during the less desirable time slots after midnight.

In an attempt to compete with foreign films in the television market, in 1977 Embrafilme signed contracts for the production of nineteen pilots for television series (see Appendix E). None of the projects were even shown on television, much less transformed into regular series. Some of them were released theatrically, and others remain on the shelves in Embrafilme's distributor. Rather than buy series from film producers, TV Globo, Brazil's strongest network and the fourth largest in the world, began producing its own (e.g., *Plantão de Polícia* [Police On-Call], *Carga Pesada* [Heavy Load]).

The response of the film industry to this situation has been to call for legislation guaranteeing national films exhibition on television. In the 1972 congress, it may be recalled, both directors and exhibitors called for a screen quota for national films on televi-

Table 28. Nationality of Films Shown on Brazilian Television, 1973–1976, 1980

	1973	1974	1975	1976	1980
United States	1,064	1,262	878	917	1,325
England	170	217	262	132	161
Italy	147	111	93	94	152
BRAZIL	10	34	6	70	32

Source: 1973–1976, Cinemateca, Museu de Arte Moderna (Rio de Janeiro), "Estatísticas 76" (n.d.); 1980, Embrafilme, *Cinejornal* 4 (1984), 44.

sion. This idea has been repeated with some frequency since that time. In 1980, for example, participants in a festival of short films held in Salvador, Bahia, signed a manifesto saying:

Television imposes consumerist and inflationary values and standards of behavior, thus decharacterizing the identity and consciousness of the Brazilian people, impeding them from exercising a critical vision of their own reality and of the contradictions of the country's development.

In this moment of redemocratization, filmmakers consider essential society's broad discussion of the Brazilian audiovisual situation and propose the transformation of the impositional model into a democratic system open to the independent manifestations of all of its sectors. . . .

[Brazilian cinema], with a diversified audiovisual patrimony, demands its space in this vehicle of mass communication, because . . . it remains absent from television while television continues to open its doors to foreign films.[6]

In less tendentious terms, other film industry professionals have called for the revision of the government's "audiovisual policy" in such a way that Brazilian cinema would be able to create a larger market in television.[7] In other words, some sectors of Brazilian cinema are attempting to hang on to television's coattails and achieve through legislative imposition what they have not been able to achieve through other avenues. Given the economic strength and political power of Brazilian television, especially the Globo network, it seems unlikely that the government will impose a screen quota of any sort in support of Brazilian cinema.

PRODUCTION COSTS

The crisis in the Brazilian film industry, characterized most dramatically by the decline in exhibition, is compounded by increased costs of production for national films. By 1982 the average cost of a film co-produced by Embrafilme was approaching $500,000, a high figure especially when contrasted with the independently produced pornochanchada, which could be made for around $80,000.[8] The average film with Embrafilme's participation requires around 1.2 million spectators to pay for itself.[9] According to Embrafilme head Roberto Parreira, of fifty films co-produced by the enterprise, only fifteen pay for themselves, and only five produce a reasonable margin of profit.[10]

Between January 1980 and March 1984, Embrafilme released 109 films. Using the 1.2 million spectators as a basis, one can assume that of that number, only twelve had paid for themselves during the period (see table 29). Films with proven critical success like *Gaijin* and *Inocência (Innocence)* have thus far been unable to recoup investment costs in the domestic market alone,

Table 29. Top-Drawing Films Released by Embrafilme,
January 1980–March 1984

	Date of Release	Spectators
Os Saltimbancos Trapalhões	12/81	5,197,936
Os Trapalhões na Serra Pelada	12/82	5,005,434
Eu te Amo	4/81	3,471,935
Pixote	10/80	2,511,378
Menino do Rio	1/82	2,104,980
O Trapalhão na Arca de Noé	12/83	2,056,029
Os Sete Gatinhos	4/80	1,936,613
Convite ao Prazer	5/80	1,841,515
Luz del Fuego	4/82	1,745,399
Bye Bye Brasil	2/80	1,487,655
Eles Não Usam Black-Tie	9/81	1,357,199
Estrada da Vida	2/81	1,261,548
Eros, o Deus do Amor	11/81	1,140,295
Aventuras da Turma da Mônica	12/82	1,127,554
Amor Estranho Amor	10/82	1,123,208
Parahyba Mulher Macho	9/83	1,115,844
Rio Babilônia	5/83	959,850
Beijo no Asfalto	6/81	877,331
Contos Eróticos	3/80	841,903
Gaijin	3/80	743,084
Terror e Êxtase	8/80	688,629
Inocência	6/83	655,046
Índia, A Filha do Sol	8/82	639,150
Engraçadinha	10/81	594,089
Garota Dourada	12/83	578,559

Source: Sindicato da Indústria Cinematográfica do Estado de São Paulo, based on data supplied by Embrafilme.

and the vast majority of Brazilian films, especially those co-produced by Embrafilme, simply do not pay for themselves.[11]

There are of course many reasons for the increased costs of film production in Brazil, many of which derive from the general economic crisis with high inflation rates, a constant devaluation of the cruzeiro, and increasing import restrictions. Two concrete reasons for increased production costs are the increased cost of imported raw film stock and of processing in Brazilian laboratories. The cost of a 1,000-foot roll of 35mm Eastmancolor Negative II film increased from 4,830 cruzeiros in January 1978 to 55,100 cruzeiros in July 1981, an increase of over 1,000 percent in a period of slightly over three years. Total inflation during this period was less than 400 percent. This situation has caused laboratories to use the less expensive Orwo stock, even though it is of lesser quality and has a shorter exhibition life.[12]

The cost of film processing has also increased substantially during the same period, although not quite as much as that of film stock itself (see table 30). Aluísio Raulino, President of the Associação Paulista de Cinema (São Paulo Film Association) calculates that in 1984 lab costs alone (material plus developing fees) for a 100-minute, 35mm color film cost 70 million cruzeiros (over U.S. $43,000), assuming that it is filmed in a five-to-one proportion (five takes for each one used).[13] The situation is compounded by the fact that despite compulsory copying laws, which were designed to strengthen laboratories and the industry's infrastructure,

Table 30. Cost of Developing 35mm Film, 1977–July 1981
(in cruzeiros per meter)

	1977	1978	1979	1980	July 1981
35mm Color Negative	2.13	2.48	3.79	6.42	8.61
35mm Color Positive (2 to 5 copies, short subjects)	6.50	7.66	12.72	36.62	46.14
35mm Color Positive (2–5 copies, feature)	5.63	7.03	11.67	34.21	46.14

Source: Filme Cultura, no. 38/39 (August–November 1981), p. 31.

the Líder Laboratories are now the only ones in operation and thus have a monopoly on film developing. Competition might allow for some reduction in the cost of lab work.

An additional aggravation to the problem of increasing production costs versus diminishing returns is the price of theater tickets. The average price of tickets rose from 8.99 cruzeiros in 1977 to 38.63 cruzeiros in 1980, an increase of 329 percent. Inflation during this period was approximately 387 percent. Ticket prices did not keep up with inflation, while production costs greatly exceeded the inflation rate. In reality ticket prices varied widely. In 1980, for example, the average price in the city of São Paulo (Brazil's largest film market) was 54.66 cruzeiros, whereas in Salvador, Bahia, it was 40.18 cruzeiros and in the State of Alagoas it was a mere 20.88 cruzeiros.[14]

Even more telling is the relationship of ticket prices to the minimum wage. In May 1981 the average ticket price had risen to the equivalent of U.S. $1.00, with the most expensive (in São Paulo) costing around $2.00. The average wage for an unskilled worker (minimum wage) was at the same time under $100 per month. That means that to go to the movies cost an unskilled worker 1 percent of his or her monthly wage. Despite low prices by U.S. standards, where a movie costs 0.4 percent of the average monthly wage, the cinema is an expensive form of entertainment in Brazil, especially when one considers that in a city like Rio de Janeiro nearly 50 percent of the working population earns the minimum wage or less.[15]

FOREIGN CINEMAS

In 1977 Jack Valenti, president of the Motion Pictures Association of America, visited Brazil. The official reason for his visit was to participate in a "Week of American Cinema" held in Brasília. His visit raised the specter of U.S. domination of the Brazilian market and caused many film industry professionals to unite in a "permanent assembly" for the defense of Brazilian cinema. The underlying reason for his visit was to try to stave off further decline in the American industry's revenue from the Brazilian market, and to argue against increasing protection of the national industry. Brazilian cinema's increased share of its own market (to over 30 percent in 1980) automatically implies its opposite, a decrease in the market share for foreign cinemas. Valenti's arguments, in discussions with several ministers of state, were well known, favoring a free and open market as the only way to attain industrial development.[16] Prior to Valenti's visit, CONCINE had modified the compulsory exhibition law, making it more difficult for theaters to remove Brazilian films from exhibition, and had implemented a new compulsory exhibition law for the national short subject (both of these changes will be discussed in the next section of this chapter).

By 1981, Brazil was considered Latin America's biggest headache for non-Brazilian producers and distributors.[17] The country had fallen to third in billings for U.S. films, ranking behind Mexico and Argentina. Owing to currency restrictions, only around 41 percent of the foreign distributors' income was remittable. United Artists' Latin American head, Tony Manne, is quoted as having said that in 1980 Central America billed as much as Brazil, because operational costs were 10 percent less and Brazil had imposed strict profit remittance restrictions.[18] In the words of Condor's Wenceslau Verde:

There's no solution for us. We've been losing coin for the past three years. The government has been piling taxes on taxes. On a film like *The Muppet Show*, for example, you have to pay 5 percent on the short, another 5 percent as a turnover tax on all rentals, plus a 25 percent income tax on billings. Then you can only remit 60 percent of revenue, and, on top of this, you have to pay an additional 15 percent on the remaining 40 percent.[19]

Distributors are forced to pay a censorship tax of $2,100 per film, and prints, which by law must be made in Brazil, cost around $2,000 each.[20]

Income of U.S. majors rose from slightly over one billion cruzeiros in 1980 to 1.9 billion in 1981. In real terms, however, those figures represent a decline of over 10 percent, given the 96 percent devaluation of Brazilian currency during the same period.[21] The general economic crisis in Latin America reduced the region to some 2 to 3 percent of total U.S. film revenues, down from the 12 to 15 percent of a decade earlier.[22] Harry Stone, vice-president of the Motion Pictures Export Association of America and long-time representative of the MPEAA in Brazil, indicates that Brazil has fallen from the sixth most important market for American films some twenty years ago to the twenty-first market in 1984. His strategy, and that of those he represents, is to pull all films except virtually guaranteed blockbusters out of the interior of the country, where profit margins are small, and concentrate on large cities, while at the same time intensifying the presence of American cinema on Brazilian television.[23]

Although such a situation has certainly hurt U.S. majors and other large distributors, it has hurt small distributors and independent producers even more. Censorship taxes, which used to be levied according to the linear meterage of all copies of a given film, are now collected by title. This tends to favor films that will be released with more than fifteen copies, since their return is greater than a film released with only one or more copies. The result has been the importation of fewer non-U.S. foreign films, especially those of a high artistic or experimental nature.[24]

Imports of foreign films declined by over 78 percent between 1975 and 1983 (see table 31). The decrease in imports and the slackening presence of foreign films in the domestic market also represents one of the ironies of the Brazilian film industry. Long accused, justly, of being one of the major impediments to the local

Table 31. Imports of Foreign Films, 1975–1980

Year	Imports
1975	595
1976	463
1977	421
1978	389
1979	190
1980	152
1981	158
1982	164
1983	127

Source: Variety, 8 August 1984.

industry's development, the crisis of the early 1980s reveals just how intertwined and interdependent these traditionally antagonistic industries are. A large part of Embrafilme's budget, for example, derives first, from a "contribution" (tax) to the development of the industry paid by all producers exhibiting their films in the country (9 percent of the enterprise's budget), and, second, from a portion of income tax due on profit remittances (26 percent).[25] The decrease in the number of foreign films entering the country and the subsequent decrease in revenue translate into a loss for Embrafilme's budget, diminishing even further the already limited funds available for its financing programs.

Even more serious, however, is the effect of the foreign film decrease on the exhibition sector. In mid-1984, Columbia, Fox, and Warner Brothers announced plans to close their offices in Curitiba (State of Paraná), Belo Horizonte (Minas Gerais), Botucatu (São Paulo), and Ribeirão Preto (São Paulo). UIP (CIC plus United Artists) had already closed offices in Salvador, Curitiba, and Belo Horizonte. All foreign distributors have eliminated films in 16mm, thus narrowing even further their area of activity. The consequence is that theaters in the interior have fewer films to choose from, generate less profit, and are compelled to close. It was estimated that the announced closing of Columbia, Fox, and Warner Brothers in the interior would force the closure of some 100 theaters in the state of Minas Gerais.[26]

The single foreign distributor to adopt an aggressive and to a large degree positive attitude toward the situation in Brazil is the French company Gaumont, which in 1982 acquired the Serrador circuit in São Paulo, composed of twenty-five theaters, including twelve first-run sites. The Gaumont move was considered a major breakthrough since it had been trying to acquire theaters in the country for some time, but had been stymied, presumably owing to pressure mounted by the ruling Severiano Ribeiro circuit in Rio de Janeiro.[27] In July of 1983 Gaumont reopened the Belas Artes theater in São Paulo, which had been gutted by fire the year before, and transformed it from a three screen to a six screen site. Gaumont also acquired its first theaters in Rio de Janeiro (Studio Catete and Studio Copacabana) at about the same time.[28]

Gaumont has also begun investing in Brazilian production,

with Carlos Diegues's *Quilombo* (1984) as its initial experiment. The production scheme of *Quilombo* represents a potentially fruitful avenue for Brazilian cinema, especially given its recent success in foreign markets. Based on Gaumont's guarantee of international distribution for the film, Diegues and Augusto Arraes, co-owners of CDK Productions, secured production-financing loans from two banks (Banco Nacional and Banespa). Gaumont agreed to cover the costs of the loans upon receipt of the first copy. Embrafilme contributed some 350 million cruzeiros, or 20 percent of the film's total cost, in the form of an advance on national distribution.[29] This is an example, albeit on a very small scale, of what Peter Evans calls a "triple alliance," or cooperation between private, state, and transnational capital.[30] Things seem to have come full circle since the early 1960s. Rather than combating foreign investments in the Brazilian film industry, some producers and directors, previously associated with the "nationalist" faction of the industry, actively court foreign participation.

THE EXHIBITION SECTOR

Although all of these factors have contributed to the crisis faced by Brazilian cinema in the 1980s, none is as decisive as the traditionally antagonistic relationship between the exhibition sector, on the one hand, and the state-supported production sector on the other. As one exhibitor has said, the silver lining in the current crisis, if there is one, is that exhibitors and producers seemed to have reached a mutual understanding that they have the same ultimate goal: to fill theaters with spectators.[31]

The antagonism between exhibition and production goes back to the end of the Bela Época of the early 1900s. Prior to that time, as seen in the first chapter, producers and exhibitors were normally one and the same. The development of independent distributors drove a wedge between producers and exhibitors, and the exhibition sector began to function almost exclusively for the benefit of foreign cinemas. In the 1930s, exhibitors fought legislation initiating a timid screen quota for Brazilian short films, just as they have fought every attempt to expand the quota until today.

The arguments used by exhibitors are familiar, and are clearly

outlined in an interview granted by exhibition magnate Luiz
Severiano Ribeiro:

[The screen quota], which drastically intervenes in the freedom of choice
of programs . . . goes against the most basic principles of free enterprise,
the law of supply and demand, and competition, which are indispensable
in a business where fluctuations are unpredictable. . . . In the final analysis it is the exhibitor, who sells directly to the public, who knows what he
should buy according to the preferences of his public. It should be noted
that Brazilian production is still of poor quality, but producers are constantly attempting to impose films that are rejected by the public by way
of supportive laws designed to protect Brazilian cinema but which frequently serve only to guarantee films with no possibility whatsoever of
success.[32]

This statement, which could have been made today, was in fact
made in 1952 in reference to the proposed creation of a National
Film Institute and the increased screen quota it would bring with
it. The argument, used then and now, concerns free trade and
open markets in opposition to state intervention and manipula-
tion of the rules of the marketplace.

To fully understand the implications of the division between
exhibitors and producers for the current crisis, it is necessary to
review state measures relative to the exhibition sector to see exactly how it has been affected over the last two decades. It is also
important to recognize that the interests of the sector have in fact
been historically tied to those of foreign distributors and, by
extension, have been in conflict with those of Brazilian cinema. It
is a difficult question to deal with, for both sides are obviously
correct in their arguments. Without a screen quota and other protectionist measures, Brazilian cinema would very likely not exist
or would exist only on the most crass commercial basis. At the
same time, state protection of the production sector has clearly led
to a loss of profits and is at least partially responsible for the
current decline of the exhibition sector, which is pernicious for
the Brazilian film industry as a whole.

The most visible area of conflict between exhibitors and the
state is the screen quota. Although information concerning the
quota has been provided throughout this study, it is important at

this point to recapitulate. The screen quota for national films was first established in 1932, mandating the compulsory exhibition of short films with each program of foreign films, and has since expanded to 144 days per year of compulsory exhibition of national films (see table 32).

Although exhibitors had always opposed the screen quota on the grounds that it interfered with their, and their audiences' freedom of choice, the conflict was exacerbated in 1970, when the Instituto Nacional do Cinema attempted to double the quota from 56 to 112 days per year starting in 1971. Exhibitors argued that they were losing money showing Brazilian films 56 days per year and would be unable to survive at 112 days per year.[33] Through intense lobbying efforts, presumably in cooperation with foreign distributors, exhibitors managed to have the quota rolled back to 84 days per year before the 112-day quota took effect.

The conflict worsened in 1972 when INC closed twenty-eight theaters in São Paulo, many of them first-run sites.[34] The theaters

Table 32. Evolution of the Screen Quota for Brazilian Films, 1932–1980

	Legislation	Quota
1932	Decree 21,240	One short for each program of foreign films
1939	Decree-law 1,494	One feature per year
1946	Decree 20,493	Three features per year
1951	Decree 30,179	One feature for every eight foreign films
1959	Decree 47,466	42 days per year
1963	Decree 52,745	56 days per year
1969	INC Res. 31	63 days per year (provisional)
1970	INC Res. 35	77 days per year (provisional)
1970	INC Res. 38	112 days per year (not implemented)
1970	INC Res. 49	98 days per year (not implemented)
1971	INC Res. 69	84 days per year
1975	INC Res. 106	112 days per year
1978	CONCINE Res. 23	133 days per year
1980	CONCINE Res. 62	140 days per year

Source: Alcino Teixeira de Mello, *Legislação do Cinema Brasileiro* (Rio de Janeiro: Embrafilme, 1978); Embrafilme, *Cinejornal* 3 (September 1981).

in question had been fined for not having fulfilled their obligations under the compulsory exhibition law in 1970 and 1971. When they refused to pay the fines, they were closed for two days. The closing occurred on the eve of a state holiday in São Paulo (January 25, commemorating the founding of the city), causing the theaters to lose an estimated 500,000 cruzeiros (slightly under U.S. $100,000). The twenty-eight interdicted sites accounted for some 70 percent of the total filmgoing public in the city. Exhibitors argued, on this and other occasions, that they were not opposed to showing Brazilian films, just to showing poor-quality films on which they had little chance to profit.

Jorge Schnitman suggests that "historically, whenever and wherever exhibitors were forced to exhibit a large number of national films, they attempted to produce their own, in many cases as inexpensively as possible."[35] British film historian Ivor Montague refers to such films as "quota quickies."[36] In 1971 a number of Brazilian exhibition groups joined together to form a company with the expressed intention of producing films to meet the requirements of the compulsory exhibition law.[37] They also began joining with independent producers, resulting in the rash of poor-quality pornochanchadas that began to flood the reserve market in 1972–1973, leaving even less room for more culturally serious films.[38] Producers associated with Embrafilme were quick to respond, calling the exhibitors' formation of a production company "disloyal combat," as if state-backed producers were the only ones with a right to make films.[39] Although Embrafilme has never attempted to censor the pornochanchada, it did transform it into one of its primary targets of attack through the 1970s.

As noted in chapter 6, in late 1972 exhibitors participated in the 1 Congresso da Indústria Cinematográfica sponsored by the Instituto Nacional do Cinema. There they presented a twenty-one-point proposal. One of their proposals, and one that has been repeated with some frequency over the years, is the classification of Brazilian films into three categories according to quality and box-office appeal. Category "A" would include films with broad commercial appeal. For these films exhibitors would pay 50 percent of net income. Films in category "B" would be those with a lesser commercial appeal and would receive 40 percent of box-office receipts, while those classified as "C," with little commercial potential, would receive only 30 percent and their exhibition would not be mandatory.[40] Since 1942 exhibitors have been obligated by law to pay 50 percent of net billings to the producer and distributor of national films. The amount paid for foreign films is negotiable, ranging from 70 percent for blockbusters to flat rates for lesser films. Exhibitors have frequently called for some flexibility in the amount paid for national films.

None of the proposals submitted by the exhibitors was accepted by the congress or implemented by the government. From that point on, the conflict between the exhibitors and the state began to escalate rapidly, especially after Roberto Farias became Embrafilme's director in 1974. In that year, in fact, *O Estado de São Paulo* ran an article with the headline "The Great Duel of National Cinema," referring to the duel between exhibitors and state-supported producers.[41] The article begins by developing the Western metaphor:

The situation of Brazilian cinema can be compared to a Western movie. The hero, who comes out of any situation looking good, is the producer. He has his film financed and 50 percent of box-office receipts guaranteed. The villain, who always comes out for the worse and with the blame, is the exhibitor, obligated to show national films eighty-four days per year and give half the income to the producer. The sheriff, who always comes to the aid of the producer, is the Instituto Nacional do Cinema, which finances the film and obligates the exhibitor to show it, regardless of the production's quality.

The "duel" would by 1980 become a "war."[42]

Two revisions in compulsory exhibition statutes provoked a further esclation of the conflict in 1977. CONCINE Resolution 10 (15 March 1977) confirmed the screen quota for Brazilian films at 112 days per year and modified the law's provisions, stipulating that exhibitors were prohibited from removing a Brazilian film from exhibition if it was attracting the average weekly audience in that theater based on average attendance figures of the previous year. Exhibitors were further prohibited from removing the film if after two weeks its audience total was 60 percent or more of the previous year's average attendance, and so on. It also stipulated that regardless of the number of weeks a Brazilian film was exhibited, only its first four weeks would count as satisfying the quota. The "holdover" provision further decreased foreign cinemas' freedom of action in the market, and the latter stipulation effectively increased the screen quota for Brazilian films in some theaters.

Exhibitors protested the new measures strenuously, but ineffectively, arguing that it would make it impossible for them to plan their programming ahead of time, especially since they had to present their scheduled programs to federal censors for approval at least forty-eight hours in advance. They were particularly upset for two reasons: first, they would theoretically be forced to continue exhibiting a film on which they were losing money, and, second, they could exhibit Brazilian films well over the number of days required by law and still be behind in their compulsory exhibition obligations. There was no provision giving them credit for showing national films more than the required number of days, and no carryover from one quarter or year to the next.[43] It is reported that some exhibitors subsequently began to show a preference for exhibiting national films with little commercial potential so that they would be able to plan their exhibition of foreign films with more certainty.

Another measure that affected compulsory exhibition statutes (and, it is said, provoked Valenti's visit to Brazil) was CONCINE Resolution 18 (24 August 1977), which mandated the compulsory exhibition of a national short subject as part of each program of foreign films. The short was to receive 5 percent of the gross box-office income, of which 40 percent would be returned to the exhibitor and 60 percent would go to the producer and distributor (of the short, not the foreign feature). Of a gross income of 100,000 cruzeiros, therefore, the producer and distributor would share 3,000 usually along an 80/20 split.[44]

The result of this law was that exhibitors began producing their own short subjects, frequently of poor quality, to accompany foreign features and fulfill the requirements of the law. Little space remained in the market for the short films of "independent" filmmakers associated with Embrafilme, and the public increasingly complained about having to endure poor-quality short subjects before a foreign feature, which further damaged the image of Brazilian cinema. In 1984 a thirteen-person jury was established to choose the films that would qualify for compulsory exhibition under this law, in the hope that the general level of quality would improve.[45]

By the mid- to late-1970s, exhibition groups, sometimes in conjunction with distribution groups, took their complaints about state cinematic policy to the courts, frequently obtaining at least temporary injunctions against various aspects of that policy. The major targets of exhibitors' legal action have been the forced purchase, from Embrafilme, of standardized tickets (for which they pay much more than the market price), the holdover provision of the compulsory exhibition law, the compulsory exhibition law itself, and the obligatory exhibition of short films. In the latter case, exhibition groups filed suit not because they were opposed to showing national short subjects, but because distribution groups, which were forced to pay the lion's share of the percentage destined to the short, had filed suit against the law, and exhibitors feared that if distributors won, the burden would fall entirely on them.[46]

By 1980, as I have suggested, the "duel" between exhibitors and the state escalated into a "war." In January, two exhibition firms obtained an injunction against the compulsory exhibition law. In April another company managed to impede the exhibition of Wladimir Carvalho's *O País de São Saruê* by arguing in court that the reserve market had not been legally regulated. Then, in June, several exhibition circuits, including the largest two in São Paulo (Hawai and Serrador), won a preliminary injunction against the quota, arguing (incorrectly) that there was no legal definition of "Brazilian film" and that they were thus unable to comply with the terms of the quota.[47] The following month they won a temporary injunction against the obligatory purchase of standardized ticket rolls.[48]

In 1983 three exhibition circuits, two of which were also foreign-based distributors (Gaumont and CIC), obtained an injunction lowering the quota from 140 to 28 days per year, alleging that CONCINE was not legally empowered to set the quota and that, regardless, Brazilian cinema did not produce a sufficient number

of films for them to comply with the law. Gaumont, which had
entered the exhibition market only the previous year, later withdrew its name from the suit.[49] Although all of these injunctions
were subsequently overturned by higher courts, they are symptomatic of the deteriorating relationship—and this was never
good—between exhibitors and the state, which has never taken
the exhibitors' interests into consideration.

Although Embrafilme has acquired or leased a number of theaters that were in financial difficulties, including a circuit in Rio
de Janeiro that had been operated by a cooperative of independent
filmmakers, it has not attempted to enter the sector on a large
scale. An Embrafilme official has been quoted as saying that the
enterprise "only got involved in exhibition where private entrepreneurs refused to go. Our policy is not to become exhibitors,
and we feel exhibition should remain in private hands."[50]
Embrafilme's activity in exhibition has been on such a small scale
(it owns one theater and leases four others) that it hardly represents a new form of state-led vertical integration.[51]

To recapitulate, Brazilian cinematic legislation stipulates that
exhibitors must show national films at least 140 days per year, that
they must pay a minimum of 50 percent of net income for those
films, that they must make payments within fifteen days of exhibition, that they must show a national short subject as part of each
program of foreign films, that they purchase standardized tickets
and box-office reporting sheets from Embrafilme at inflated
prices, and that they keep national films in exhibition as long as
total spectators (for two weeks or more) equal 60 percent of the
previous year's average. In return, they have received nothing
from the state. All of these items combined have caused a decline
in income, which led to the closing of many theaters, especially in
the interior of the country, and to the crisis described statistically
in table 26.

CONCLUSION

Given the severity of the film industry's crisis, a reformulation
of state policy toward it is inevitable, and yet the divisions outlined in chapter 6 (cultural versus commercial, industrial versus

concentrationist) continue to exist, perhaps now in even more exacerbated fashion than in the late 1970s, making a consensus concerning the future of state policy difficult to achieve. Some filmmakers, including some who had previously supported Embrafilme, now see the enterprise as a drain on the industry and call for the "privatization" of its distributor, the transfer of its cultural activities to the Ministry of Education and Culture (now, after March 1985, to the Ministry of Culture), and its transformation into a minor agency that collects funds from the various cinematic taxes and redistributes them to the industry.[52]

Aware that the current structure of the state cinematic apparatus is inadequate to guarantee future industry development, film professionals from all sectors met continuously throughout 1984 and 1985 to devise a set of proposals to overcome the difficulties of the situation. Special attention has been given to exhibition, the expansion of the film market in the areas of television and home video, and revisions in Embrafilme's financing programs.[53]

Proposals concerning exhibition include the construction of new theaters in government housing projects, tax incentives for the construction of new sites elsewhere, the revitalization of parallel circuits (museums, school auditoriums, etc.), exemption for all theaters from service taxes, and the revision of statutes concerning the compulsory purchase by exhibitors of standardized tickets in cities of under 200,000 inhabitants. Embrafilme and CONCINE have also shown for the first time a degree of flexibility with regard to the screen quota, putting them more in tune with the real necessities of the market, especially in the new "multiplex" sites.[54]

Film industry professionals now recognize that the domestic market, especially in its reduced dimensions, is no longer sufficient to guarantee an adequate return on the average Brazilian film, so proposals have been made that will expand markets and increase producers' income. Early in 1984 CONCINE passed two resolutions (98 and 99) regulating the sale of videocassettes in the country. Among the provisions of these resolutions is a 25 percent quota for national films. That is, 25 percent of all recorded videocassettes in dealers' catalogues or stocks must be national, theatrical films. The stipulation that they be theatrical precludes films made originally for television from participating in the quota. In addition, 15 percent of the 25 percent must be composed of national short subjects.[55] Although these resolutions indicate a recognition of the growing importance of video markets in Brazil, they may also be impossible to enforce or may have little effect, since no legislation can force consumers to rent or purchase national films on video.

With regard to television, it has been proposed that networks be permitted to televise no more than two foreign films per day and then only those whose censorship certificates (valid for five years) have expired. These provisions are intended to reduce the number of foreign films available to networks and hopefully create a space for national films on television.

In reference to production, proposals request that the government provide incentives for the implantation in Brazil of a producer of raw film stock (a proposal first made in the early 1930s), that tax breaks be given to public or private enterprises that invest in film production, and that Embrafilme be restructured in such a way as to make it more agile and capable of lending assistance to the industry as a whole. Embrafilme's director Roberto Parreira (1982–1985) announced that in the future the enterprise's financing programs will be limited to advances on distribution (as in the case of *Quilombo*), and that the state will no longer be directly involved in film production, as in the co-production program.[56] A proposal has also been made to concentrate Embrafilme's cultural activities under a special agency (CENTROCINE) with financial and administrative autonomy, and with a flat 15 percent of Embrafilme's current budget. By this proposal, industry professionals hope to make Embrafilme per se responsible only for commercial activities. It remains to be seen whether any of these proposals will be implemented, or what effect they will have.

Other areas of society have their own ideas about the future of the Brazilian film industry. The first law approved by acting President José Sarney during the ultimately fatal illness of Tancredo Neves, was Law 7,300, formulated by his son José Sarney Filho, a federal deputy from the state of Maranhão. Law 7,300, which ultimately did not take effect, would have prohibited foreign participation in the production, distribution, or exhibition of films in Brazil, thus effectively nationalizing the industry. Such a law, symptomatically proposed and approved without consulting industry professionals, would neutralize the positive efforts of a firm like Gaumont, and could have a drastic effect on the Brazilian film industry as a whole.[57]

Regardless of the outcome of these proposals, it is clear that the federal government has yet to formulate a comprehensive plan for the development of the film industry. State intervention in the industry, which increased gradually from the early thirties until the mid-1960s before accelerating rapidly, has not conformed to any preconceived design, but rather has taken shape, as Alberto Ruy Sánchez suggests concerning the Mexican industry, in accordance with the rhythms of the industry's crises. This has led to inevitable distortions, such as the antagonistic relationship between the state and exhibitors, and to perhaps unresolvable contradictions, such as that reflected in the 1980s crisis.

How does one assess the performance of the state in relation to the film industry in Brazil? Justifications for state intervention fall into two broad categories, one economic and the other cultural. Economically, it is argued that state intervention is necessary to curb imports and reduce the outward flow of currency reserves, as well as to stimulate an adequate level of sustained growth in the national industry through the correction of market imbalances and through the provision of production capital in a traditionally undercapitalized industry.

The first part of the economic argument is somewhat less than compelling. The amount lost in foreign exchange owing to the importation of foreign films is considered, by a former finance minister, to be insignificant.[58] Although the film industry is very small and is not a key sector of the economy, the second half of the argument is more to the point. Without some sort of state assistance, whether purely protectionist or more supportive, the film industry would have little chance to compete successfully in the domestic market against highly organized foreign concerns, and without the ability to compete, it would have no chance to attain even minimal levels of stability and sustained growth.

Culturally, it is argued that the cinema is an instrument of national integration (although it pales by comparison with the integrative power of television). It transmits and reinforces cultural and social values viewed as essential to national development. It may also provide a kind of "prestige value." Filmmaker and former head of Embrafilme's distribution Gustavo Dahl once remarked that "every great nation has a great cinema." If we accept Dahl's perhaps overstated assertion, the cinema becomes a subjective measure of a country's development. It also transmits a national self-image both at home and abroad, so it is not surprising that the state would see it as a legitimate area of concern, especially when one considers the state's incorporative predilections.

Despite the frequently rhetorical nature of such justifications for state intervention, the state does in fact have a dual task. It must support films of an adequate technical and cultural quality, and it must at the same time support the industry's economic development. The history of state intervention over the last twenty years suggests that it has not always been able to reconcile the dichotomy between the two aspects of its mandated duties. In this sense the cultural/commercial dichotomy within the industry is reflected in the state cinematic apparatus itself.

There can be little doubt about the state's success in cultural terms. It has made viable many film projects that otherwise might not have been completed, as it has contributed decisively to Brazilian cinema's becoming the premier cinema in Latin America. It has supported films of a wide variety of genres, styles, and political persuasions—with remarkably few direct ideological constraints—and has helped increase the international prestige of Brazilian cinema. Under Embrafilme's aegis, Brazilian films have garnered over ninety awards in international festivals (Appendix F). In short, Embrafilme is largely responsible for the best that Brazilian cinema has had to offer in the last decade and a half.

On the other hand, although Embrafilme has helped Brazilian cinema gain an ever-increasing share of its own market, its (and CONCINE's) policies have not led to the consolidation of Brazilian cinema as a self-sustaining industry. Its program of co-productions, which has led to so many excellent films, has allowed the bulk of Brazilian cinema, or at least that cinema which it supports, to remain an essentially *auteur* cinema in which many directors have almost complete control over the final shape of their film projects. Although this has given Brazilian cinema a multiplicity of themes and styles unmatched in Latin America, it has also made independent filmmakers almost totally dependent on the state for production financing.

Government officials have claimed that the state's policy toward the industry has been to make the cinema more competitive in its own market, but the screen quota and the various forms of financial assistance the state has provided have in fact suspended the rules of the market for Brazilian films, which no longer compete against foreign films in the domestic market, but rather against each other in the reserve market. The goals of Embrafilme's production programs, furthermore, have not always dovetailed with those of its distributor, creating a paradoxical situation in which the enterprise has co-produced films for which the distributor sees little commercial potential. The result has been that many films spend more time on the dusty shelves of the distributor than in exhibition. Since Embrafilme has become the major if not the sole source of much production financing, it has itself become a marketplace where filmmakers compete against each other for the right to make films, thus exacerbating tensions within the industry and creating a situation in which the play of influences is often more important than the talent of the filmmaker or producer.

In a number of ways Embrafilme has repeated the errors of the Vera Cruz studios of the early 1950s. Vera Cruz, it may be recalled, was the last major attempt at concentrated industrialization in Brazilian cinema. It improved the quality of national production, but did so by elevating production costs way above the potential for return in the domestic market. At the same time, it concentrated solely on production, ignoring the infrastructure of Brazilian cinema and leaving distribution in the hands of American companies. Consequently, its films were not exhibited as widely as necessary, and the company was forced into bankruptcy.

Although Embrafilme has tended to support a different production model from that of Vera Cruz (an atomized, relatively artisan model, as opposed to a studio model), and although it created its own distributor rather than entrust films to foreign concerns, it too improved the technical quality of Brazilian cinema by inflating production costs to levels far above the market potential for return. It too has done little to improve and strengthen the industry's infrastructure. And this is even less acceptable in Embrafilme's case, since it was created precisely to support the development of the film industry as a whole. Embrafilme, along with the Instituto Nacional do Cinema and CONCINE, has placed onerous demands on the exhibition sector while offering nothing in return.

Embrafilme has helped increase Brazilian cinema's share of its own market, but at the same time state policies, formulated by CONCINE with Embrafilme's participation, have contributed to a drastic decline in the dimensions of that market. In 1975, for example, Brazilian cinema accounted for 17.7 percent of the domestic market. In 1983 it controlled over 30 percent. But 15 million *more* spectators saw national films in 1975 than in 1983 (see tables 22, 25, and information accompanying table 26). Brazilian cinema now receives a larger slice of a much smaller pie.

In the introduction I summarized Jorge Schnitman's distinction between restrictive, supportive, and comprehensive protectionist policies. A restrictive policy limits foreign films' access to the market through screen quotas, import quotas, and high tariffs and duties. A supportive policy includes various forms of direct support of the industry, while a comprehensive policy includes both restrictive and supportive measures. According to Schnitman's definitions, Brazil has clearly developed a comprehensive policy toward the national industry. But our discussion of the 1980s crisis suggests that a comprehensive policy is not comprehensive enough if it does not attempt to strengthen all areas of the industry and not merely production. Embrafilme and CONCINE's major failure has been not the policies of support for film production, but rather the lack of support for the exhibition sector.

State intervention in the Brazilian film industry is clearly a double-edged sword. In reference to its inability to reconcile cultural and economic responsibilities, Embrafilme's director Roberto Parreira distinguishes between cultural and economic "profit," arguing that one should not attempt to quantify cultural production. If Embrafilme is in the red economically, it has certainly been profitable in cultural terms. By supporting the most talented Brazilian directors in the production of films such as *Bye Bye Brasil, Pixote, Eles Não Usam Black-Tie, Inocência,* and *Memórias do Cárcere (Prison Memories)*, among many others, Embrafilme, despite its shortcomings, has performed an invaluable service for Brazil and its culture.

APPENDICES

NOTES

BIBLIOGRAPHY

INDEX

APPENDIX A

Brazilian Feature Film Production, 1930–1985

Year	No.	Year	No.	Year	No.	Year	No.
1930	18	1944	9	1958	44	1972	70
1931	17	1945	8	1959	34	1973	58
1932	14	1946	10	1960	34	1975	85
1933	10	1947	11	1961	30	1976	84
1934	7	1948	15	1962	27	1977	72
1935	6	1949	21	1963	32	1978	101
1936	7	1950	20	1964	27	1979	96
1937	6	1951	22	1965	33	1980	102
1938	8	1952	34	1966	28	1981	80
1939	7	1953	29	1967	44	1982	86
1940	13	1954	25	1968	54	1983	84
1941	4	1955	28	1969	53	1984	90
1942	8	1956	29	1970	83	1985	86
1943	8	1957	36	1971	94		

Sources: Alcino Teixeira de Mello, Legislação do Cinema Brasileiro (Rio de Janeiro: Embrafilme, 1978); Embrafilme, annual reports, 1978, 1979, 1980; Variety, 17 March 1982, 4 May 1983, 21 March 1984; Assessoria de Imprensa, Embrafilme.

Appendix B

Films Made Under INC-Administered Co-production Program

Film	Director(s)	Producer(s)	Co-Producer(s)
1968			
Adorável Trapalhão	J. B. Tanko	J. B. Produções	Condor Filmes
As Amorosas	Walter Hugo Khoury	Kamera Filmes	Columbia Pictures
As Armas	Astolfo Araújo	Data Filmes	Allied Artists
Até que o Casamento nos Separe	Flávio Tambellini	Data Filmes	Rank Films
Como Matar um Playboy	Carlos Hugo Christensen	Atlântida	Fox Films
A Doce Mulher Amada	Ruy Santos	Euro Filmes	Royal Films
Os Herdeiros	Carlos Diegues	C. J. Diegues & Jarbas Barbosa	Condor Filmes
O Homem Nu	Roberto Santos	Wallfilmes	Pelmex
O Homem que Comprou o Mundo	E. Coutinho	Mapa	Columbia Pictures
Jovem Cão[a]	Maurício G. Leite	Tekla	Franco-Brasileira
Macunaíma	Joaquim Pedro de Andrade	Grupo Filmes & Filmes do Serro	Condor Filmes
Madona de Cedro	Carlos Coimbra	Cinedistri	M-G-M
Os Marginais	M. Kendler & A. C. Prates Correia	Mariana Filmes	Columbia Pictures
O Quarto	Rubem Biáfora	Data Filmes	Columbia Pictures

Film	Director(s)	Producer(s)	Co-Producer(s)
Quelé do Pajeú	Anselmo Duarte	Procine & Arro Filme	Columbia Pictures
Relato da História de um Mundo Novo (unfinished)	—	Bolivar Madruga Duarte	Screen Gems
Trilogia do Terror	José M. Marins et al.	P.N.F.	Franco-Brasileira

1969

Film	Director(s)	Producer(s)	Co-Producer(s)
Anjos e Demônios	C. H. Christensen	C. H. Christensen	Paramount
Um Anjo Mau	Roberto Santos	Vera Cruz	Fox Films
A Arte de Amar Bem	Fernando de Barros	Wallfilmes	Paramount
Assalto à Brasileira	Flávio Migliaccio	Adolpho Chadler	Royal Films & Art Filmes
Um Certo Capitão Rodrigo	Anselmo Duarte	Vera Cruz	United Artists
Cômicos e Mais Cômicos	Jurandir Noronha	Cine-Sul	Pelmex
Como era Gostoso o meu Frances	N. P. dos Santos	L. C. Barreto	Condor Filmes
Cordélia Cordélia	Rodolfo Nanni	Rodolfo Nanni	Screen Gems
Dentro e Fora de Casa (unfinished)	—	Data Filmes	Allied Artists
As Gatinhas	Astolfo Araújo	Servicine & Fama Filmes	Gália Filmes
O Homem das Estrelas	J. Daniel Poulet	L. C. Barreto	Condor Filmes
Memórias de um Gigolô	Alberto Pieralisi	Magnus Filmes	Paramount & Franco-Brasileira
A Moreninha	Glauco M. Laurelli	Lauper Filmes	CBS
Uma Mulher para Sábado	Maurício Rittner	Kinetos & Assessoria Cine.	Columbia Pictures & Telesistema Filmes
As Noites de Iemanjá	Maurício Capovilla	Data Filmes	Paramount
Palácio dos Anjos	Walter Hugo Khoury	Vera Cruz	M-G-M

Film	Director(s)	Producer(s)	Co-Producer(s)
1969			
Pindorama	Arnaldo Jabor	Kamera Filmes	Screen Gems & Columbia Pictures
Juliana do Amor Perdido	Sérgio Ricardo	Entrefilmes	Brascontinental
Verão de Fogo	Pierre Kalfon	Vera Cruz	M-G-M & Les Films Number One
Viver de Morrer	Jorge Ileli	Entrefilmes	M-G-M

Source: *Filme Cultura* 3, no. 14 (April–May 1970), 55.

Note: Films are classified by the year co-production funds were released.
a. Not completed with this title.

Appendix C

Films Financed Under Embrafilme's Loan Program, 1974–1979

Film	Director	Producer
1974		
O Caçador de Fantasmas	Flávio Migliaccio	Circus Produções Cinematográficas
Cada Um Dá o Que Tem	Adriano Stuart et al.	Cinedistri
52 Filmetes Coloridos	—	Ciencine Didático Brasileiro
Efigênia Dá Tudo Que Tem	Olivier Perroy	Olho Filmes
A Estrela Sobe	Bruno Barreto	L. C. Barreto
A Extorsão	Flávio Tambellini	Flávio Tambellini
A Força de Xangô	Iberê Cavalcânti	Cine TV e Audiovisual
Gargalhada Final	Xavier de Oliveira	Lestepe Produções Cinematográficas
Guerra Conjugal	Joaquim Pedro de Andrade	Filmes do Serro
Ipanema Adeus	Paulo Roberto Martins	Totem Filmes
O Leão do Norte	Carlos del Pino	Boavista Cinematográfica
A Lenda de Ubirajara	André Luiz de Oliveira	André Luiz de Oliveira Produções
O Marginal	Carlos Manga	Carlos Manga Produções
A Ovelha Negra	Haroldo Marinho Barbosa	Nove Produções Cinematográficas
O Padre que Queria Pecar	Lenine Otoni	Bênnio Produções Cinematográficas
O Pistoleiro	Oscar Santana	Sani Filmes
Pureza Prohibida	Alfredo Sternheim	Rossanna Ghessa Produções
Quem Tem Medo do Lobisomem?	Reginaldo Farias	Ipanema Filmes
Quando as Mulheres Querem Provas	Cláudio McDowell	Vydia Produções Cinematográficas

Film	Director	Producer
1974		
Robin Hood, O Trapalhão na Floresta	J. B. Tanko	J. B. Tanko Produções
O Trapalhão na Ilha do Tesouro	J. B. Tanko	J. B. Tanko Produções
Um Varão Entre as Mulheres	Victor di Mello	Di Mello Produções
1975		
Essa Mulher é Minha	Alberto Pieralisi	Alberto Pieralisi Filmes
Esse Rio Muito Louco	Denoy de Oliveira et al.	L. M. Produções Cinematográficas
Kung-Fu Contra as Bonecas	Adriano Stuart	Servicine
Marília e Marina	Luiz Fernando Goulart	Alter Filmes
Primavera dos Enforcados	Alberto Salvá	Herbert Richers
1976		
O Crime do Zé Bigorna	Anselmo Duarte	Fidelíssima Produções
Como Matar uma Sogra	Luiz Maximiniano	L. M. Produções Cinematográficas
Gente Fina é Outra Coisa	Antônio Calmon	Sincrocine
Simbad, O Marujo Trapalhão	J. B. Tanko	J. B. Tanko Produções
1977		
As Filhas do Fogo	Walter Hugo Khoury	Lynxfilme
Essa Freira é Uma Parada	Roberto Machado	Roberto Machado Produções
O Ituano	Adriano Stuart	Cinedistri
1978		
Anjo Só no Céu	J. B. Tanko	J. B. Tanko Produções
Embalos de Ipanema	Antônio Calmon	Sincrocine
A Pantera Nua	Luiz Miranda Correia	Rossanna Ghessa Produções

Film	Director	Producer
1979		
Bye Bye Brasil	Carlos Diegues	L. C. Barreto
52 Filmes Coloridos (contract extended)	—	Ciencine Didático Brasileiro
Pequeno Polegar	Victor Lima	Ve-Victor Éboli Produções

Source: Embrafilme.

APPENDIX D

Films Released by Embrafilme, 1974–1984

1974

O Sítio do Picapau Amarelo
Uirá, um Índio em Busca de Deus
Como nos Livrar do Saca
As Moças Daquela Hora
Os Condenados
Noite do Espantalho
O Leito da Mulher Amada
O Último Malandro
Karla, Sedenta de Amor
A Noiva da Cidade
Amor e Medo

Sedução, Qualquer Coisa a Respeito do Amor
Brutos Inocentes
O Forte
Ovelha Negra, Uma Despedida de Solteiro
O Segredo da Rosa
Pureza Proibida
A Cartomante
O Amuleto de Ogum
O Comprador de Fazendas
Sinfonia Brasileira

1975

Um Homem Célebre
Uma Tarde, Outra Tarde
O Leão do Norte
Um Varão entre as Mulheres
Nós os Canalhas
O Padre que Queria Pecar
Lucíola, o Anjo Pecador
O Trapalhão na Ilha do Tesouro
O Caçador de Fantasmas
A Lenda de Ubirajara

O Filho do Chefão
O Resgate (Nem os Bruxos Escapam)
Ana a Libertina
O Casal
Ipanema Adeus
Alegres Vigaristas
Confissões de uma Viúva Moça
Nordeste: Cordel, Repente, Canção
O Pistoleiro

1976

As Aventuras Amorosas de um Padeiro
O Sósia da Morte

Pedro Bó, O Caçador de Cangaceiros
Perdida
Lição de Amor

1976

Um Soutien Para Papai	Desquitadas em Lua de Mel
O Rei da Noite	Soledade
O Desejo	Pecado na Sacristia
Simbad, o Marujo Trapalhão	Aleluia Gretchen
O Casamento	Dona Flor e Seus Dois Maridos
O Esquadrão da Morte	Fogo Morto
Ritmo Alucinante	Marcados para Viver
Xica da Silva	Noite das Fêmeas

1977

Os Trapalhões no Planalto dos Macacos	Ajuricaba
	O Crime do Zé Bigorna
As Granfinas e o Camelô	Tenda dos Milagres
A Mulher do Desejo	Ódio
Uma Aventura na Floresta Encantada	Marília e Marina
Ibraim do Subúrbio	Quem Matou Pacífico?
As Aventuras de um Detetive Português	Casa das Tentações
	Os Amores da Pantera
Pontal da Solidão	Crueldade Mortal
O Seminarista	Fruto Proibido
Ladrões de Cinema	O Jogo da Vida
Na Ponta da Faca	Paixão e Sombras
A Noite dos Assassinos	

1978

Cordão de Ouro	Doramundo
Os Trapalhões nas Minas do Rei Salomão	A Queda
	Um Marido Contagiante
Sinfonia Brasileira	O Monstro de Santa Teresa
Gordos e Magros	Um Brasileiro Chamado Rosaflor
Mar de Rosas	Parada 88, o Limite de Alerta
Barra Pesada	Se Segura Malandro
Diamante Bruto	Paraíso no Inferno
Morte e Vida Severina	O Desconhecido
O Cortiço	Tudo Bem
A Dama do Lotação	Amor Bandido
Chuvas de Verão	A Lira do Delírio
Lúcio Flávio, o Passageiro da Agonia	

1979

Na Boca do Mundo	A Morte Transparente
Anchieta, José do Brasil	A Força de Xangô

1979

O Amante da Minha Mulher
As Filhas do Fogo
Coronel Delmiro Gouvéia
Os Muckers
Fim de Festa
A Deusa Negra
O Coronel e o Lobisomem
Iracema, A Virgem dos Lábios de Mel
Cabeças Cortadas
Gargalhada Final
Raoni
Canudos
Inquietações de uma Mulher Casada

O Guarani
Revólver de Brinquedo
Vamos Cantar Disco Baby
Diário da Província
Essa Freira é uma Parada
Macunaíma (re-release)
A Noiva da Cidade (re-release)
O País de São Saruê
Amante Latino
Terra dos Índios
Princípio do Prazer
Os Noivos
O Sol dos Amantes

1980

Maneco Super Tio
Muito Prazer
Curumim
A Volta do Filho Pródigo
Bye Bye Brasil
O Namorador
J. S. Brown
Contos Eróticos
Parceiros da Aventura
Os Trombadinhas
Gaijin
Crônica de um Industrial
Os Sete Gatinhos
Tinha Bububu no Bobobo
Convite ao Prazer
Matou a Família e Foi ao Cinema
O Bandido Antônio Dó
A Dama de Branco
A Intrusa
Ele, Ela, Quem?
Flamengo Paixão
Samba da Criação do Mundo
Lerfa-Mu

Os Anos JK: Uma Trajetória Política
Terror e Êxtase
Amantes da Chuva
Dona Flor e Seus Dois Maridos (re-release)
O Caçador de Esmeraldas
Viagem ao Mundo da Língua Portuguesa
O Grande Palhaço
Pixote, A Lei do Mais Fraco
Até a Última Gota
A Revolução de 30
Música Para Sempre
Paula
A Dama do Lotação (re-release)
Teu, Tua
A Idade da Terra
Abismo
Agonia
Iracema
O Gigante da América
O Homem que Virou Suco

1981

O Boi de Prata
Estrada da Vida

Fruto do Amor
Cabaret Mineiro

1981

Ato de Violência
Eu te Amo
Santo Sudário
Xica da Silva (re-release)
Beijo no Asfalto
Rainha do Rádio
O Mundo Mágico dos Trapalhões
Lúcio Flávio, o Passageiro da Agonia
(re-release)

Filha de Iemanjá
Abrigo Nuclear
Maldita Consciência
Eles Não Usam Black-Tie
Engraçadinha
Eros, o Deus do Amor
Os Saltimbancos Trapalhões

1982

Menino do Rio
Pixote, A Lei do Mais Fraco (re-
release)
O Homem do Pau-Brasil
Amor e Traição
Jânio a 24 Horas
Luz del Fuego
Asa Branca
O Sonho não Acabou
Índia
In Vino Veritas
Eu te Amo (re-release)

Manelão, o Caçador de Orelhas
Prova de Fogo
O Rei da Noite
Beijo na Boca
O Homem de Areia
O Segredo da Múmia
Das Tripas Coração
Amor Estranho Amor
Caminho das Índias
Os Trapalhões na Serra Pelada
As Aventuras da Turma da Mônica

1983

As Aventuras do Tio Maneco
Pra Frente Brasil
Aventuras de um Paraíba
Toda Nudez Será Castigada (re-
release)
Corações a Mil
Tabu
Dora, Doralina
Egungun
A República Guarani
Bar Esperança
Prata Palomares
Tormenta
Sargento Getúlio
Rio Babilônia

Sete Dias de Agonia
Inocência
O Bom Burguês
A Difícil Viagem
Janete
Parahyba Mulher Macho
Terra
Nasce uma Mulher
A Próxima Vítima
Idolatrada
Ao Sul do Meu Corpo
O Último Vôo do Condor
O Trapalhão na Arca de Noé
Garota Dourada

1984

A Princesa e o Robô
Agüenta Coração
Águia na Cabeça
Filho Adotivo
O Mágico e o Delegado
Para Viver um Grande Amor
Quilombo
Memórias do Cárcere
O Mágico de Oróz

Nunca Fomos Tão Felizes
Bete Balanço
O Rei da Vela
Baiano Fantasma
Erendira
Amor Voraz
Noites do Sertão
O Cavalinho Azul
A Filha dos Trapalhões

1985

Tensão no Rio
Abrasasas
Patriamada
Muda Brasil
Jeitosa
Os Bons Tempos Voltaram
Além da Paixão

Os Trapalhões no Reino da Fantasia
A Estrela Nua
Espelho de Carne
Avaeté
O Rei do Rio
Boi Aruã

Source: Embrafilme.

APPENDIX E

Films Co-produced by Embrafilme (by year of completion)

Film	Producer	Director
1974		
O Amuleto de Ogum	Regina Filmes	Nelson P. dos Santos
O Comprador de Fazendas	Alberto Pieralisi	Alberto Pieralisi
O Filho do Chefão	Distrifilmes	Víctor Lima
Um Homem Célebre	Zoom Cinematográfica	Miguel Faria, Jr.
Sinfonia Brasileira	Jaime Prades	Jaime Prades
1975		
Aventuras Amorosas de um Padeiro	Regina Filmes	Waldir Onofre
Confissões de uma Viúva Moça	Di Mello Produções	Víctor di Mello
O Desejo	W. H. Khouri	W. H. Khouri
O Ladrão de Bagdá	Ve-Victor Eboli	Víctor Lima
Lição de Amor	L. C. Barreto	Eduardo Escorel
Lucíola, Um Anjo Pecador	Servicine	Alfredo Sternheim
O Monstro de Santa Teresa	William Cobbett	William Cobbett
A Mulher do Desejo	C. H. Christensen	C. H. Christensen
Nós, os Canalhas	Magnus Filmes	Jece Valadão
Perdida	Mapa	C. A. Prates Correa
O Sósia da Morte	L. M. Produções Cinematográficas	Luís Miranda
Um Soutien para Papai	CASB Produções Cinematográficas	C. A. Souza Barros

213

Film	Producer	Director
1976		
Aleluia Gretchen	Sílvio Back	Sílvio Back
Crueldade Mortal	Sincrocine	Luís P. dos Santos
Fogo Morto	Miguel Borges	Marcos Farias
Fruto Proibido	Di Mello	Egídio Éccio
O Ibraim do Subúrbio	Sincrocine	Cecil Thiré
A Noite dos Assassinos	Magnus	Jece Valadão
O Resgate	Filmes Três	Valdi Ercolani
O Seminarista	Vila Rica	G. Santos Pereira
Soledade	Paulo Thiago	Paulo Thiago
Xica da Silva	J. B. Produções Cinematográficas	Carlos Diegues
1977		
Ajuricaba	Oswaldo Caldeira	Oswaldo Caldeira
Um Brasileiro Chamado Rosaflor	OPF	Geraldo Miranda
Cordão de Ouro	Lanterna Mágica	A. Carlos Fontoura
O Desconhecido	Scorpius	Ruy Santos
Diamante Bruto	Pilar Filmes	Orlando Senna
Ela, Ele, Quem?	A. P. Sampaio	Luís de Barros
A Força de Xangô	Cine TV e Áudio-Visual	Iberê Cavalcânti
Gordos e Magros	Filmes do Serro	Mário Carneiro
O Jogo da Vida	Documenta	Maurício Capovilla
Ladrões de Cinema	Lente Filmes	Fernando C. Campos
Mar de Rosas	Área Produções Cinematográficas	Ana Carolina
Um Marido Contagiante	CASB	C. A. Souza Barros
Os Mistérios do Sexo	Palmares	Denoy de Oliveira
Morte e Vida Severina	Mapa	Zelito Viana
Ódio	Vidya	Carlos Mossy
Paixão e Sombras	W. H. Khoury	W. H. Khoury
Parada 88	NAM	José Anchieta Costa
Paraíso no Inferno	Rosário	Joel Barcelos
Quem Matou Pacífico?	Vila Rica	Renato Santos Pereira
Revólver de Brinquedo	Battaglin Produções	Antônio Calmon
Teu, Tua	Empresas Associação J. R.	Domingos de Oliveira

Film	Producer	Director
1978		
Anchieta, José do Brasil	Sant'Anna Produções	P. César Saraceni
Na Boca do Mundo	Lente Filmes	Antônio Pitanga
Chuvas de Verão	Alter Filmes	Carlos Diegues
Coronel Delmiro Gouveia	Saruê Filmes	Geraldo Sarno
A Dama do Lotação	Regina Filmes	Neville d' Almeida
Doramundo	Raiz Produções Cinematográficas	J. Batista de Andrade
Fim de Festa	Ventania	Paulo Porto
Inquietações de uma Mulher Casada	Thor Filmes	Alberto Salvá
A Lira do Delírio	Walter Lima, Jr.	Walter Lima, Jr.
A Morte Transparente	C. H. Christensen	C. H. Christensen
O Namorador	Di Mello	Lenine Otoni
Se Segura Malandro	Zoom Cinematográfica	Hugo Carvana
Só Restam as Estrelas	Wilson Silva	Wilson Silva
As Trapalhadas de Dom Quixote e Sancho Pança	Kinoarte	Ary Fernandes
Tudo Bem	Sagitário	Arnaldo Jabor
A Volta do Filho Pródigo	Roland Henze	Ipojuca Pontes
1979		
O Amante da Minha Mulher	Alberto Pieralisi	Alberto Pieralisi
Os Amantes da Chuva	Oca Cinematográfica	Roberto Santos
Desenhos Animados	Briquet	Clóvis Vieira
O Guarani	Fauzi Mansur	Fauzi Mansur
A Intrusa	C. H. Christensen	C. H. Christensen
Iracema, a Virgem dos Lábios de Mel	C.S.C.	Carlos Coimbra
A Noiva da Cidade	Catavento	Alex Viany
Os Parceiros da Aventura	A. F. Sampaio	José Medeiros
O Sol dos Amantes	Lynxfilme	G. Santos Pereira
1979 television pilots		
Alice	Raiz Produções	J. Batista de Andrade
Brasil, Os Mistérios das Origens	Playtime Produções	J. M. Coelho, R. Varela

Film	Producer	Director
1979 television pilots		
Caramuru	Oca Cinematográfica	Francisco Ramalho, Jr.
O Coronel e o Lobisomem	Alcino Diniz	Alcino Diniz
Curumim	NAU	Plácido de Campos, Jr.
História dos Povos de Língua Portuguesa	Jaraguá Filmes	Ruben R. dos Santos
Os Imigrantes	Thomaz Farkas	Sérgio Muniz
João Juca, Jr., Detetive Carioca	Telemil Filmes	Denoy de Oliveira
Maneco o Super-Tio	Flávio Migliáccio	Flávio Migliáccio
Os Melhores Momentos da Literatura Brasileira	Blimp Filmes	Denoy de Oliveira
O Mudo	Lynxfilmes	Júlio Cesar Oliveira
Nosso Mundo	Regina Filmes	Nelson P. dos Santos
Orum o Vingador	Magnus Filmes	Jorge Durán Parra
A Terra dos Índios	Mapa	Zelito Viana
Tio Benício	Lente Filmes	Pedro E. Stilpen
Vida Vida	Produções J. R.	Domingos de Oliveira
Vigilante Rodoviário	Procitel	Ary Fernandes
1980		
Antônio Dó	Filmes do Valle	Paulo Leite Soares
Ato de Violência	Lynxfilme	Eduardo Escorel
Beijo no Asfalto	L. C. Barreto	Bruno Barreto
Cabaret Mineiro	Zoom Cinematográfica	C. A. Prates Correa
A Dama da Gafieira	Roberto Machado	Roberto Machado
Gaijin	CPC	Tizuka Yamasaki
O Gigante da América	Júlio Bressane	Júlio Bressane
O Grande Palhaço	William Cobbett	William Cobbett
O Homem que Virou Suco	Raiz Produções	J. Batista de Andrade
A Idade da Terra	CPC	Glauber Rocha
Maldita Consciência	Sérgio Bianchi	Sérgio Bianchi
Meu Boi de Prata	Cine-TV	Pedro Camargo
Muito Prazer	Morena Produções	David Neves
A Opção	Prodsul	Ozualdo Candeias
Paula	Oca Cinematográfica	Francisco Ramalho, Jr.
As Pequenas Taras	Rosário Produções	Maria do Rosário
Pixote	H. B. Produções	Hector Babenco
Prova de Fogo	L. C. Barreto	Marcos Altberg
A Rainha do Rádio	L. F. Goulart	Luíz F. Goulart

Film	Producer	Director
1980		
Os Sete Gatinhos	Cineville	Neville d'Almeida
Silêncio e Medo	Zoom/Forma	Alberto Graça
Tinha Bububu no Bobobó	Marcos Farias	Marcos Farias
1981		
Abrigo Nuclear	Bahia Filmes	Roberto Pires
O Caçador de Orelhas	Prodsul	Ozualdo Candeias
O Caminho das Índias	Gira Filmes	Augusto Sevá
Eles Não Usam Black-Tie	Leon Hirszman	Leon Hirszman
Engraçadinha	Encontro Produções	Haroldo M. Barbosa
O Homem do Pau-Brasil	Filmes do Serro	Joaquim P. de Andrade
Insônia	Cooperativa Mista	Emmanoel Cavalcânti
Jânio a 24 Horas	Thomaz Farkas	Luiz A. M. Pereira
Um Marciano na Minha Cama	Cipal	Mário Jorge
O Menino e o Rei	Start Filmes	Walberci Ribas
A Pele do Bicho	Cine-TV	Pedro Camargo
Os Saltimbancos Trapalhões	Renato Aragão	J. B. Tanko
1982		
Ao Sul do Meu Corpo	Sant 'Anna Produções	Paulo César Saraceni
Asa Branca	Roberto Santos	Djalma Batista
As Aventuras da Turma da Mônica	Maurício de Souza	Maurício de Souza
As Aventuras de um Paraíba no Rio	Lucy Barreto	Marcos Altberg
Beijo na Boca	Encontro Produções	Paulo Sérgio Almeida
Das Tripas Coração	Crystal Cinematográfica	Ana Carolina
Dora, Doralina	Scorpius	Perry Salles
Luz del Fuego	Morena Filmes	David Neves
Noites Paraguaias	Atalante Produções	Aloysio Raulino
Pra Frente Brasil	R. F. Farias	Roberto Farias
Rio Babilônia	CPC	Neville d' Almeida
Sargento Getúlio	Hermano Penna	Hermano Penna
O Segredo da Múmia	Super 8 Produções	Ivan Cardoso
Sete Dias de Agonia	Denoy de Oliveira	Denoy de Oliveira
O Sonho não Acabou	Morena Filmes	Sérgio Resende

Film	Producer	Director
1982		
Tabu	Júlio Bressane	Júlio Bressane
Os Trapalhões na Serra Pelada	Renato Aragão	J. B. Tanko
O Último Vôo do Condor	Emílio Fontana	Emílio Fontana
Vivos ou Mortos	Filmes do Valle	Paulo Leite Soares
1983		
Agüenta Coração	R. F. Farias	Reginaldo Farias
Águia na Cabeça	Morena Produções	Paulo Thiago
Bar Esperança	CPC	Hugo Carvana
O Bom Burguês	Encontro Produções	Oswaldo Caldeira
Diacuí	Alto Filmes	Ivan Kurdna
A Difícil Viagem	A & B Produções	Geraldo Moraes
Egungun	Sociedade da Cultura Negra	Carlos Basblat
Garota Dourada	Fábio Barreto	Antônio Calmon
Idolatrada	Grupo Novo de Cinema	Paulo Augusto Gomes
Inocência	L. C. Barreto	Walter Lima, Jr.
Janete	Tatu Filmes	Chico Botelho
O Mágico e o Delegado	Sani Filmes	Fernando Coni Campos
Nasce uma Mulher	Roberto Santos	Roberto Santos
Nunca Fomos Tão Felizes	Salles e Salles	Murilo Salles
Parahyba Mulher Macho	CPC	Tizuka Yamasaki
A Princesa e o Robô	Maurício de Souza	Maurício de Souza
A Próxima Vítima	Raiz Produções	J. Batista de Andrade
O Rei da Vela	5° Tempo	José Celso M. Correia
Os Trapalhões na Arca de Noé	Renato Aragão	J. B. Tanko

1984 (co-production and/or advance on distribution)

Assunto Muito Particular	N.D.R. Filmes	Nello de Rossi
Ela e os Homens	Filmes do Valle	Schubert Magalhães
Abrasasas	Gira Filmes	Reinaldo Volpato
O Baiano Fantasma	Palmares Produções Cinematográficas	Denoy de Oliveira

Film	Producer	Director
1984 (co-production and/or advance on distribution)		
Noites do Sertão	Grupo Novo de Cinema	Carlos A. Prates Correia
Amor Voraz	Cinema Centro do Brasil	Walter Hugo Khoury
Filho Adotivo	Madial Filmes	Deni Cavalcânti
Memórias do Cárcere	L. C. Barreto	Nelson P. dos Santos
Quilombo	C.D.K. Produções	Carlos Diegues
Tensão no Rio	Sombra Cinema e Comunicação	Gustavo Dahl
Para Viver um Grande Amor	Bastidores Produções	Miguel Farias
Bete Balanço	CPC	Lael Rodrigues
Cavalinho Azul	Cinefilmes	Eduardo Escorel
Exu-Piá, Coração de Macunaíma	Corcina	Paulo Veríssimo
Os Trapalhões e o Mágico de Oróz	Renato Aragão Produções	Dedê Santana
Noite	Morena Filmes	Gilberto Loureiro
Espelho de Carne	Enigma	Antônio Carlos Fontoura
A Estrela Nua	Olympus Filmes	José Antônio & Ícaro Martins
Além da Paixão	L. C. Barreto	Bruno Barreto
A Filha dos Trapalhões	Renato Aragão Produções	Dedê Santana
Os Bons Tempos Voltaram . . .	Cinearte Produções Cinematográficas	Ivan Cardoso & John Herbert
O Beijo da Mulher Aranha	H. B. Filmes	Hector Babenco
1985 (co-production and/or advance on distribution)		
Patriamada	CPC	Tizuka Yamazaki
A Marvada Carne	Tatu Filmes	André Klotzel
Muda Brasil	Encontro Produções Cinematográficas	Oswaldo Caldeira
Pedro Mico	Ipojuca Pontes Produções	Ipojuca Pontes
Avaeté—A Semente da Vingança	Produções Cinematográficas Mapa	Zelito Viana
Um Filme 100% Brasileiro	Grupo Novo de Cinema	José Sette de Barros
Os Trapalhões no Reino da Fantasia	Renato Aragão Produções	Dedê Santana

Film	Producer	Director
1985 (co-production and/or advance on distribution)		
Eu Sei que Vou te Amar	Sagitário Produções Cinematográficas	Arnaldo Jabor
O Rei do Rio	L. C. Barreto	Fábio Barreto
Chico Rei	Art-4 Produções	Walter Lima, Jr.
Amenic	Amenic Produções Cinematográficas	Fernando Silva
A Hora da Estrela	Raiz Produções Cinematográficas	Suzana Amaral
Tigipió	Grupo Novo de Cinema	Pedro Jorge Castro
Brás Cubas	Júlio Bressane Produções	Júlio Bressane
Nem Tudo É Verdade	Rogério Sganzerla	Rogério Sganzerla
Rock Estrela	CPC	Lael Rodrigues
Com Licença, Eu Vou à Luta	R. F. Farias	Lui Farias
Filha Demência	E. M. Cinematográfica	Carlos Reichenbach
A Igreja dos Oprimidos	L. C. Barreto	Jorge Bodansky
Sonho sem Fim	Cinefilmes	Lauro Escorel

Source: Embrafilme.

International Awards Won by Brazilian Films, 1970–1984

Film	Award	Location
1970		
Tostão, A Fera de Ouro	Silver Medal	Cortina d' Ampezzo
Azzylo Muito Louco	Luis Buñuel Prize	Cannes
Memória de Helena	Honorable Mention	Locarno Festival
Tarzan (short)	Silver Medal	Sitges
Marcelo Zona Sul	Silver Plaque	San Sebastián
1971		
Pecado Mortal	Critics' Prize	Venice
Pecado Mortal	Best Film	Grenoble
Brasil Ano 2000	Best Film	Cartegena
Em Família	Silver Medal	Moscow
Meu Pé de Laranja Lima	Asturias Trophy	Gijón
Os Deuses e os Mortos	Best Color	Barcelona
Os Deuses e os Mortos	Best Direction	Grenoble
Os Deuses e os Mortos	Silver Plaque	San Sebastián
Guerra dos Pelados	Honorable Mention	Benalmadena
1972		
A Culpa	Dama das Paraguas	Barcelona
A Casa Assassinada	Esfinge Award	Panamá
Esta Noite Encarnarei no Teu Cadáver	Gold Medal	Sitges
Toda Nudez Será Castigada	Silver Bear	Berlin
Os Inconfidentes	Arts and Letters Award	Venice

Film	Award	Location
1972		
Sonhos e Pesadelos (short)	Gold Medal	Cannes
Brasil Retrato de um País	First Prize	Marseille
1973		
As Deusas	Best Color	Barcelona
1974		
O Anjo da Noite	Special Jury Prize	Sitges
A Noite do Espantalho	Best Music	Toulon
Vai Trabalhar Vegabundo	Gold Cariddi	Taormina
Os Condenados	Silver Peacock	New Delhi
1975		
Pilar (short)	Bronze Medal	Madrid
Guerra Conjugal	Honorable Mention	Barcelona
1977		
Di Cavalcânti (short)	Special Jury Prize	Cannes
Dona Flor e Seus Dois Maridos	Special Jury Prize	Taormina
1978		
A Queda	Silver Bear	Berlin
Lúcio Flávio	Best Actor	Taormina
Chuvas de Verão	Colón de Oro	Huelva
A Força de Xangô	Best Research	Panamá
A Força de Xangô	Best Cinematography	Panamá
A Força de Xangô	Best Supporting Actor	Panamá
1979		
Braços Cruzados, Máquinas Paradas	Fomento Award	Leipzig
Coronel Delmiro Gouvéia	Grand Prize	Havana
Greve	Jury's Special Mention	Havana

Film	Award	Location
1980		
Gaijin	Honorable Mention	Cannes
Gaijin	Georges Sadoul Award	Cannes
Gaijin	Grand Prize	Havana
Tudo Bem	Best Actress	Taormina
Até a Última Gota	Best Film	Mannheim
A Menina e a Casa da Menina (short)	Ecumenical Jury Award	Nyon
O Grande Palhaço	Crystal Goblet	Tashkent
Crônica de um Industrial	Honorable Mention	New Delhi
A Volta do Filho Pródigo	Honorable Mention	New Delhi
Ajuricaba	Honorable Mention	Tashkent
A Lenda de Ubirajara	Honorable Mention	Tashkent
Os Mucker	Honorable Mention	Filmex/Los Angeles
Chuvas de Verão	Honorable Mention	Filmex/Los Angeles
Parada 88	Honorable Mention	Tashkent
1981		
República dos Assassinos	Second Place for Best Film	Cartagena
República dos Assassinos	Best Actor	Cartagena
O Homem que Virou Suco	Gold Medal	Lille
O Homem que Virou Suco	Special Mention	Huelva
O Homem que Virou Suco	Best Actor	Huelva
A Menina e a Casa da Menina (short)	Honorable Mention	Lille
Em Nome da Razão (short)	Honorable Mention	Lille
Pixote	Special Festival Award	Lucerne
Pixote	Silver Leopard	Lucerne
Pixote	Special Jury's Prize	San Sebastián
Pixote	Gold Makhila	Biarritz
Pixote	Public's Grand Prize	Biarritz
Pixote	Honorable Mention	Filmex/Los Angeles
Pixote	Best Foreign Film	New York Film Critics

Film	Award	Location
1981		
Pixote	Best Actress	National Critics Association, U.S.A.
A Opção	Jury's Grand Prize	Lucerne
A Opção	Bronze Leopard	Lucerne
Gaijin	Public's Award	Brussels
Gaijin	Honorable Mention	Filmex/Los Angeles
Eles Não Usam Black-Tie	First Special Jury Award	Venice
Eles Não Usam Black-Tie	Golden Lion (co-winner)	Venice
Eles Não Usam Black-Tie	Second Prize, International Critics	Venice
Eles Não Usam Black-Tie	Third Agis Prize	Venice
Eles Não Usam Black-Tie	Fourth Prize, OCIC	Venice
Eles Não Usam Black-Tie	Best Film	Valladolid
Eles Não Usam Black-Tie	Grand Prize	Nantes
Eles Não Usam Black-Tie	Grand Prize	Havana
Se Segura, Malandro	Second Prize	Cadiz
1982		
Nada Levarei Quando Morrer, Aqueles que a Mim Devem, Cobrarei no Inferno (short)	Special Jury Award	Lille
Sete Dias de Agonia	Quijote Prize	Havana
O Segredo da Múmia	Grand Critics Prize	Madrid
Meow (short)	Special Jury Award	Cannes
Pixote	Best Film	Sidney
Das Tripas Coração	Best Screenplay	Cartagena
Asa Branca	Special Prize	Nantes
O Homem do Pau Brasil	Special Mention	Huelva
Índia, A Filha do Sol	Second Mention of Jury	Havana

Film	Award	Location
1983		
Pra Frente Brasil	OCIC	Berlin
Pra Frente Brasil	Jury of Association of Art Theaters	Berlin
A Idade da Terra	Special Award of Museum of Modern Art	Cartagena
Eles Não Usam Black-Tie	Critics' Award	Cartegena
Tzubra Tzuma (short)	Second Prize for Animation	Murcia
Parahyba Mulher Macho	Best Director	Cartagena
Parahyba Mulher Macho	Best Actress	Cartagena
Parahyba Mulher Macho	Special Theater Award	Cartagena
Parahyba Mulher Macho	Best Actress	Havana
Parahyba Mulher Macho	Special Jury's Award	Huelva
Parahyba Mulher Macho	Andalusian Writers' Award	Huelva
Parahyba Mulher Macho	Spanish Film Societies' Award	Huelva
Animando (short)	Diploma of Merit	Melbourne
Animando	Best Didactic Film	Espinho, Portugal
Sargento Getúlio	Bronze Leopard	Lucerne
Sargento Getúlio	Special Jury's Award	Lucerne
Sargento Getúlio	UNESCO Award	Nantes
Sargento Getúlio	Best Actor	Havana
O Homem que Virou Suco	Special Critics' Award	Nevers
Bar Esperança	First Prize	Cadiz
Bar Esperança	UNEAC Award	Havana
Inocência	Second Prize	Havana
Terceiro Milênio	3 Worlds Award	Cinéma du Réel, Paris
1984		
Cangaceiros Trapalhões	Best Children's Film	Tomar, Portugal
Vagabundos Trapalhões	Second Prize	Tomar, Portugal

Film	Award	Location
1984		
Araucária (medium-length film)	Award from United Nations Organization for Agriculture	Festival of Agricultural Films, Berlin
Fala Mangueira (medium-length film)	Honorable Mention	Murcia
Fala Mangueira	3 Worlds Award	Cinéma du Réel, Paris
Memórias do Cárcere	International Critics Award	Cannes
Noites do Sertão	Best Photography	Cartagena
Noites do Sertaõ	Best Actress	Cartagena
Quilombo	Best Artistic Contribution to Latin American Cinema	Cartagena

Source: Embrafilme.

NOTES

INTRODUCTION

1. See, for example; Peter Evans, *Dependent Development: The Alliance of Multinational, State, and Local Capital in Brazil* (Princeton, N.J.: Princeton University Press, 1979); and Thomas J. Trebat, *Brazil's State-Owned Enterprises: A Case Study of the State as Entrepreneur* (Cambridge: Cambridge University Press, 1983).

2. Antônio Cândido, *Literatura e Sociedade* (São Paulo: Editora Nacional, 1975), pp. 77–88.

3. J. M. Taylor, "The Politics of Aesthetic Debate: The Case of Brazilian Carnival," *Ethnology* 21, no. 4 (October 1982), 303.

4. Janet Lever, *Soccer Madness* (Chicago: University of Chicago Press, 1983), pp. 52, 56.

5. *Jornal do Brasil,* 2 April 1982; *Correio Braziliense,* 3 April 1982; *Veja,* 14 July 1982.

6. Thomas Guback, *The International Film Industry: Western Europe and America Since 1945* (Bloomington: Indiana University Press, 1969), pp. 142–43.

7. Ibid., p. 144.

8. Ibid.

9. Jorge Schnitman, *Film Industries in Latin America: Dependency and Development* (Norwood, N.J.: Ablex Publishing Company, 1984), pp. 39–40.

10. Alberto Ruy Sánchez, *Mitología de un cine en crisis* (Mexico City: Premia, 1981), See also Carl Mora, *Mexican Cinema* (Berkeley and Los Angeles: University of California Press, 1982).

11. U.S. Department of Commerce, Business, and Defense Services Administration, "World Survey of Motion Picture Theater Facilities," (1960).

12. Teotônio dos Santos, "Brazil," in *Latin America: The Struggle with*

Dependency and Beyond, ed. Ronald H. Chilcote and Joel C. Edelstein (New York: Wiley, 1974); Schnitman, pp. 16–26, 66–75; and Sérgio Caparelli, *Televisão e Capitalismo no Brasil* (Porto Alegre: L&PM Editores, 1982), p. 10.

13. Schnitman, esp. ch. 4.

14. Sánchez, p. 46.

15. Michael Chanan, *The Dream that Kicks: The Prehistory and Early Years of Cinema in Britain* (London: Routledge & Kegan Paul, 1980), p. 27.

16. Ibid., p. 23.

17. Schnitman, p. 1.

18. Ibid., p. 46.

19. Randal Johnson, "State Policy Toward the Film Industry in Brazil," Technical Papers Series, no. 36, Office for Public Sector Studies, Institute of Latin American Studies, University of Texas, Austin (1982).

20. Ibid.; Schnitman, p. 6.

21. Carlos Drummond de Andrade, *Passeios na Ilha*; cited by Sérgio Miceli, *Intelectuais e Classe Dirigente no Brasil (1920–1945)* (São Paulo: Difel, 1979), p. 129.

22. Carlos Nelson Coutinho, "O Significado de Lima Barreto na Literatura Brasileira," in *Realismo e Anti-Realismo na Literatura Brasileira* (Rio de Janeiro: Paz e Terra, 1974), pp. 4–6; see also "Cultura e Democracia," in his *Democracia como Valor Universal* (São Paulo: Livraria Editora Ciências Humanas, 1980), pp. 71–77.

23. Jean-Claude Bernardet, *Cinema Brasileiro: Propostas para uma História* (Rio de Janeiro: Paz e Terra, 1979), p. 46.

24. Octavio Paz, *El ogro filantrópico: historia y política, 1971–1978* (Mexico City: Juan Mortiz, 1979), p. 306.

25. Ibid., p. 314.

26. Bernardet, p. 57.

27. The following definitions borrowed from Fernando Henrique Cardoso, "On the Characterization of Authoritarian Regimes in Latin America," in *The New Authoritarianism in Latin America*; ed. David Collier (Princeton, N.J.: Princeton University Press, 1979), pp. 33–57; in the same volume see also, Julio Cotler, "State and Regime: Comparative Notes on the Southern Cone and 'Enclave' Societies," pp. 255–82.

28. Riordan Roett, *Brazil: Politics in a Patrimonial Society* (Boston: Allyn and Bacon, 1972), p. 51.

29. See note 27; other analysts have described this same state as bureaucratic-authoritarian (O'Donnell), as a sinecure state (*estado cartorial*—Jaguaribe), and as a patrimonial state (Roett).

30. Howard J. Wiarda, *Corporatism and National Development in Latin America* (Boulder, Colo.: Westview Press, 1981), p. 34. For discussions of corporatism in different contexts, see Douglas A. Chalmers, ed., *Changing Latin America* (New York: Academy of Political Science, Columbia University, 1972); Kenneth Paul Erikson, *The Brazilian Corporative State and Working-Class Politics* (Berkeley and Los Angeles: University of California Press, 1977); Collier, ed.; James M. Malloy, ed., *Authoritarianism and Corporatism in Latin America* (Pittsburgh, Pa.: University of Pittsburgh Press, 1977); Guillermo O'Donnell, *Modernization and Bureaucratic Authoritarianism* (Berkeley, Calif.: Institute of International Studies, 1973); Frederick B. Pike and Thomas Stritch, eds., *The New Corporatism: Social-Political Structures in the Iberian World* (South Bend, Ind.: University of Notre Dame Press, 1974); Roett; Alfred Stepan, ed., *Authoritarian Brazil: Origins, Policies, and Future* (New Haven, Conn.: Yale University Press, 1973).

31. The idea of the state as a site of contradiction is borrowed from Nicos Poulantzas, *State, Power, Socialism* (London: Verso, 1980).

32. Wiarda, p. 47.

33. Alfred Stepan, *State and Society: Peru in Comparative Perspective* (Princeton, N.J.: Princeton University Press, 1978), p. 47.

34. Wiarda, p. 128; also Erikson, p. 46; and James M. Malloy, "Authoritarianism and Corporatism in Latin America," p. 12.

CHAPTER 1. THE EARLY DEVELOPMENT OF BRAZILIAN CINEMA, 1896–1930

1. Peter Evans, *Dependent Development: The Alliance of Multinational, State, and Local Capital in Brazil* (Princeton, N.J.: Princeton University Press, 1979), p. 10.

2. Juarez Rubens Brandão Lopes, *Desenvolvimento e Mudança Social: Formação da sociedade urbano-industrial no Brasil* (São Paulo: Companhia Editora Nacional, 1971), pp. 3–9.

3. Ibid.

4. Warren Dean, *The Industrialization of São Paulo: 1880–1945* (Austin: University of Texas Press, 1969), p. 9.

5. Lopes, p. 6.

6. Ibid., p. 14.

7. José Mária Bello, *A History of Modern Brazil: 1889–1964*, trans. James L. Taylor (Stanford, Calif.: Stanford University Press, 1966), p. 177.

8. Vicente de Paula Araújo, *A Bela Época do Cinema Brasileiro* (São

Paulo: Perspectiva, 1976), p. 74. Subsequent references to this work will be given in the text.

9. Ismail Xavier, "Allegories of Underdevelopment: From the 'Aesthetics of Hunger' to the 'Aesthetics of Garbage,'" Ph.D. diss., New York University, 1982, p. 17.

10. Dean, p. 10; see also Jean-Claude Bernardet, Cinema Brasileiro: Propostas para uma História (Rio de Janeiro: Paz e Terra, 1979), pp. 37–38.

11. Sérgio Miceli, Poder, Sexo, e Letras na Republica Velha (Estudo Clínico dos Anatolianos) (São Paulo: Perspectiva, 1977), pp. 80–81; also José Inácio de Melo Souza, "Congressos, Patriotas, e Illusões: Subsídios para uma História dos Congressos de Cinema" unpublished, 1981, p. 11.

12. Souza, p. 12.

13. Francisco de Assis Barbosa, A Vida de Lima Barreto, 3d ed. (Rio de Janeiro: Civilização Brasileira, 1964), p. 169.

14. Vicente de Paula Araújo, Salões, Circos, e Cinemas de São Paulo (São Paulo: Perspectiva, 1981), p. 208.

15. According to Antônio Noronha Santos, " 'One night, France was in the company of [José] Veríssimo and other bigwigs of the Academia [Brasileira de Letras] taking a stroll down the Avenue when his attention was drawn toward the exhibition hall that Paschoal Segreto has installed beside his cabaret . . . . He was walking toward it when a warning issued from the scandalized group that it was a 'free' cinema. Anatole shrugged his shoulders and entered. The films . . . were so horrendous in their base abjection that they seemed more like warnings against the dangers of veneral disease. France, who accepted everything as a matter of ethics, simply smiled.' " Cited by Barbosa, p. 183, n. 4.

16. Carlos Roberto de Souza, A Fascinante Aventura do Cinema Brasileiro (São Paulo: Fundação Cinemateca Brasileira, 1981), p. 7.

17. Paulo Emílio Salles Gomes, "Panorma do Cinema Brasileiro: 1896/1966," in Cinema: Trajetória no Subdesenvolvimento (Rio de Janeiro: Paz e Terra, 1980), p. 42.

18. Alex Viany, Introdução ao Cinema Brasileiro (Rio de Janeiro: Instituto Nacional do Livro, 1959), p. 33.

19. Araken Campos Pereira, Jr., Cinema Brasileiro, 1908–1978 (Santos: Editora Casa do Cinema Ltda., 1979), 1:81–98.

20. See Jean-Claude Bernardet, Filmografia do Cinema Brasileiro, 1900–1935: Jornal O Estado de São Paulo (São Paulo: Governo do Estado de São Paulo, Secretaria da Cultura, Comissão de Cinema, 1979).

21. Maria Rita Eliezer Galvão, Crônica do Cinema Paulistano (São Paulo: Ática, 1975), p. 21.

22. Ibid., p. 22. Further information concerning Serrador is drawn from this source and Araújo, *A Bela Época do Cinema Brasileiro* and *Salões, Circos, e Cinemas de São Paulo*.

23. This figure may be misleading. Many of Serrador's films have Italian titles (e.g., *La Donna e Mobile, Questo e Quello, I Pagliacci*). It is not known if he produced local versions of the operatic excerpts or if he imported them and used Brazilian lyric singers behind the screen.

24. Bernardet, *Filmografia*.

25. Araújo, *Salões*. Subsequent references will be given in the text.

26. Bernardet, *Filmografia*.

27. U.S. Department of Commerce, Bureau of Foreign and Domestic Commerce, *Motion Pictures in Argentina and Brazil*, Trade Information Bulletin, no. 630 (1929).

28. Araken Campos Pereira, Jr., provides different production figures for this period. According to his research, Brazilian production levels were slightly higher, averaging nineteen films per year. This in no way modifies the argument. See note following table 1.

29. Based on films listed in Araken Campos Pereira, Jr.

30. Bernardet, *Cinema Brasileiro*, pp. 23–28.

31. Paulo Emílio Salles Gomes, *Humberto Mauro, Cataguases, Cinearte* (São Paulo: Perspectiva, 1974), p. 302.

32. Ibid., p. 297.

33. Ibid., p. 316.

34. Cited in ibid., p. 322.

35. U.S. Department of Commerce, *Motion Pictures*.

Chapter 2. Sound, Studios, and the State, 1930–1950

1. Thomas E. Skidmore, *Politics in Brazil, 1930–1964: An Experiment in Democracy* (New York: Oxford University Press, 1967), pp. 3–12.

2. Ibid., pp. 9–12.

3. For an excellent and detailed discussion of the Prestes column, see Neil Macaulay, *The Prestes Column: Revolution in Brazil* (New York: New Viewpoints, 1974).

4. Skidmore, pp. 9–10.

5. Ibid., p. 12.

6. Octávio Ianni, *Estado e Planejamento Econômico no Brasil (1930–1970)*, 3d ed. (Rio de Janeiro: Civilização Brasileira, 1979), pp. 13–14.

7. Skidmore, pp. 7-8.

8. Ibid., pp. 39-40; Ianni, pp. 34-43; for a broader historical view, see Kenneth Paul Erikson, *The Brazilian Corporative State and Working-Class Politics* (Berkeley and Los Angeles: University of California Press, 1977).

9. Skidmore, p. 15.

10. An English version of Vargas's suicide letter was published in *The New York Times*, 25 August 1954; reprinted in *A Documentary History of Brazil*, ed. E. Bradford Burns, (New York: Alfred A. Knopf, 1966), pp. 368-71.

11. Carlos Diegues, "As esperanças do cinema brasileiro," *Opinião*, 26 September 1975, p. 21.

12. Ismail Xavier, *Sétima Arte: Um Culto Moderno* (São Paulo: Perspectiva, 1977), pp. 199-263.

13. Gaizka Usabel, "American Film in Latin America: The Case History of United Artists Corporation, 1919-1951," Ph.D. diss., University of Wisconsin, Madison, 1975, p. 146.

14. *Diário Nacional*, 17 January 1929; cited in Jean-Claude Bernardet and Maria Rita Galvão, *Cinema: Repercussões em Caixa de Eco Ideológica (As idéias de "nacional" e "popular" no pensamento cinematográfico brasileiro)* (São Paulo: Brasiliense, Embrafilme, Secretaria da Cultura, MEC, 1983), p. 46.

15. Usabel, p. 356.

16. *Variety*, 20 January 1937.

17. Araken Campos Pereira, Jr., *Cinema Brasileiro (1908-1978)*, vol. 1 (Santos: Editora Casa do Cinema Ltda., 1979).

18. *Variety*, 15 October 1930, 14 October 1936; Usabel, pp. 225, 353.

19. *Variety*, 12 November 1930, 20 February 1934, 6 April 1938, 1 February 1939.

20. *Variety*, 10-24 July 1929; Usabel, p. 149.

21. Usabel, p. 253.

22. In Associação Cinematográfica de Produtores Brasileiros, *Relatório da Diretoria*, Secretary Armando de Moura Carijó (Rio de Janeiro: Typographo do Jornal do Commércio, 1937), pp. 66-68.

23. Usabel, p. 353.

24. Geraldo Santos Pereira, *Plano Geral do Cinema Brasileiro* (Rio de Janeiro: Borsoi, 1973, p. 300.

25. Carlos Roberto de Souza, *A Fascinante Aventura do Cinema Brasileiro* (São Paulo: Fundação Cinemateca Brasilera, 1981), p. 50.

26. *Relatório da Diretoria*, pp. 23-24.

27. *Correio da Manhã*, 30 May 1934; rpt. in *Relatório da Diretoria*, pp. 82-86.

28. *Relatório da Diretoria*, pp. 23–24.
29. Carlos Roberto de Souza, p. 51.
30. *Correio da Manhã*, 26 June 1934; rpt. in *Relatório da Diretoria*, pp. 79–82.
31. Bernardet and Galvão, p. 49.
32. *Diário Nacional*, 28 January 1928; cited in Bernardet and Galvão, p. 55.
33. Cited in Bernardet and Galvão, p. 51.
34. Carlos Roberto de Souza, p. 51.
35. *Variety*, 20 January 1937.
36. *Relatório da Diretoria*, pp. 24–27.
37. Ibid., pp. 101–05.
38. Vamireh Chacon, *Estado e Povo no Brasil* (Rio de Janeiro: José Olympio/Câmara dos Deputados, 1977), p. 97.
39. Adalberto Mário Ribeiro, "O Instituto Nacional de Cinema Educativo," *Revista do Serviço Público* 3, no. 7 (March 1944), 77; also Ana Cristina César, *Literatura não é Documento* (Rio de Janeiro: MEC/Funarte, 1980), pp. 15–21.
40. Geraldo Santos Pereira, p. 293.
41. Ibid., p. 295.
42. Ibid., p. 296.
43. Ibid.
44. *Variety*, 25 February 1942; 18 March 1942.
45. Geraldo Santos Pereira, p. 297.
46. Ibid.; see also Chacon, pp. 92–97.
47. José Inácio de Melo Souza, "Congressos, Patriotas, e Ilusões: Subsídios para uma História dos Congressos de Cinema; (Manuscript, 1981), p. 26 .
48. Based on films listed in Araken Campos Pereira, Jr.
49. Owing to the near-impossibility of gaining access to archives, Atlântida has not yet been studied fully by either Brazilian or American scholars. Economic data on the company is unavailable.
50. Geraldo Sautos Pereira, p. 298.
51. Alcino Teixeira de Mello, *Legislação do Cinema Brasileiro* (Rio de Janeiro: Embrafilme, 1978), 1:158–65.
52. *Variety*, 8 January 1947.
53. Werner Baer, *The Brazilian Economy: Its Growth and Development* (Columbus, Ohio: Grid Publishing Company, 1979), pp. 62–66.
54. *Variety*, 27 February 1946, 6 November 1946, 27 November 1946, 30 April 1947, 7 January 1948, 14 July 1948, 21 July 1948, 4 August 1948, 27 October 1948, 4 January 1950, 13 December 1950.
55. Geraldo Santos Pereira, p. 306.

56. Discussion of Vera Cruz taken from Randal Johnson, *Cinema Novo × 5: Masters of Contemporary Brazilian Film* (Austin: University of Texas Press, 1984), pp. 4–6, which draws from Maria Rita Galvão, *Cinema e Burquesia: O Caso Vera Cruz* (Rio de Janeiro: Civilização Brasileira/Embrafilme, 1981); Maria Rita Galvão, "Vera Cruz: A Brazilian Hollywood," in *Brazilian Cinema*, ed. Randal Johnson and Robert Stam (Rutherford, N.J.: Fairleigh Dickinson University Press, 1982), pp. 270–80; and Randal Johnson and Robert Stam, "The Shape of Brazilian Film History," in ibid., pp. 15–51.

57. Galvão, *Cinema e Burquesia;* "Vera Cruz: A Brazilian Hollywood."

58. José Inácio de Melo Souza, p. 28.

59. Bernardet and Galvão, p. 62.

3. Congresses, Conflicts, and State Institutions 1950–1960

1. Thomas E. Skidmore, *Politics in Brazil, 1930–1964: An Experiment in Democracy* (New York: Oxford University Press, 1967), p. 51.

2. Ibid., pp. 88–90.

3. Ibid., p. 75.

4. Ibid., p. 97.

5. Alberto Cavalcânti, *Filme e Realidade* (1953; rpt. Rio de Janeiro: Artenova/Embrafilme, 1977), p. 52.

6. *Cine Repórter*, 28 November 1953.

7. Maria Rita Galvão, "Vera Cruz: A Fábrica de Sonhos," Ph.D. diss., Universidade de São Paulo 1976, p. 762.

8. *O Globo*, 19 March 1951.

9. José Inácio de Melo Souza, "Congressos, Patriotas, e Ilusões: Subsídios para uma Historia dos Congressos de Cinema" (unpublished, Fundagao Cinemateca Brasileira, 1981), p. 54.

10. Ibid., p. 53.

11. Cited in Jean-Claude Bernardet and Maria Rita Galvão, *Cinema: Repercussões em Caixa de Eco Ideológica (As idéias de "nacional" e "popular" no pensamento cinematográfico brasileiro)* (São Paulo: Brasiliense, Embrafilme, Secretaria da Cultura, MEC, 1983), p. 67.

12. Ibid., p. 68.

13. Ibid.

14. Ibid., p. 71.

15. Ibid., p. 82

16. José Inácio de Melo Souza, p. 4.

17. Thomas H. Guback, *The International Film Industry: Western*

Europe and America Since 1945 (Bloomington: Indiana University Press, 1969), pp. 17–21.

18. *Última Hora*, 19 July 1951.

19. *Diário Carioca*, 5 September 1952.

20. Ibid.

21. *Cine Repórter*, 18 October 1952.

22. José Inácio de Melo Souza, p. 58.

23. For a discussion of *cavação*, see Carlos Roberto de Souza, *A Fascinante Aventura do Cinema Brasileiro* (São Paulo: Fundação Cinemateca Brasileira, 1981); also Maria Rita Galvão, *Crônica do Cinema Paulistano* (São Paulo: Ática, 1975).

24. José Inácio de Melo Souza, pp. 60–61.

25. For a discussion of these organizations, see Alberto Ruy Sánchez, *Mitología de un cine en crisis* (Mexico City: Premia, 1981), pp. 46–49; Guback, pp. 148–49.

26. José Inácio de Melo Souza, p. 130.

27. Alberto Ruy Sánchez, "Utopía de un cine en crisis," presented at the 44th International Congress of Americanists, Manchester, England, September 1982.

28. José Inácio de Melo Souza, p. 131.

29. Ibid., p. 66.

30. Ibid., pp. 66–67.

31. Dos Santos's thesis is discussed and reproduced in full in ibid., pp. 70–71, 159–63.

32. *Variety*, 14 November 1956.

33. José Inácio de Melo Souza, pp. 159–63.

34. Ibid., pp. 130–33.

35. Ibid., p. 74.

36. Geraldo Santos Pereira, *Plano Geral do Cinema Brasileiro* (Rio de Janeiro: Borsoi, 1973), pp. 233–39.

37. *Jornal de Cinema*, 15 November 1952; Pereira, pp. 235–39.

38. Geraldo Santos Pereira, p. 240.

39. Ibid., pp. 241–42; also Souza, pp. 98–127.

40. Sérgio Renato Villela, "Cinema Brasileiro: Capital e Estado" unpublished, CNDA/Funarte 1979, pp. 97–98; José Mário Ortiz Ramos, *Cinema, Estado, e Lutas Culturais* (Rio de Janeiro: Paz e Terra, 1983), pp. 19–23.

41. The groups and their composition are defined by both Villela and Ramos; see note 40.

42. Cited in Maria Rita Galvão, *Burguesia e Cinema: O Caso Vera Cruz* (Rio de Janeiro: Civilização Brasileira/Embrafilme, 1981), pp. 204–06.

43. *Jornal do Commércio*, 6 June 1954.

44. *Sitação Econômica e Financeira do Cinema Brasileiro* (São Paulo: Comissão Municipal de Cinema, 1955).

45. Geraldo Santos Pereira, p. 311.

46. Ramos, p. 36.

47. The production of Brasil Filmes included *Gato de Madame* (Agostinho M. Pereira, 1956), *O Sobrado* (C. Gabus Mendes and W. G. Durst, 1956), *Osso, Amor, e Papagaios* (Carlos Alberto S. Barros and Cesar Mêmolo, Jr., 1957), *Estranho Encontro* (Walter Hugo Khoury, 1958), *Paixão de Gaúcho* (W. G. Durst, 1958), *Rebelião em Vila Rica* (Geraldo and Renato Santos Pereira, 1958), *Moral em Concordata* (Fernando de Barros, 1959), and *Ravina* (Rubem Biáfora, 1959). Extracted from Araken Campos Pereira, Jr., *Cinema Brasileiro, 1908–1978* (Santos: Editora Casa do Cinema, 1979).

48. *Revista do Livro* 1, nos. 1–5 (June 1956), 58–71.

49. For a discussion of this period, see Skidmore, pp. 163–86; and Maria Victória de Mesquita Benevides, *O Governo Kubitschek* (Rio de Janeiro: Paz e Terra, 1976).

50. *Correio da Manhã*, 21 December 1956.

51. *Cine Repórter*, 1 December 1956.

52. Werner Baer, *The Brazilian Economy: Its Growth and Development* (Columbus, Ohio: Grid Publishing Company, 1979), p. 67.

53. Geraldo Santos Pereira, pp. 248–251; *Cine Repórter*, 16 February 1958; *Variety*, 30 April 1955.

54. Geraldo Santos Pereira, pp. 312–14.

55. Antônio Moniz Vianna, "A Comissão é uma Comédia (Nacional)," *Correio da Manhã*, 9 February 1957.

56. See note 40.

57. Geraldo Santos Pereira, p. 315.

58. *Projeção*, April 1955.

59. Ibid.

60. Information extracted from Araken Compos Pereira, Jr.

CHAPTER 4. CINEMA NOVO AND GEICINE, 1960–1966

1. Geraldo Santos Pereira, *Plano Geral do Cinema Brasileiro* (Rio de Janeiro: Borsoi, 1973), p. 316.

2. Ibid., p. 317.

3. *Projeção*, February 1961.

4. Thomas E. Skidmore, *Politics in Brazil, 1930–1964: An Experiment in Democracy* (New York: Oxford University Press, 1967), p. 205–13.

5. Portions of the following discussion are taken from Randal Johnson, "Brazilian Cinema Novo," *Bulletin of Latin American Research* (1985).

6. The following summary of some of the ideas of the Instituto Superior de Estudos Brasileiros was extracted from Caio Navarro de Toledo, *ISEB: Fábrica de Ideologias* (São Paulo: Ática, 1978).

7. A key essay in the theoretical development of Brazilian cinema is Paulo Emílio Salles Gomes's "Uma Situação Colonial?" in *O Estado de São Paulo*, 19 November 1960; reprinted in *Crítica de Cinema no Suplemento Literário* (Rio de Janeiro: Paz e Terra, 1982), 2:286–91.

8. For another perspective on the ISEB, see Renato Ortiz, *Cultura Brasileira e Identidade Nacional* (São Paulo: Brasiliense, 1985), pp. 45–67.

9. "Uma Estética da Fome," *Revista Civilização Brasileira* 3 (July 1965), emphasis in original; English version in *Brazilian Cinema*, ed. Randal Johnson and Robert Stam (Rutherford, N.J.: Fairleigh Dickinson University Press, 1982), pp. 68–71; reprinted in *Twenty-five Years of the New Latin American Cinema*, ed. Michael Chanan (London: British Film Institute/Channel Four Television, 1983), pp. 13–14.

10. Randal Johnson and Robert Stam, "The Shape of Brazilian Film History," in *Brazilian Cinema*, ed. Johnson and Stam, pp. 16–51.

11. For discussions of the concept of *auteur*, see *Theories of Authorship: A Reader*, ed. John Caughie (London: Routledge & Kegan Paul, 1981).

12. *Revisão Crítica do Cinema Brasileiro* (Rio de Janeiro: Civilização Brasileira, 1963), pp. 13–14.

13. Ismail Xavier, "Allegories of Underdevelopment: From the 'Aesthetics of Hunger' to the 'Aesthetics of Garbage,'" Ph.D. diss., New York University, 1982, pp. 18–21.

14. Sérgio Renato Villela, "Cinema Brasileiro: Capital e Estado" unpublished, CNDA/Funarte 1979, p. 98; José Mário Ortiz Ramos, *Cinema, Estado, e Lutas Culturais* (Rio de Janeiro: Paz e Terra, 1983), pp. 19–23.

15. Ramos, 19–23.

16. Maurice Capovilla, "GEICINE e problemas econômicos do cinema brasileiro," *Revista Brasiliense* 44 (November–December 1962), 26–32. The article is also discussed in Ramos, pp. 31–32.

17. *Revista do GEICINE* 1 (1961), 14.

18. Ibid., p. 15.

19. Ibid., pp. 16–17.

20. Ibid., p. 6.

21. *Revista do GEICINE* 2 (1964), 26–27. The films produced under

the program were *El Justicero* (*The Enforcer;* Nelson Pereira dos Santos, 1967); *O Mundo Alegre de Helô* (*The Happy World of Helô;* Carlos A. S. Barros, 1967); *O Beijo* (*The Kiss;* Flávio Tambellini, 1965); *Crônica da Cidade Amada* (*Chronicle of the Beloved City;* Carlos H. Christensen, 1965); *Amor e Desamor* (*Love and Unlove;* Gerson Taveres, 1966); *O Corpo Ardente* (*The Ardent Body;* Walter Hugo Khoury, 1966); and *Três Histórias de Amor* (*Three Love Stories;* Alberto d' Aversa, 1966). See *Filme Cultura* 6 (September 1967), 36.

22. Cited in Geraldo Santos Pereira, p. 255.

23. "Normas para financiamentos destinados a 'custeio de produção de filmes,'" Banco do Brasil, 1962.

24. Werner Baer, *Industrialization and Economic Development in Brazil* (Homewood, Ill.: Richard D. Irwin, 1965), pp. 55–58.

25. *Revista do GEICINE* 1 (1961), 18–21.

26. Resolution 269 of the Conselho de Política Aduaneira, 17 February 1962; Geraldo Santos Pereira, p. 318.

27. Geraldo Santos Pereira, p. 324.

28. *Revista do GEICINE* 1 (1961), 7–11.

29. Ibid., pp. 18–21.

30. *O Estado de São Paulo,* 1 December 1963.

31. Ibid.; Ramos, p. 278.

32. *Revisão Crítica do Cinema Brasileiro,* p. 139.

33. Ibid., p. 141.

34. *Revista do GEICINE* 1 (1961), 28.

35. Geraldo Santos Pereira, p. 258.

CHAPTER 5. THE INSTITUTO NACIONAL DO CINEMA,
1966–1975

1. Peter Evans, *Dependent Development: The Alliance of Multinational, State, and Local Capital* (Princeton, N.J.: Princeton University Press, 1979), pp. 216–17.

2. Ibid., p. 218.

3. Ibid., p. 219; Octávio Ianni, *Estado e Planejamento Econômico no Brasil: 1930–1970,* 3rd ed. (Rio de Janeiro: Civilização Brasileira, 1979), pp. 225–97.

4. Renato Ortiz, *Cultura Brasileira e Identidade Nacional* (São Paulo: Brasiliense, 1985), pp. 80–87. Ortiz lists the following state organizations in, broadly speaking, the cultural area: 1965: Embratel; 1966: Conselho Federal de Cultura, Conselho Federal de Turismo, Embratur, Instituto

Nacional do Cinema; 1967: Ministry of Telecommunications; 1969: Embrafilme; 1972: Telebrás; 1975: Funarte; Centro Nacional de Referência Cultural; 1976: CONCINE, Radiobrás; 1979: Secretaria de Patrimônio Histórico e Artístico Nacional, Fundação Pró-Memória.

5. Adonias [Aguiar] Filho, *O Conselho Federal de Cultura* (Brasília: MEC, 1978), p. 3.

6. Ortiz, pp. 90–106.

7. Cited in Adonias Filho; also in Conselho Federal de Cultura, *Aspectos da Política Cultural Brasileira* (Rio de Janeiro: MEC/CFC, 1976), pp. 21–22.

8. Harry G. Johnson, "A Theoretical Model of Economic Nationalism in New and Developing States," in *Economic Nationalism in Old and New States*, ed. Johnson (Chicago: University of Chicago Press, 1969), p. 9.

9. *Jornal do Brasil*, 24 September 1966; *O Estado de São Paulo*, 5 October 1966.

10. Thomas E. Skidmore, *Politics in Brasil, 1930–1964: An Experiment in Democracy* (New York: Oxford University Press, 1967), p. 308; Ronald M. Schneider, *The Political System of Brazil: Emergence of a "Modernizing" Authoritarian Regime, 1964–1970* (New York: Columbia University Press, 1971), pp. 125–27, 170–73.

11. Testifying before a congressional investigative committee looking into the situation of the national film industry shortly after the coup d'état of 1964, Paulo Emílio Salles Gomes referred to the history of failure to create an Instituto Nacional do Cinema and suggested that the film industry should take advantage of the present situation and the "greater powers" of the executive branch to initiate the necessary changes. Paraphrased in Rogério Costa Rodrigues, "A Indústria Cinematográfica Brasileira e a Conquista do Mercado," *Revista de Informação Legislativa* 9 (1966), pp. 209–16.

12. GEICINE's original proposal in *Revista do GEICINE* 2 (1964), 6–13; Decree-law 43 in Alcino Teixeira de Mello, *Legislação do Cinema Brasileiro* (Rio de Janeiro: Embrafilme, 1978), pp. 37–53.

13. *Diário de Notícias*, 19 October 1966.

14. *Jornal do Brasil*, 7 and 27 September 1966.

15. *Jornal do Brasil*, 8 October 1966.

16. *Jornal do Brasil*, 11 October 1966.

17. *Jornal do Commércio*, 14 October 1966.

18. *Jornal do Brasil*, 19 October 1966.

19. *Estado de São Paulo*, 5 October 1966; *Jornal do Brasil*, 19 October 1966.

20. José Mário Ortiz Ramos, Cinema, Estado, e Lutas Culturais (Rio de Janeiro: Paz e Terra, 1983), pp. 51–87.

21. Diário de Noticias, November 1966.

22. All of the Instituto Nacional do Cinema's 112 Resolutions are reprinted in Mello, Legislação do Cinema Brasileiro 2: 384–485. Resolutions discussed in the text will not be cited individually.

23. Decree-law 43, ch. 3.

24. Beatriz Wahrlich, "Controle Político das Empresas Estatais Federais no Brasil—Uma Contribuição ao seu Estudo," Revista de Administração Pública 14, no. 2 (April–June 1980), 8 n. 7.

25. Ramos, p. 72.

26. See Decree-law 862, 12 September 1969, in Mello, pp. 53–58.

27. Geraldo Santos Pereira, Plano Geral do Cinema Brasileiro (Rio de Janeiro: Borsoi, 1973), p. 94.

28. Ramos, pp. 73–74.

29. Jornal da Tarde, 28 March 1970.

30. Jornal da Tarde, 29 March 1970.

31. Jornal da Tarde, 28 March 1970.

32. The following discussion of Cinema Novo is summarized from Randal Johnson and Robert Stam, "The Shape of Brazilian Film History," in Brazilian Cinema, ed. Johnson and Stam (Rutherford, N.J.: Fairleigh Dickinson University Press, 1982); Randal Johnson, Cinema Novo x 5: Masters of Contemporary Brazilian Film (Austin: University of Texas Press, 1984); Randal Johnson, "Brazilian Cinema Novo," Bulletin of Latin American Research (1985); and Randal Johnson, "The Development of the Brazilian Film Industry," presented at the Northeastern Association of Brazilianists, Mount Holyoke College, May 4, 1985.

33. Ruy Guerra, "Popular Cinema and the State," in Brazilian Cinema, ed. Johnson and Stam, pp. 101–03.

34. Gustavo Dahl, "Cinema Novo e Estruturas Econômicas Tradicionais," Revista Civilização Brasileira 1, nos. 5–6 (March 1966), 193–204.

35. Jean-Claude Bernardet and Maria Rita Galvão, Cinema: Repercussões em Caixa de Eco Ideológica (São Paulo: Brasiliense, Embrafilme, Secretaria da Cultura, MEC, 1983), pp. 237–248.

36. Ortiz, pp. 110–11.

37. Guerra, pp. 101–03.

38. "The Luz e Ação Manifesto," in Brazilian Cinema, ed. Johnson and Stam, pp. 91–92.

39. Rubens Rodrigues dos Santos, "O MEC e o Cinema," O Estado de São Paulo, 2 and 3 June 1971.

40. *O Estado de São Paulo*, 10 September 1980.
41. *O Estado de São Paulo*, 19 October 1978.

CHAPTER 6. EMBRAFILME, CONCINE, AND A NEW DIRECTION IN STATE POLICY, 1969–1980

1. Ronald M. Schneider, *The Political System of Brazil: The Emergence of a "Modernizing" Authoritarian Regime, 1964–1970* (New York: Columbia University Press, 1971), p. 274.
2. Ibid., p. 293.
3. Beatriz Wahrlich, "Controle Político das Empresas Estatais Federais no Brasil—Uma Contribuição ao seu Estudo," *Revista de Administração Pública* 14, no. 2 (April–June 1980), 8.
4. The text of Decree-law 862 is in Alcino Teixeira de Mello, *Legislação do Cinema Brasileiro* (Rio de Janeiro: Embrafilme, 1978), 1:53–58.
5. Ibid., p. 54. Private shareholders included the Companhia Cinematográfica Vera Cruz (1,000 shares), Entrefilmes (500), Cinedistri (500), Magnus Filmes (300), Cinesul (300), J.B. Produções Cinematográficas (100), Kâmera Filmes (100), Procine (100), Arro Filmes (100), Carlos Hugo Christensen (100), Somil (100), Júlio Mendes Produções Cinematográficas (100), and Cinédia (50). See Geraldo Santos Pereira, *Plano Geral do Cinema Brasileiro* (Rio de Janeiro: Borsoi, 1973), p. 336.
6. Legislation concerning both of these organizations is found in Mello. See also Randal Johnson, "State Policy Toward the Film Industry in Brazil," Technical Papers Series, no. 36, Office for Public Sector Studies, Institute of Latin American Studies, University of Texas, Austin, 1982.
7. Geraldo Santos Pereira, p. 265.
8. *Jornal do Brasil*, 18 December 1969; portions reprinted in Geraldo Sautos Pereira, pp. 265–66.
9. Bulletin of the 5th Brasília Festival of Brazilian Films; portions are reprinted in Geraldo Santos Pereira, pp. 265–66.
10. *Gazeta Mercantil*, 9–11 January 1982.
11. Mello, p. 54.
12. In late 1969, in fact, the president of INC asked the minister of education and culture to remove film financing from INC's attributes. See ibid.
13. Ibid., p. 57.
14. Johnson, "State Policy."
15. Dieter Goebel and Carlos Roberto Rodrigues de Souza, "A Economia Cinematográfica Brasileira" (São Paulo, Mimeographed) pp. 6–7.

16. Ibid., pp. 9–10.

17. It should be remembered that at this time the INC was still granting subsidies based on box-office performance as well as additional awards for quality. Taking the latter into consideration would give us a higher percentage of films with state support.

18. O Estado de São Paulo, 2 June 1971.

19. O Estado de São Paulo, 28 January 1972.

20. In Randal Johnson, "Toward a Popular Cinema: An Interview with Nelson Pereira dos Santos," Studies in Latin American Popular Culture 1 (1982), 228.

21. Geraldo Santos Pereira, p. 270.

22. José Mário Ortiz Ramos, Cinema, Estado, e Lutas Culturais (Rio de Janeiro: Paz e Terra, 1983), p. 111.

23. For a summary of the discussions of the congress, see Filme Cultura 22 (November–December 1972), 11–20.

24. Ramos, pp. 109–10.

25. For a discussion of Brazil's labor policy, see Kenneth Paul Erikson, The Brazilian Corporative State and Working-Class Politics (Berkeley and Los Angeles: University of California Press, 1977).

26. Jornal da Tarde, 20 February 1978.

27. Jornal da Tarde, 26 January 1972.

28. In 1983 three exhibition groups—Gaumont, Haway, and CIC—filed suit to have the screen quota reduced to twenty-eight days per year, alleging a shortage of good-quality Brazilian films. See A Folha de Sãa Paulo, 8 April 1983.

29. Geraldo Santos Pereira, pp. 278–79.

30. Ibid., pp. 271–79.

31. Johnson, "State Policy."

32. Mello 1:16.

33. The text of Decree-law 77,299 is in Mello 1: 59–68.

34. Ministério de Educação e Cultura, "Política Nacional de Cultura," (1976).

35. Ramos, pp. 147–56.

36. Embrafilme, Annual reports, 1973 and 1974.

37. In 1983 the Cinema International Corporation merged with United Artists to form United International Pictures, or UIP. Variety, 26 January 1983.

38. Gazeta Mercantil, 9–11 January 1982; Johnson, "State Policy."

39. Johnson, "State Policy."

40. Ibid.

41. Embrafilme, Cinejornal 1 (July 1980), 36–43.

42. On the *Iracema* affair, see *Veja*, 19 May 1976; *A Folha de São Paulo*, 25 July and 20 November 1980. For a review of the film, see the *New York Times*, 25 May 1982. Roberto Parreira quoted in *Veja*, 28 April 1982.

43. *Veja*, 8 March 1978.

44. For critics' views of state policy, see Jean-Claude Bernardet, *Cinema Brasileiro: Propostas para uma História* (Rio de Janeiro: Paz e Terra, 1979), especially chapter 4; and Ramos.

45. *Tribuna da Imprensa*, 21 September 1978 and 10 October 1978.

46. For a definition and discussion of co-optation, see Phillipe C. Schmitter, *Interest Conflict and Political Change in Brazil* (Stanford, Calif.: Stanford University Press, 1971), esp. pp. 72—73. See also Ramos, ch. 4.

47. Renato Ortiz, *Cultura Brasileira e Identidade Nacional* (São Paulo: Brasiliense, 1985), p. 82.

48. Jorge Schnitman, *Film Industries in Latin America: Dependency and Development* (Norwood, N.J.: Ablex Publishing Company, 1984), p. 66.

49. In an interview granted to Sílvio Tendler, in "Cinema e Estado: Em Defesa do Miúra," M.A. thesis, Pontifícia Universidade Católica, Rio de Janeiro, 1982, p. 164.

50. Ibid., p. 10.

51. Quoted in Bernardet, *Cinema Brasileiro*, p. 57.

52. In an extensive interview granted after the release of the internationally acclaimed *Pixote*, director Hector Babenco said the following: "My standard of living is this: I have a sandwich for lunch and I eat out once a week . . . . My office is shameful. I have a typewriter I'm still making payments on and two telephone lines. I am the perfect picture of the Brazilian producer's improvisation. I don't have anything, not even a lease. . . . But the image that people have, because *Lúcio Flávio* [1977] was a success, is that I have a commercial structure behind me. 'HB Filmes'! In fact it's just me, an office and a secretary. When I'm sick, HB is sick; when I'm broke, HB is broke. . . . It doesn't exist, it's not a production company; it's just me, made viable as a juridical entity in order to exist. In *Cinema 5* (Fundação Cinemateca Brasileira, Spring 1980), 15.

53. *Jornal de Brasília*, 20 September 1978; *O Estado de São Paulo*, 22 September 1978.

54. Ramos, pp. 91—92.

55. Johnson, "State Policy."

56. "Lei Básica do Cinema Brasileiro," *Filme Cultura*, 33 (May 1979), 114—16.

57. See Randal Johnson, "Popular Cinema in Brazil," *Studies in Latin American Popular Culture* 3 (1984), 86–96.

CHAPTER 7. MOVING TOWARD CRISIS, 1980–1984

1. Alberto Ruy Sánchez, *Mitología de un cine en crisis* (Mexico City: Premia, 1981), p. 46. Subsequent quotes taken from same volume.
2. Data from Embrafilme.
3. See Randal Johnson, "Film, Television and Traditional Folk Culture in *Bye Bye Brasil*," *Journal of Popular Culture* 18, no. 1 (1984), pp. 121–132.
4. Sérgio Mattos, *The Impact of the 1964 Revolution on Brazilian Television* (San Antonio: V. Klingensmith, 1982), pp. 41–60.
5. Ibid., p. 2.
6. *Jornal do Brasil*, 23 September 1980.
7. See, for example, *O Globo*, 28 March 1981; also Jom Tob Azulay, "Panorama da Indústria Cinematográfica Brasileira," *Jornal do Brasil*, 13 July 1980, and, by the same author, "Cinema Brasileiro e Comunicação Social," *Jornal do Brasil*, 11 January 1981.
8. *Variety*, 29 December 1982.
9. *O Globo*, 3 June 1984; other sources place the figure at 700,000 or 1.5 million spectators.
10. Quoted in *Isto É*, 23 May 1984.
11. These figures can be misleading. A film like *Terror e Êxtase*, for example, no doubt cost much less than *Rio Babilônia*. Therefore it may have had fewer spectators and generated a larger profit. But the average is what matters, and it conforms to the situation described.
12. *Filme Cultura* 38–39 (August–November 1981), 30.
13. *O Estado de São Paulo*, 27 May 1984.
14. Embrafilme, *Cinejornal* 4 (September 1982), 22.
15. The calculation concerning the minimum wage versus ticket prices was done by Claudia Springer, "Brazilian Policies for a National Film Industry" (manuscript, 1982). The figure concerning the percentage of working-class people earning less than minimum wage comes from Aílton Benedito de Souza, "Violência no Rio de Janeiro: Outro nome para a luta de classe," *Comunicação e Política*, 2, nos. 1–2 (March–June 1984), 99.
16. *Correio Braziliense*, 15 October 1977, 26 October 1977.
17. *Variety*, 25 March 1981.
18. Ibid.
19. Ibid.
20. Ibid.; see also *Variety*, 13 May 1981.

21. *Variety*, 17 March 1982.

22. *Variety*, 3 November 1982.

23. *Jornal do Brasil*, 7 August 1984.

24. Sérgio Augusto, "O cinema de arte volta à tona," *A Folha de São Paulo*, 20 May 1984.

25. *O Estado de São Paulo*," 8 September 1983.

26. *Jornal do Brasil*, 10 August 1984; *Variety*, 8 August 1984.

27. *Variety*, 17 March 1982, 19 May 1982.

28. *Variety*, 6 July 1983.

29. Sérgio Augusto, "Em cartaz, a crise do cinema," *A Folha de São Paulo*, 10 May 1984.

30. Peter Evans, *Dependent Development: The Alliance of Multinational, State, and Local Capital in Brazil* (Princeton, N.J.: Princeton University Press, 1979).

31. Interview with Ugo Sorrentino, 10 August 1984.

32. *Diário Carioca*, 5 September 1952.

33. *Jornal da Tarde*, 10 July 1970, 27 July 1970, 11 September 1970.

34. *Jornal da Tarde*, 26 January 1972.

35. Jorge Schnitman, *Film Industries in Latin America: Dependency and Development* (Norwood, N.J.: Ablex Publishing Company, 1984), p. 67, n. 1.

36. Ivor Montague, *Film World* (Baltimore: Penguin Books, 1967), p. 254.

37. *Projeção* 30, no. 136 (September 1971), 3; also *Jornal da Tarde*, 15 July 1971.

38. See Randal Johnson, "Popular Cinema in Brazil," *Studies in Latin American Popular Culture* 3 (1984), 86–96.

39. *Jornal da Tarde*, 22 July 1971.

40. *O Estado de São Paulo*, 2 July 1975.

41. *O Estado de São Paulo*, 13 January 1974.

42. "A Guerra do Cinema," *Jornal da Tarde*, 26 June 1980.

43. *Correio do Povo*, 10 June 1977.

44. Alcino Teixeira de Mello, *Legislação do Cinema Brasileiro* (Rio de Janeiro: Embrafilme, 1978), 1:217–27.

45. *Jornal do Brasil*, 10 August 1984.

46. *O Estado de São Paulo*, 1 November 1978.

47. *A Folha de São Paulo*, 30 January 1980, 31 January 1980; *Jornal do Brasil*, 23 June 1980, 25 June 1980; *Jornal da Tarde*, 26 June 1980; *O Estado de São Paulo*, 29 June 1980; *Visão*, 14 June 1980.

48. *Jornal do Brasil*, 22 September 1980.

49. *A Folha de São Paulo*, 8 April 1983.

50. *Variety*, 25 March 1981; cited by Springer.

51. Embrafilme, Annual Report, 1982.

52. Marcos Farias, "É hora de privatizar a Embrafilme," *Jornal do Brasil*, 8 January 1984.

53. This information, unless otherwise noted, is condensed from the draft of a document prepared by film industry professionals for submission to the minister of education and culture, August 1984.

54. *Variety*, 21 March 1984.

55. Ibid.

56. Ibid.

57. *Jornal do Brasil*, 29 March 1985; *Veja*, 3 April 1985. Due to the uncertainty caused by the law, Gaumont sold its theaters to a national exhibition group in mid-1985.

58. Mário Henrique Simonsen, *Jornal do Brasil*, 27 July 1976; cited by Azulay, "Panorama."

BIBLIOGRAPHY

BOOKS AND ARTICLES

Aguiar Filho, Adonias. *O Conselho Federal de Cultura.* Brasília: MEC, 1978.

Araújo, Vicente de Paula. *A Bela Época do Cinema Brasileiro.* São Paulo: Perspectiva, 1976. Debates no. 116.

————. *Salões, Circos e Cinemas de São Paulo.* São Paulo: Perspectiva, 1981. Debates no. 163.

Augusto, Sérgio. "O cinema de arte volta à tona." *A Folha de São Paulo,* 20 May 1984.

————. "Em cartaz, a crise do cinema." *A Folha de São Paulo,* 10 May 1984.

Azulay, Jom Tob. "Cinema Brasileiro e Comunicação Social." *Jornal do Brasil,* 11 January 1981.

————. "Panorama da Indústria Cinematográfica Brasileira." *Jornal do Brasil,* 13 July 1980.

Baer, Werner. *The Brazilian Economy: Its Growth and Development.* Columbus, Ohio: Grid Publishing Company, 1979.

————. *Industrialization and Economic Development in Brazil.* Homewood, Ill.: Richard D. Irwin, 1965.

Banco do Brasil. "Normas para financiamentos destinados a 'custeio de produção de filmes'" Banco do Brasil, 1982.

Barbosa, Francisco de Assis. *A Vida de Lima Barreto.* 3d ed. Rio de Janeiro: Editora Civilização Brasileira, 1964.

Bello, José Mária. *A History of Modern Brazil: 1889–1964.* Trans. James L. Taylor. Stanford, Calif.: Stanford University Press, 1966.

Benevides, Maria Victória de Mesquita. *O Governo Kubitschek.* Rio de Janeiro: Paz e Terra, 1976.

Bernardet, Jean-Claude. *Cinema Brasileiro: Propostas para uma História.* Rio de Janeiro: Paz e Terra, 1979.

_____. "Cinema e Estado." *A Folha de São Paulo (Folhetim)*, 4 September 1983.

_____. *Filmografia do Cinema Brasileiro, 1900–1935: Jornal O Estado de São Paulo*. São Paulo: Governo do Estado de São Paulo, Secretaria da Cultura, Comissão de Cinema, 1979.

Bernadet, Jean-Claude, and Maria Rita Galvão. *Cinema: Repercussões em Caixa de Eco Ideológica (As idéias de "nacional" e "popular" no pensamento cinematográfico brasileiro)*. São Paulo: Brasiliense, Embrafilme, Secretaria da Cultura, MEC, 1983.

Broca, Brito. *A Vida Literária no Brasil–1900*. 3d ed. Rio de Janeiro: José Olympio Editora, 1975.

Burns, E. Bradford, ed. *A Documentary History of Brazil*. New York: Alfred A. Knopf, 1966.

Cândido, Antônio. *Literatura e Sociedade: ensaios de teoria e história literária*. 4th rev. ed. São Paulo: Editora Nacional, 1975.

Caparelli, Sérgio. *Televisão e Capitalismo no Brasil*. Porto Alegre: L&M Editores, 1982.

Capovilla, Maurice. "GEICINE e problemas econômicos do cinema brasileiro." *Revista Brasiliense* 44 (November–December 1962), 26–32.

Cardoso, Fernando Henrique. "On the Characterization of Authoritarian Regimes in Latin America." In *The New Authoritarianism in Latin America*, ed. David Collier, 33–57. Princeton, N.J.: Princeton University Press, 1979.

Caughie, John, ed. *Theories of Authorship: A Reader*. London: Routledge & Kegan Paul, 1981.

Cavalcânti, Alberto. *Filme e Realidade*. 1933; rpt. Rio de Janeiro: Artenova/Embrafilme, 1977.

César, Ana Cristina. *Literatura não é Documento*. Rio de Janeiro: MEC/Funarte, 1980.

Chacon, Vamireh. *Estado e Povo no Brasil*. Rio de Janeiro: José Olympio Editora/Câmara dos Deputados, 1977.

Chalmers, Douglas A., ed. *Changing Latin America*. New York: Academy of Political Science, Columbia University, 1972.

_____. "The Politicized State in Latin America." In *Authoritarianism and Corporatism in Latin America*, ed. James M. Malloy, 23–45. Pittsburgh: University of Pittsburgh Press, 1977.

Chanan, Michael. *The Dream That Kicks: The Prehistory and Early Years of Cinema in Britain*. London: Routledge & Kegan Paul, 1980.

_____. *Labour Power in the British Film Industry*. London: British Film Institute, 1976.

Le Cinema et L'État. Strasbourg: Conseil de l'Europe, 1979. Cahiers JEB 3/79.

Chilcote, Ronald H., and Joel C. Edelstein, eds. Latin America: The Struggle with Dependency and Beyond. New York: Wiley, 1984.

Collier, David, ed. The New Authoritarianism in Latin America. Princeton, N.J.: Princeton University Press, 1979.

Conselho Federal de Cultura. Aspectos da Política Cultural Brasileira. Rio de Janeiro: MEC/CFC, 1979.

Cotler, Júlio. "State and Regime: Comparative Notes on the Southern Cone and 'Enclave' Societies." In The New Authoritarianism in Latin America, ed. David Collier, 255–82. Princeton, N.J.: Princeton University Press, 1979.

Coutinho, Carlos Nelson. A Democracia como Valor Universal. São Paulo: Livraria Editora Ciências Humanas, 1980.

————. "O Significado de Lima Barreto na Literatura Brasileira." In Coutinho, et al. Realismo e Anti-Realismo na Literatura Brasileira, 1–56. Rio de Janeiro: Paz e Terra, 1974.

Dean, Warren. The Industrialization of São Paulo: 1880–1945. Austin: University of Texas Press, 1969.

Diegues, Carlos. "As esperanças do cinema brasileiro." Opinião 26 (September 1975), 21.

Dos Santos, Theotônio. "Brazil." In Latin America: The Struggle with Dependency and Beyond, ed. Ronald Chilcote and Joel Edelstein. New York: Wiley, 1984.

Erikson, Kenneth Paul. The Brazilian Corporative State and Working-Class Politics. Berkeley and Los Angeles: University of California Press, 1977.

Evans, Peter. Dependent Development: The Alliance of Multinational, State, and Local Capital in Brazil. Princeton, N.J.: Princeton University Press, 1979.

Farias, Marcos. "É hora de privatizar a Embrafilme." Jornal do Brasil, 8 January 1984.

Galvão, Maria Rita Eliezer. Burquesia e Cinema: O Caso Vera Cruz. Rio de Janeiro: Civilização Brasileira/Embrafilme, 1981.

————. Crônica do Cinema Paulistano. São Paulo: Ática, 1975.

————. "Vera Cruz: A Brazilian Hollywood." Brazilian Cinema, ed. Johnson and Stam, 270–80. Rutherford, N.J.: Fairleigh Dickinson University Press, 1982.

————. "Vera Cruz: A Fábrica de Sonhos." Ph.D.diss., Universidade de São Paulo, 1976.

Goebel, Dieter and Carlos Roberto Rodrigues de Souza. "A Economia Cinematográfica Brasileira." São Paulo, 1975. Mimeo.

Gomes, Paulo Emílio Salles. *Cinema: Trajetória no Subdesenvolvimento.* Rio de Janeiro: Paz e Terra, 1980.

————. *Humberto Mauro, Cataguases, Cinearte.* São Paulo: Perspectiva, 1974. Estudos 22.

————. "Uma Situação Colonial?" *O Estado de São Paulo,* 19 November 1960. Rpt. in *Crítica de Cinema no Suplemento Literário.* Rio de Janeiro: Paz e Terra, 1982, pp. 286–91.

Guback, Thomas H. *The International Film Industry: Western Europe and America Since 1945.* Bloomington: Indiana University Press, 1969.

Guerra, Ruy. "Popular Cinema and the State." In *Brazilian Cinema,* ed. Johnson and Stam, 101–03. Rutherford, N.J.: Fairleigh Dickinson University Press, 1982.

Ianni, Octávio. *Estado e Planejamento Econômico no Brasil (1930–1970).* 3d ed. Rio de Janeiro: Civilização Brasileira, 1979.

Jaguaribe, Hélio. *O Nacionalismo na Atualidade Brasileira.* Rio de Janeiro: Instituto Superior de Estudos Brasileiros, 1958.

Johnson, Harry G. "A Theoretical Model of Economic Nationalism in New and Developing States." In *Economic Nationalism in Old and New States,* ed. H. G. Johnson. Chicago: University of Chicago Press, 1969.

Johnson, Randal. "Brazilian Cinema Novo." *Bulletin of Latin American Research* 3, no. 2 (1984), 95–106.

————. *Cinema Novo × 5: Masters of Contemporary Brazilian Film.* Austin: University of Texas Press, 1984.

————. "The Development of the Brazilian Film Industry." Presented at the Northeastern Association of Brazilianists, Mount Holyoke College, 1985.

————. "Film, Television, and Traditional Folk Culture in *Bye Bye Brasil.*" *Journal of Popular Culture* 18, no. 1 (1984), 121–32.

————. "Popular Cinema in Brazil." *Studies in Latin American Popular Culture* 3 (1984), 86–96.

————. "State Policy Toward the Film Industry in Brazil." Technical Papers Series, no. 36. Office for Public Sector Studies, Institute of Latin American Studies, University of Texas, Austin, 1982.

————. "Toward a Popular Cinema: An Interview with Nelson Pereira dos Santos." *Studies in Latin American Popular Culture* 1 (1982), 225–36.

Johnson, Randal, and Robert Stam, eds. *Brazilian Cinema*. Rutherford, N.J.: Fairleigh Dickinson University Press, 1982.

"Lei Básica do Cinema Brasileiro." *Filme Cultura* 33 (May 1979), 114–16.

Lever, Janet. *Soccer Madness*. Chicago: University of Chicago Press, 1983.

Lima, Antônio Augusto de Cavalheiro. "Cinema: Problema do Governo." *Revista do Livro* 1, 1–2 (June 1956), 58–71.

Lopes, Juarez Rubens Brandão. *Desenvolvimento e Mudança Social: Formação da sociedade urbano-industrial no Brasil*. São Paulo: Editora Nacional, 1971.

"The *Luz e Ação* Manifesto." In *Brazilian Cinema*, ed. Johnson and Stam, 91–92. Rutherford, N.J.: Fairleigh Dickinson University Press, 1982.

Macaulay, Neil. *The Prestes Column: Revolution in Brazil*. New York: New Viewpoints, 1974.

Malloy, James M., ed. *Authoritarianism and Corporatism in Latin America*. Pittsburgh, Pa.: University of Pittsburgh Press, 1977.

————. "Authoritarianism and Corporatism in Latin America: The Modal Pattern." In *Authoritarianism and Corporatism in Latin America*, ed. Malloy, 3–19. Pittsburgh: University of Pittsburgh Press, 1977.

Martins, Carlos Estevam. *Capitalismo de Estado e Modelo Político no Brasil*. Rio de Janeiro: Graal, 1977.

Mattos, Sérgio. *The Impact of the 1964 Revolution on Brazilian Television*. San Antonio: V. Klingensmith, 1982.

Mello, Alcino Teixeira de. *Legislação do Cinema Brasileiro*. 2 vols. Rio de Janeiro: Embrafilme, 1978.

Miceli, Sérgio. *Intelectuais e Classe Dirigente no Brasil (1920–1945)*. São Paulo: Difel, 1979.

————. *Poder, Sexo e Letras na República Velha (Estudo Clínico dos Anatolianos)*. São Paulo: Perspectiva, 1977.

Ministério de Educação e Cultura. "Política Nacional de Cultura." Brasilia: MEC, 1976.

Montague, Ivor. *Film World*. Baltimore: Penguin Books, 1967.

Mora, Carl. *Mexican Cinema*. Berkeley and Los Angeles: University of California Press, 1982.

Morel, Regina Lúcia de Moraes. *Ciência e Estado: A política científica no Brasil*. São Paulo: Thomas A. Queiroz, 1979.

Naves, Sylvia Bahiense, et al. "Hector Babenco." *Cinema* (Fundação Cinemateca Brasileira) 5 (Spring 1980), 9–22.

O'Donnell, Guillermo A. *Modernization and Bureaucratic Authoritarianism*. Berkeley: Institute of International Studies, 1973.

Ortiz, Renato. *Cultura Brasileira e Identidade Nacional*. São Paulo: Brasiliense, 1985.

Paz, Octavio. *El Ogro Filantrópico: Historia y Política, 1971–1978*. Mexico City: Editorial Juan Mortiz, 1979.

Pereira, Araken Campos, Jr. *Cinema Brasileiro (1908–1978)*. 2 vols. Santos: Editora Casa do Cinema, 1978.

Pereira, Geraldo Santos. *Plano Geral do Cinema Brasileiro*. Rio de Janeiro: Borsoi, 1973.

Pike, Frederick B. and Thomas Stritch, ed. *The New Corporatism: Social-Political Structures in the Iberian World*. West Bend: Notre Dame University Press, 1974.

Poulantzas, Nicos. *State, Power, Socialism*. London: Verso, 1980.

5 (Quinto) Festival de Brasília de Cinema Brasileiro. *Boletim* (1969).

Ramos, José Mário Ortiz. *Cinema, Estado, e Lutas Culturais*. Rio de Janeiro: Paz e Terra, 1983.

Relatório da Diretoria. Associação Cinematográfica de Produtores Brasileiros. Rio de Janeiro: Typographo do Jornal do Commércio, 1937.

Ribeiro, Adalberto Mário. "O Instituto Nacional de Cinema Educativo." *Revista do Serviço Público* 3 no. 7 (March 1944), 67–90.

Rocha, Glauber. "Uma Estética da Fome." *Revista Civilização Brasileira* 3 (July 1965). Translation in *Brazilian Cinema*, ed. Johnson and Stam, 68–71. Rutherford, N.J.: Fairleigh Dickinson University Press, 1982.

———. *Revisão Crítica do Cinema Brasilerio*. Rio de Janeiro: Civilização Brasileira, 1963.

Rodrigues, Rogério Costa. "A Indústria Cinematográfica Brasileira e a Conquista do Mercado." *Revista de Informação Legislativa* 9 (1966), 209–16.

Roett, Riordan, ed. *Brazil in the Sixties*. Nashville: Vanderbilt University Press, 1972.

———. *Brazil: Politics in a Patrimonial Society*. Boston: Allyn and Bacon, 1972.

Sanchez, Alberto Ruy. *Mitología de un cine en crisis*. Mexico City: Premia, 1981.

———. "Utopía de un cine en crisis." Presented at the 44th International Congress of Americanists, Manchester, England, September 1982.

Santos, Rubens Rodrigues dos. "O MEC e o Cinema." *O Estado de São Paulo*, 2 and 3 June 1971.

Schmitter, Phillipe C. *Interest Conflict and Political Change in Brazil*. Stanford: Stanford University Press, 1971.

————. "Still the Century of Corporatism?" In *The New Corporatism: Social-Political Structures in the Iberian World*, ed. Pike and Stritch, 85–131. West Bend, Ind.: Notre Dame University Press, 1974.

Schneider, Ronald M. *The Political System of Brazil: The Emergence of a "Modernizing" Authoritarian Regime, 1964–1970*. New York: Columbia University Press, 1971.

Schnitman, Jorge A. "The Argentine Film Industry: A Contextual Study." Ph.D.diss., Stanford University, 1979.

————. *Film Industries in Latin America: Dependency and Development*. Norwood, N.J.: Ablex Publishing Company, 1984.

————. "State Protectionism and Film Industry Development: A Comparative View of Argentina and Mexico." Presented at the Conference of World Communications: Decisions for the 80's, University of Pennsylvania, 12–14 May 1980.

Situação Econômica e Financeira do Cinema Brasileiro. São Paulo: Comissão Municipal do Cinema, 1955.

Skidmore, Thomas E. *Politics in Brazil, 1930–1964: An Experiment in Democracy*. New York: Oxford University Press, 1967.

Souza, Aílton Benedito de. "Violência no Rio de Janeiro: Outro nome para a luta de classes." *Comunicação e Política* 2, nos. 1–2 (March–June 1984), 93–106.

Souza, Carlos Roberto de. *A Fascinante Aventura do Cinema Brasileiro*. São Paulo: Fundação Cinemateca Brasileira, 1981.

Souza, José Inácio de Melo. "Congressos, Patriotas e Ilusões: Subsidios para uma História dos Congressos de Cinema." Unpublished, Fundaçao Cinemateca Brasileira, 1981.

Springer, Claudia. "Brazilian Policies for a National Film Industry." Unpublished, 1982.

Stepan, Alfred, ed. *Authoritarian Brazil: Origins, Policies, and Future*. New Haven, Conn.: Yale University Press, 1973.

————. *State and Society: Peru in Contemporary Perspective*. Princeton, N.J.: Princeton University Press, 1978.

Taylor, J. M. "The Politics of Aesthetic Debate: The Case of Brazilian Carnival." *Ethnology* 21, no. 4 (October 1982), 301–11.

Tendler, Sílvio. "Cinema e Estado: Em Defesa do Miúra." M.A. Thesis, Pontifícia Universidade Católica, Rio de Janeiro, 1982.

Toledo, Caio Navarro de. *ISEB: Fábrica de Ideologias*. São Paulo: Ática, 1978.

Topik, Steven. "The Evolution of the Economic Role of the Brazilian State, 1889–1930." *Journal of Latin American Studies* 2, no. 2 (1979), 325–42.

Trebat, Thomas J. *Brazil's State-Owned Enterprises: A Case Study of the State as an Entrepreneur.* Cambridge: Cambridge University Press, 1983.

United States Department of Commerce, Bureau of Foreign and Domestic Commerce. "Motion Pictures in Argentina and Brazil." *Trade Information Bulletin,* no. 630 (1929).

United States Department of Commerce, Business and Defense Services Administration. *World Survey of Motion Picture Theater Facilities* Washington, D.C.: GPO, 1960.

Usabel, Gaizka. "American Films in Latin America: The Case History of United Artists Corporation, 1919–1951." Ph.D. diss., University of Wisconsin, Madison, 1975.

Viany, Alex. *Introdução ao Cinema Brasileiro.* Rio de Janeiro: Instituto Nacional do Livro, 1959.

Villela, Sérgio Renato Víctor. "Cinema Brasileiro: Capital e Estado. Unpublished, CNDA/Funarte [1979].

Wahrlich, Beatriz. "Controle Político das Empresas Estatais Federais Brasil—Uma Contribuição ao seu Estudo." *Revista de Administração Pública* 14, no. 2 (April–June 1980).

Wiarda, Howard J. *Corporatism and National Development in Latin America.* Boulder, Colo.: Westview Press, 1981.

Wirth, John D. *The Politics of Brazilian Development: 1930–1954.* Stanford, Calif.: Stanford University Press, 1970.

Xavier, Ismail. "Allegories of Underdevelopment: From the 'Aesthetics of Hunger' to the 'Aesthetics of Garbage'." Ph.D. diss., New York University, 1982.

_____. *Sétima Arte: Un Culto Moderno.* Sao Paulo: Perspectiva, 1977. Debates no. 142.

NEWSPAPERS

Brasília
  Correio Braziliense
  Jornal de Brasília
Porto Alegre
  Correio do Povo
Rio de Janeiro
  Correio da Manhã
  Diário Carioca
  Diário de Notícias
  O Globo
  Jornal do Brasil
  Jornal do Commércio
  Tribuna da Imprensa
São Paulo
  O Estado de São Paulo
  A Folha de São Paulo
  Gazeta Mercantil
  Jornal da Tarde

PERIODICALS (SÃO PAULO)

  Isto É
  Veja
  Visão

INDUSTRY PUBLICATIONS

New York
  Variety
Rio de Janeiro
  Brasil Cinema
  Cinejornal
  Filme Cultura
  Guia de Filmes
  Jornal de Cinema
  Revista do GEICINE
São Paulo
  Cine Repórter
  O Exibidor
  Projeção

INDEX

Pitt Latin American Series

Cole Blasier, Editor

ARGENTINA

Argentina in the Twentieth Century
David Rock, Editor

Discreet Partners: Argentina and the USSR Since 1917
Aldo César Vacs

Juan Perón and the Reshaping of Argentina
Frederick C. Turner and José Enrique Miguens, Editors

The Life, Music, and Times of Carlos Gardel
Simon Collier

BRAZIL

The Film Industry in Brazil: Culture and the State
Randal Johnson

The Politics of Social Security in Brazil
James M. Malloy

Urban Politics in Brazil: The Rise of Populism, 1925–1945
Michael L. Conniff

COLOMBIA

Gaitan of Colombia: A Political Biography
Richard E. Sharpless

Roads to Reason: Transportation, Administration, and Rationality in Colombia
Richard E. Hartwig

CUBA

Army Politics in Cuba, 1898–1958
Louis A. Pérez, Jr.

Cuba Between Empires, 1878–1902
Louis A. Pérez, Jr.

Cuba, Castro, and the United States
Philip W. Bonsal

Cuba in the World
Cole Blasier and Carmelo Mesa-Lago, Editors

Cuba Under the Platt Amendment
Louis A. Pérez, Jr.

Cuban Studies, Vol. 16
Carmelo Mesa-Lago, Editor

Intervention, Revolution, and Politics in Cuba, 1913–1921
Louis A. Pérez, Jr.

Revolutionary Change in Cuba
Carmelo Mesa-Lago, Editor

The United States and Cuba: Hegemony and Dependent Development,
1880–1934
Jules Robert Benjamin

MEXICO

Essays on Mexican Kinship
Hugo G. Nutini, Pedro Carrasco, and James M. Taggart, Editors

The Mexican Republic: The First Decade, 1823–1832
Stanley C. Green

The Politics of Mexican Oil
George W. Grayson

Voices, Visions, and a New Reality: Mexican Fiction Since 1970
J. Ann Duncan

US POLICIES

Cuba, Castro, and the United States
Philip W. Bonsal

The Hovering Giant: U.S. Responses to Revolutionary Change in Latin America
Cole Blasier

Illusions of Conflict: Anglo-American Diplomacy Toward Latin America
Joseph Smith

Puerto Rico and the United States, 1917–1933
Truman R. Clark

The United States and Cuba: Hegemony and Dependent Development,
1880–1934
Jules Robert Benjamin

The United States and Latin America in the 1980s: Contending Perspectives on
a Decade of Crisis
Kevin J. Middlebrook and Carlos Rico, Editors

USSR POLICIES

Discreet Partners: Argentina and the USSR Since 1917
Aldo César Vacs

The Giant's Rival: The USSR and Latin America
Cole Blasier